CW00522040

YOU WILL BE ABLE TO GARDEN BY THE END OF THIS BOOK

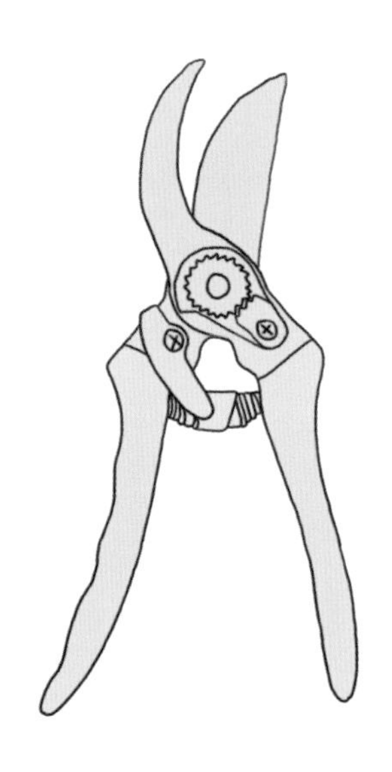

First published in Great Britain in 2023 by Mitchell Beazley, an imprint of
Octopus Publishing Group Ltd in association with The Royal Horticultural Society
Carmelite House, 50 Victoria Embankment, London EC4Y 0DZ
www.octopusbooks.co.uk

An Hachette UK Company www.hachette.co.uk

Distributed in the US by Hachette Book Group, 1290 Avenue of the Americas,
4th and 5th Floors, New York, NY 10104

Distributed in Canada by Canadian Manda Group, 664 Annette St., Toronto, Ontario, Canada M6S 2C8

ISBN 978 1 78472 840 3
A CIP catalogue record for this book is available from the British Library.

Printed and bound in China
3 5 7 9 10 8 6 4 2

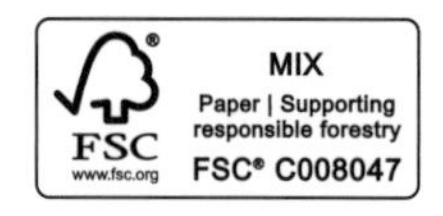

Publisher: Alison Starling
Senior Managing Editor: Sybella Stephens
Copy Editor: Caroline West
Art Director: Juliette Norsworthy
Designer: Rachel Cross
Colour Illustrator: Claire Rollet
Black and White Illustrator: Claire Huntley
Picture Research Managers: Giulia Hetherington and Jennifer Veall
Production Controllers: Lucy Carter and Nic Jones

RHS Consultant Editor: Simon Maughan
RHS Head of Editorial: Tom Howard

The Royal Horticultural Society is the UK's leading gardening charity dedicated to advancing horticulture and promoting good gardening. Its charitable work includes providing expert advice and information, training the next generation of gardeners, creating hands-on opportunities for children to grow plants and conducting research into plants, pests and environmental issues affecting gardeners.

For more information visit www.rhs.org.uk or call 0845 130 4646

YOU WILL BE ABLE TO GARDEN BY THE END OF THIS BOOK

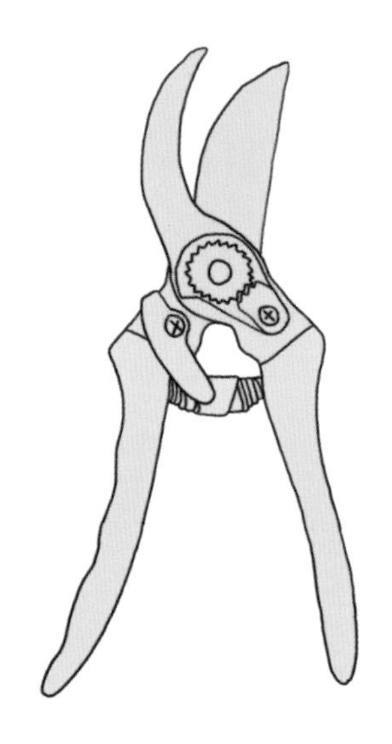

SIMON AKEROYD

MITCHELL BEAZLEY

CONTENTS

Introduction

Welcome to *You Will Be Able To Garden By The End Of This Book*. Containing 12 chapters, it is packed to the rafters with gardening advice – like an overcrowded potting shed – so you can create and maintain your garden. Whether you have a tiny courtyard or something larger, everything you need to know to create the garden of your dreams can be found within these pages.

The book takes you on a horticultural journey, starting by helping you to assess your garden and providing advice and inspiration for how to design your ideal outdoor space. There is then guidance on everything from how to plant beds and borders to how to sow and propagate plants. As well as information on looking after ornamental plants you will find advice on growing your own vegetables, herbs and fruit. You will learn how to establish and maintain a lawn, discover tips on encouraging wildlife, and find information on creating water features, as well as how to care for the plants you have nurtured and deal with pests and diseases to keep them healthy.

As you undergo your horticultural odyssey, you'll also pick up many practical skills along the way, as you learn to prune, cut hedges and sow seeds. The world of gardening is such a fascinating place and you will find yourself constantly expanding your knowledge and skill set, just as the trunk of a tree expands as it grows. Gardening also teaches you to be creative and to look at the importance of colour, texture and shape, and how these can be combined to create a place of beauty.

You will even be able to impress your friends with a basic knowledge of Latin because botanical plant names use this fascinating language. There is some soil science and plant anatomy to learn too. Finally, a glossary at the back of the book will help you with those key gardening terms that at first glance only make sense to the horticulturally initiated. But, perhaps most importantly, gardening will help keep both your mind and body active and healthy.

However, perhaps this book should come with a warning, because once you start gardening, it is very hard to stop. Having a garden that you have created with your own hands will make you feel great about yourself and the world. Your garden will beguile and fascinate you. It will open up an exciting world of wonder where every day you will step outside and your senses will be bombarded with natural beauty, whether this is the amazing aromas of flowers or a new seedling as it sends out its first shoots. It might be a plant erupting into colour or a fruit bush burgeoning with fresh berries. You will enjoy the satisfaction of biting into a crunchy apple or a sweet strawberry, knowing you made that possible. The air will be filled with the sound of bird song and the soporific sound of buzzing bees. You will look forward to seeing the seasons change, and the plants with them as they adapt to nature's rhythms.

Gardening is a very positive pastime and gardeners like to plan for the future. In fact, gardening never stays still. It is always looking forwards and will take you on a rewarding horticultural rollercoaster ride. Once you have begun gardening, you will find yourself always anticipating what the future holds. With hope, passion and anticipation for great things to come – because what you have planted will one day flower and give joy to yourself and others.

I hope you enjoy this book and that it will help you master the basics of how to create your own garden haven. Good luck and happy gardening

CHAPTER 1

BASICS

If you have been thinking of donning a pair of gardening gloves and getting out into the garden for the first time, then this chapter will help you make the transition from garden novice to garden guru in next to no time, providing advice on the basics of gardening and everything you need to know to get started. To motivate and inspire you to go outside and begin gardening, this chapter first looks at the many benefits it can have for yourself, your family and the environment.

This chapter also explains how a plant grows and what it requires to thrive in your garden. After all, just like us, plants have their own preferences as to where they prefer to live. They will sulk or worse if grown in an environment that they are not happy with. There is also information on the basic anatomy of a plant because understanding a plant's different parts will help you make informed decisions about planting, pruning and training.

Finally, this chapter includes a list of tools and other pieces of equipment that will help you garden more successfully, as well as a useful seasonal chart, so you have an idea of which jobs to do when.

Gardening is good for you

There are numerous reasons people choose to take up gardening, joining millions of others as they cultivate their plants and surrounding landscapes. In many countries around the world, gardening is the number one pastime and activity. There has never been a better time to pick up a trowel and join the burgeoning community of people from all walks of life who are discovering the joy to be found in gardening.

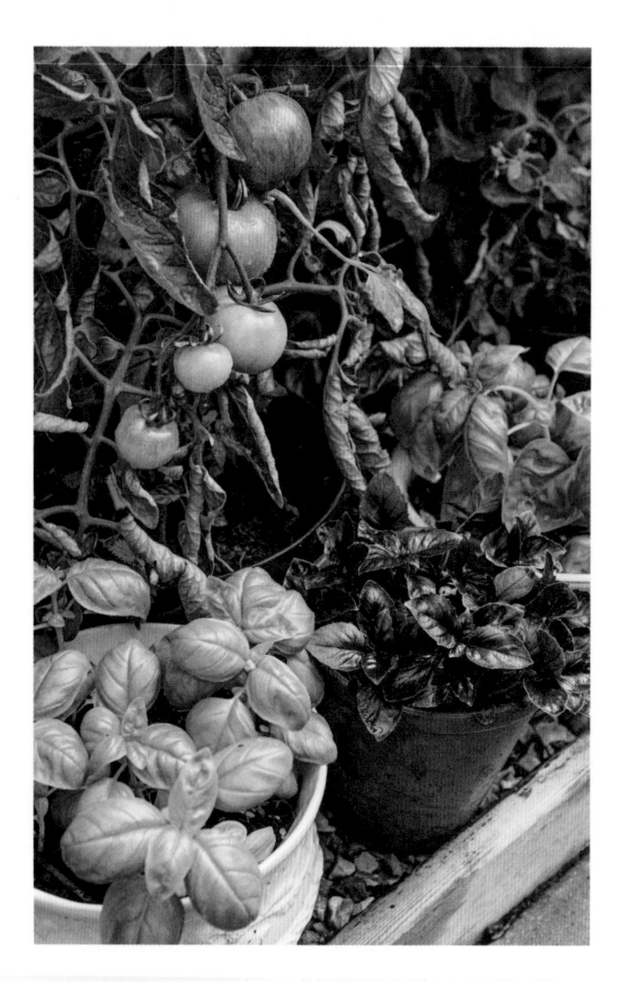

IMPROVE MENTAL WELL-BEING

Research has shown that gardening is good for our mental health and that people can benefit from the healing power of nature. Gardening is a relaxing and calming pursuit – since it is not an intense pastime, it doesn't overstimulate or cause anxiety. Instead, being surrounded by plants has a restorative effect and has been shown to improve people's mood. Being outside in the sunshine, and among plants, is also thought to lower blood pressure. Some psychologists are even prescribing 'green therapy' as a method for alleviating depression and stress.

GROW YOUR OWN FOOD

Growing your own food is another great reason for starting to garden. This doesn't require much space. In fact, many people living in towns and cities are growing edible crops in containers or windowboxes on balconies and rooftops, in porches and on patios. Growing your own crops means that not only will you reduce food miles to literally nothing, but you can also save money and rest assured that your fruit and vegetables haven't been genetically modified, sprayed with chemicals or fed artificial fertilizers. It can also give you some food security when there are so many uncertainties about global food supplies.

CREATE BEAUTIFUL SPACES

Growing plants in your garden and immediate surroundings increases the beauty of the area, and this is something that everybody in the vicinity will benefit from and enjoy. Not only does admiring a beautiful front or back garden make us feel good, but these spaces can also increase the value of your house and that of neighbouring homes. Areas of housing where there are trees and other plants create a much more attractive environment than what would otherwise be little more than a concrete jungle.

ATTRACT WILDLIFE

Creating a garden will inevitably encourage a range of wildlife such as birds, insects, bats and many others into the space. Not only is watching wildlife up close a fascinating and rewarding hobby, but a garden also increases the biodiversity of an area, which is good news for the environment.

WHY TAKE UP GARDENING?

* Plants contribute to clean, healthy air.
* Gardens provide valuable habitats for wildlife.
* Gardening keeps you fit and active.
* Sunlight provides you with vitamin D.
* You can grow your own food.
* It stimulates all the senses.

Opposite: *Growing your own food is very rewarding, and the crops also taste so much better than those you can buy in the shops.* ***Right:*** *Growing plants will not only make your space more beautiful, but a well-tended garden can also increase the value of your home.*

What plants need to grow

When starting a garden, no matter what the size, it is useful to have a basic understanding of the plants' growing requirements, so you can nurture them and help them to thrive under your care. Their two basic requirements are light and water, but you'll also need to understand their different types, sizes and habits to ensure they will fit your space.

LET THERE BE LIGHT

Plants require light to make the energy they need to grow in a process called photosynthesis, in which sunlight is captured by chlorophyll (a green pigment) in the leaves to convert water and carbon dioxide (and minerals) into sugar (glucose) and oxygen. The sugar not needed to provide energy or build cellulose is converted to starch and stored for later use. Plants have adapted to varying light levels, depending on where they grow in the wild. For example, woodland plants, like some ferns, need shady conditions, while desert plants or those from North America's prairies need hot, sunny conditions. So, always read plant labels to check how much light a plant needs. If you inherit plants, identify them and check their requirements to be sure they will receive the right amount of light in your garden.

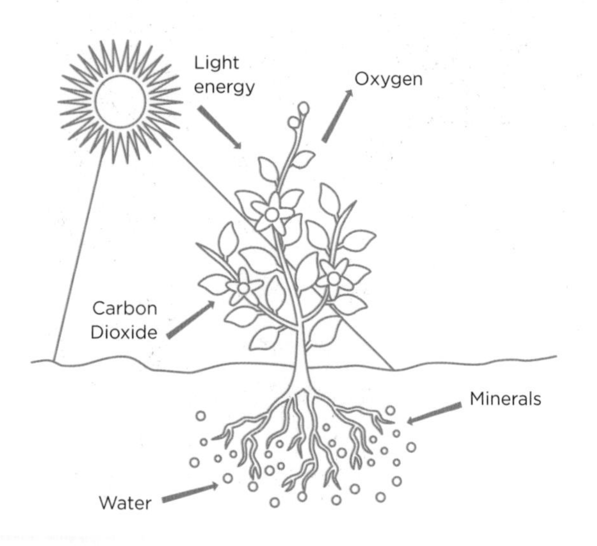

HOW PLANTS GROW

Plants have different growth 'habits', so it is helpful to understand how they grow before you plant them. Climbers, for example, should be grown on a fence, wall or trellis. But even if you know a plant is a climber, be aware that some are self-clinging with tendrils, while others need regular tying in as they grow. Other plants have a prostrate habit, which makes them ideal for ground cover. If you purchase or propagate a plant, check the growth habit, including the eventual size, to be sure you have the space to grow it. Even trees are different shapes and sizes – tall, thin, wide, pendulous, and so on.

ENJOY CLEANER AIR

Plants absorb carbon dioxide and pump out oxygen when they photosynthesize, so your air is cleaner if you have plants nearby.

TYPES OF PLANTS

You can grow different types of plants in a garden, ranging in size and shape. Listed below are the most common ones you will come across.

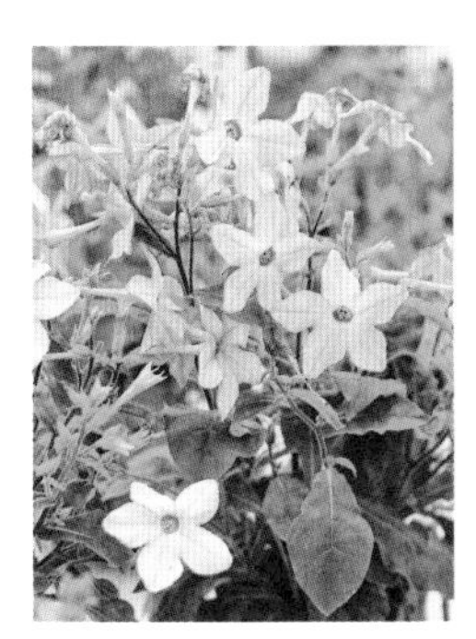

Annuals Plants that only live for one year. Within that time, they flower, produce seed and die. This category also includes bedding plants, which are treated as annuals in areas where they will not survive cold winters.

Biennials Plants that live for two years. Within that time, they will produce flowers, go to seed and die.

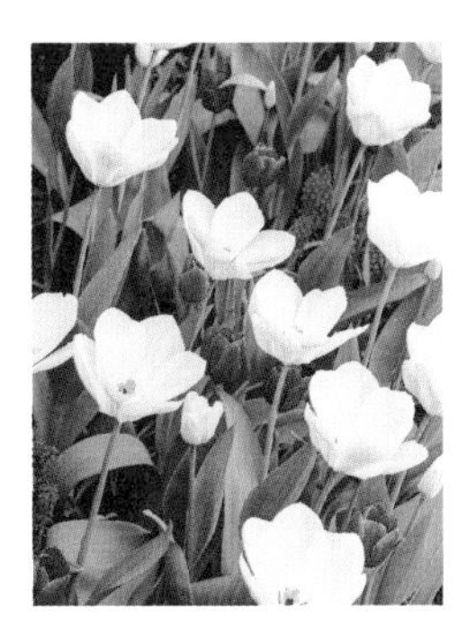

Bulbs This category includes true bulbs, tubers, rhizomes and corms, which all store energy in a swollen organ below ground, as opposed to relying only on a system of roots.

Herbaceous perennials Perennial means that a plant will live for more than two years, while herbaceous indicates it is made of soft material (non-woody). Perennials usually die back when it gets cold, only to reappear in the spring.

Shrubs A deciduous or evergreen plant that has woody stems or branches. There is no clear-cut way to differentiate between a tree and a shrub, but shrubs are generally smaller and also multi-stemmed.

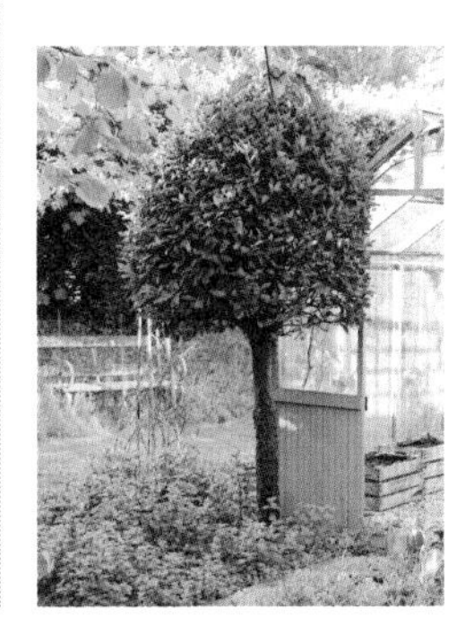

Trees A plant with a single woody trunk, but can also be multi-stemmed. Like shrubs, trees can be deciduous or evergreen. There are trees suitable for small gardens and some specimens can even be grown in a container.

Plant anatomy and names

A basic knowledge of the various parts of a plant is helpful to understanding how they grow. Recognizing the various parts and why they are important can help us appreciate what plants need to thrive. All plants are slightly different, but below are some of the key parts of their anatomy.

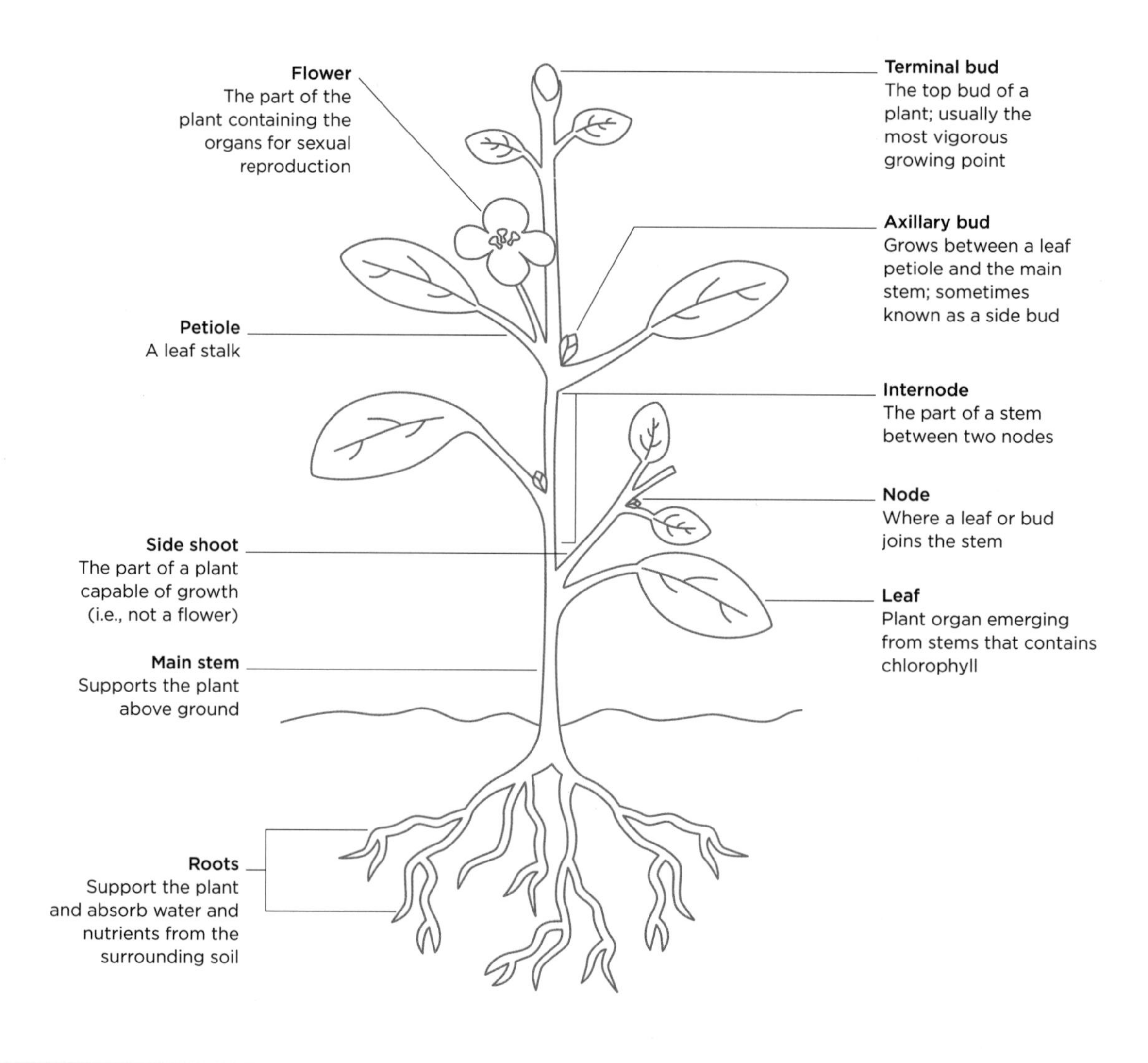

PLANT NAMES

In gardening there are two types of names for plants, the common name and the botanical name. For example, below are the common names of three well-known plants followed by the corresponding botanical names:
Common names – stinging nettle, foxglove, English oak tree
Botanical names – *Urtica dioica, Digitalis purpurea, Quercus robur*

While common names are useful, they can also be confusing because different countries, indeed even different regions in the same country, have different colloquial names for the same plants.

To avoid confusion, in the 18th century the Swedish botanist Carl Linnaeus developed an international method for naming different plants, which was based on Latin and categorized plants into groups based on common botanical traits. This means that wherever you are in the world, you can refer to a plant without the risk of confusion caused by variations in common names.

The three key parts of this botanical naming system that are relevant to most gardeners when buying or talking about plants are the genus, species and cultivar – for example, *Malus* (genus) *domestica* (species) 'Granny Smith' (cultivar).

HOW TO WRITE BOTANICAL NAMES

The genus and species names of plants always appear in italics. The genus name starts with a capital letter and the species name starts in lowercase. The cultivar name is always in inverted commas, non-italic and begins with a capital. For example, *Salvia nemorosa* 'Caradonna' or *Acer palmatum* 'Bloodgood'. Not all plants have a cultivar name, however – for example, *Crocus sativus* or *Echinacea purpurea*.

DIFFERENCE BETWEEN VARIETY AND CULTIVAR

A cultivar is a plant developed or bred through cross cultivation with another plant. In other words, a 'cultivar' has been cultivated or specifically bred for horticulturists or agriculturists, although sometimes it is an accidental crossing – for example, at a plant nursery. A variety is something that has occurred naturally in the wild.

NOTE A hybrid occurs when two species are crossed, while a cross is when two cultivars or varieties are crossed with each other.

Botanical or Latin names can seem quite daunting at first, but once you get the hang of them, they can be very useful, as they can tell you something about the plant. For example:
alba/albus – white flowers
campestris – grows in fields
grandiflora – large-flowered
odorata – perfumed
reptans – creeping habit
scandens – climbing habit
sinensis – from China

Sustainable gardening

Gardening involves creating beautiful outdoor areas and caring for plants. You can use a garden to have a positive impact on your local environment, creating a space that attracts wildlife, and to improve your physical and mental health. Gardening can help you contribute to a greener and healthier planet if you garden responsibly and sustainably. Following sustainable horticultural practices and a few simple guidelines can turn your garden into a truly eco-friendly haven.

WHAT IS SUSTAINABLE GARDENING?
Sustainable gardening is first and foremost a mindset and way of thinking. Understanding that a garden is a place where the natural world meets the home environment will help you approach it in an eco-friendly way. Think twice before introducing any non-biodegradable materials, such as plastic, into your garden and accept that there will be the occasional weed and outbreak of pests and disease. Try to recycle objects, build a compost heap to reuse as much garden waste as possible, include a pond to attract wildlife, and practise waterwise gardening, being careful with the amount of water you use and choosing drought-tolerant plants.

One of the most important steps you can take to create a healthy and sustainable environment is to avoid using chemicals and artificial fertilizers. Many insecticides and fungicides are toxic to wildlife and can destroy natural ecosystems. Instead, use natural remedies and plant feeds that won't harm the environment or wildlife. Even spraying plants with water will remove blackfly, and beer traps can help control slugs. Natural fertilizers can be made from plants such as nettles and comfrey to avoid the need for artificial fertilizers (see pages 104–5) – they are free too. You can also use green manures by sowing nutrient-rich plants near crops to increase the fertility of the soil.

Look at other solutions for managing weeds instead of reaching for a bottle of weedkiller. Most can be tolerated and will benefit the environment. If they must be removed, many can be pulled out by hand without resorting to chemicals. Mulching over bare soil with a natural material such as cornstarch landscaping fabric or even standard garden compost will reduce the number of germinating weeds.

WORK WITH YOUR ENVIRONMENT

Choose plants that suit the existing conditions. If you have acidic soil in the shade, then do your best to select plants that are suitable. This reduces the need to import lots of soil, composts and other materials to maintain them, keeps air miles to a minimum and helps reduce your carbon footprint.

FOR PEAT'S SAKE

Always use peat-free potting compost. Peat is a non-sustainable and ever-diminishing resource which is excavated from peatland habitats that sustain a unique diversity of fauna and flora. There are alternatives to peat-based composts, so look for 'Peat Free' labels.

TIPS ON SUSTAINABLE GARDENING

* Work with your natural environment.
* Recycle materials whenever possible.
* Harvest rainwater in water butts to conserve water.
* Use peat-free potting compost.
* Make your own garden compost.
* Avoid plastic products, including pots and plant labels.
* Make homemade liquid plant feeds.
* Avoid using chemicals such as artificial insecticides, pesticides and fungicides.
* Use hand tools or petrol-free machinery.
* Create areas to encourage wildlife.
* Buy local.

Opposite: *A water butt need not be obtrusive and installing one can help you conserve water.*
Right: *Composting uses up kitchen and garden waste and the compost can then be applied to flowerbeds.*

Tools needed to garden

Having the correct gardening tools can make the world of difference to efficiency and what you can achieve in your garden. It will also lead to less muscle strain and ensure a better result overall. When purchasing tools, it is worth considering where they are going to be stored, as they can take up quite a lot of room. They can also be expensive, so ensure any storage solution is secure.

SPADE

Used for cultivating the soil, digging holes and planting, spades are a key tool in the garden. They usually have a T- or D-shaped handle which can be of varying lengths. Choose a spade that feels comfortable and balanced when you use it. Spades with stainless-steel blades are best because the soil tends not to stick to them, and they are nice and light to use. For smaller areas, a 'border' spade can be used instead, which has a smaller blade and handle and is useful for working in confined gardens.

SHOVEL

These look similar to a spade, but have a blunter and wider blade. A shovel is not used for digging, but for moving loose material such as soil and wood chip.

FORK

Used for loosening and cultivating the soil. There are other types of forks available such as pitchforks and potato forks. Smaller border forks are easier for working in confined spaces.

HOE

Hoes are used for removing annual weeds among beds and borders. The blade is usually pushed or pulled just below the surface of the soil, severing the plant from the roots. For small spaces, an onion hoe can be used, which has a shorter handle.

THREE-PRONGED CULTIVATOR

A useful tool for breaking up the soil. It is dragged over or just below the surface, breaking any capping or mild compaction which might be preventing moisture and fertilizers/plant feed from penetrating into the root zone. There are both short and long-handled versions available.

RAKES

There are lots of different rakes available, but they are generally used to level the ground and cultivate a fine tilth. Some spring-tine or plastic rakes are used for collecting leaves or scarifying (removing thatch or dead grass) from a lawn.

Wider, landscape rakes are good for levelling the ground, while standard garden rakes can be used to create a fine, level tilth for sowing and to remove stones and other unwanted material from beds. Softer, rubber rakes are used to brush topdressing into aerated holes on lawns.

HAND FORK

Used for weeding among confined spaces and cultivating small areas of soil, such as in a raised bed or containers.

HAND TROWEL

Trowels are used for planting small plants or bulbs. Those with longer handles are helpful if you suffer from back problems.

DIBBER

Used when propagating plants by pushing it into the compost to make a preliminary hole before inserting seeds or cuttings.

WATERING CAN

Used for watering plants in small areas. For larger areas you may need a garden hose attached to a reel to keep it neat and tidy. Ideally, if you have room, there should be water butts too, to harvest rainwater and use it on the garden.

If you are watering newly planted seedlings or young plants, attach a rose to the end of the watering can or garden hose. The finer spray stops them being damaged.

TIPS ON ADDITIONAL TOOLS

You may need to equip yourself with some extra gardening clothing and items such as:

* Kneeler or knee pads
* Gardening gloves
* Stout pair of boots
* Tool belt or holster for secateurs
* Hat, to keep off the sun
* Sunscreen
* Waterproof coat and trousers

SECATEURS

Used for pruning woody stems and herbaceous material. There are two different types: bypass and anvil. The former give a better cut, using a scissor action, whereas the latter tend to crush down onto the plant.

HAND SHEARS

Used for cutting small hedges, instead of a mechanized hedge trimmer, or cutting back herbaceous plants when there is too much material to use secateurs.

LOPPERS

Helpful for cutting back thicker stems than those that are cut with secateurs. Loppers with extendable or telescopic handles give move leverage when cutting thicker stems, whereas ratchet systems exert even more pressure. There are both short- and long-handled versions available.

PRUNING SAWS

These are designed specifically for cutting small branches. They are long and narrow, enabling the saw to fit into awkward angles. Some can be folded away safely and kept in a pocket. Larger types have covers over the blade and can often be hung from a tool belt.

WHEELBARROW

Essential in larger gardens for moving material from one area of a garden to another. It is much easier to move things in a wheelbarrow, and will save any back strain.

HEDGE TRIMMER

Instead of hand-held shears, a hedge trimmer can be used to cut hedges. The advantage of a hedge trimmer is that it has a cutting bar which helps you keep a straight line when cutting. It is also slightly easier to reach higher than with hand shears. There are petrol or electric/battery versions available.

LAWN MOWER

You'll need a mower if you have a lawn, although these days people are cutting their lawns less often to encourage biodiversity and wildlife. Rotary mowers are used for rougher grass, whereas cylinder mowers are for fine lawns. For those with a decent budget and a large garden, there are remote-controlled mowers and also mowers with sensors that can be programmed to cut in a certain area, meaning you can relax in a deckchair while the machine takes the strain.

STRING TRIMMER

Also known as a Strimmer®, electric/battery-powered string trimmers are available as well as petrol ones. They are used to cut long grass with a rotating nylon string and to trim up to the edges of decking and patios. If the trimmer is turned on its side, then it can also be used to edge the lawn after it has been mown.

HALF MOON EDGING TOOL

Used to cut the edges of a lawn. This tool has a flat blade, so should give a better finish than a spade which is slightly curved. When edging a lawn, use strings tied behind two posts to act as a guide for where to cut.

EDGING SHEARS

Used to trim the edges of the lawn, clipping back stray blades of grass and keeping it neat and tidy. Edging shears have long handles, saving on having to bend down, and the cutting action is like a pair of scissors, where one blade cuts across another.

TIDY UP GRASS CLIPPINGS

Always pick up grass clippings at the edge of beds and borders after edging because they can end up seeding where they land. Some edging shears collect the clippings in a container as you work.

Spring

Spring is an exciting time in the garden, as it erupts into colour. It is also usually a busy time, with some gardeners referring to the month of May (or late spring) in the gardening calendar as 'mayhem'. However, with a bit of planning, it need not be too manic. Mowing can start, as can seed sowing and planting out bedding after all risk of frost has passed.

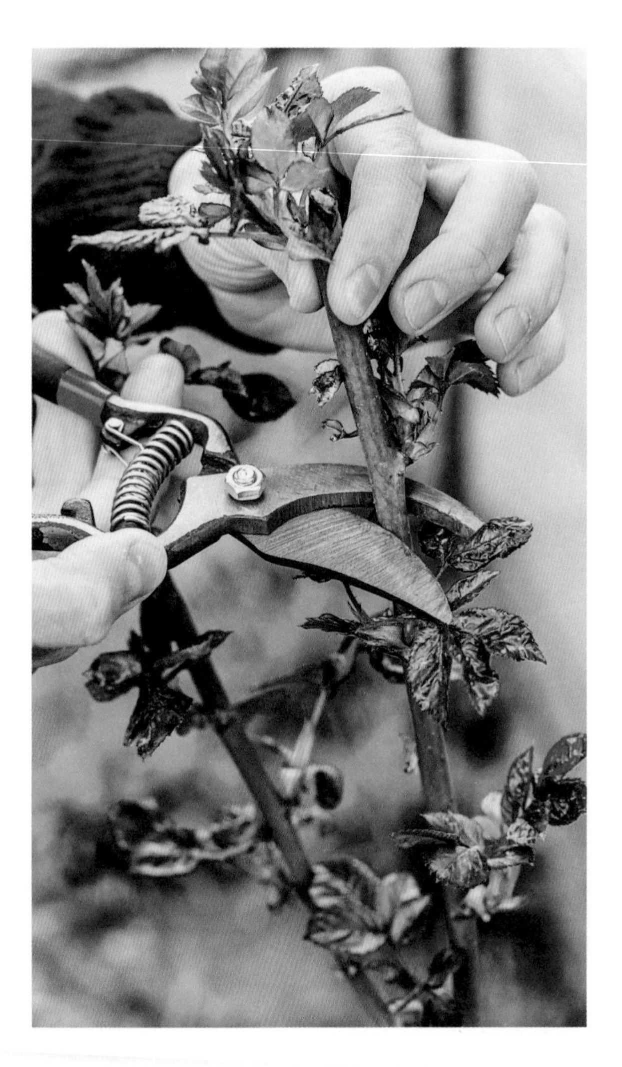

* Plant summer- and autumn-flowering bulbs.
* Lift and divide herbaceous perennials before they start actively growing.
* Herbaceous plants and shrubs can be planted if this was not already done in autumn.
* Prune roses in early spring.
* Sow half-hardy annuals in a heated propagator and then plant them out after all risk of frost has passed.
* Check for weeds and remove if necessary.
* Mulch around newly emerging herbaceous perennials. Try to keep the material off the crowns of the plants.
* Mulch around trees and shrubs, keeping it off the trunk.
* Mowing can start, but use a high setting to begin with.
* Prune late-flowering shrubs.
* Lawns can be laid with turf or sown with seed.
* Tender plants will need covering with some horticultural fleece if there is a risk of frost.

Prune shrubs that flower in late summer to maintain their shape.

Summer

The garden should be in full swing by now. Summer is when the garden starts to knit together nicely. If you have a lawn, then mowing can start regularly, although do not forget to leave some areas long for wildlife. Keep adding grass clippings to the compost heap, if you have one, and do not forget to turn the compost every few weeks to speed up decomposition.

* Prune early-flowering shrubs after they have finished flowering.
* Get support stakes in early for annuals and herbaceous perennials before they flop over.
* Keep plants well watered, particularly recently planted seedlings.
* Take semi-ripe and soft stem cuttings of shrubs and perennials.
* Fruit trees and some vegetable plants may need feeding weekly once they start to blossom/flower.
* Deadhead bedding plants, repeat-flowering roses and a few other shrubs and herbaceous perennials to ensure they continue to flower.
* Cut the lawn regularly at its usual height but avoid cutting in prolonged periods of drought.
* Prune hedges but only up until the nesting season for birds.

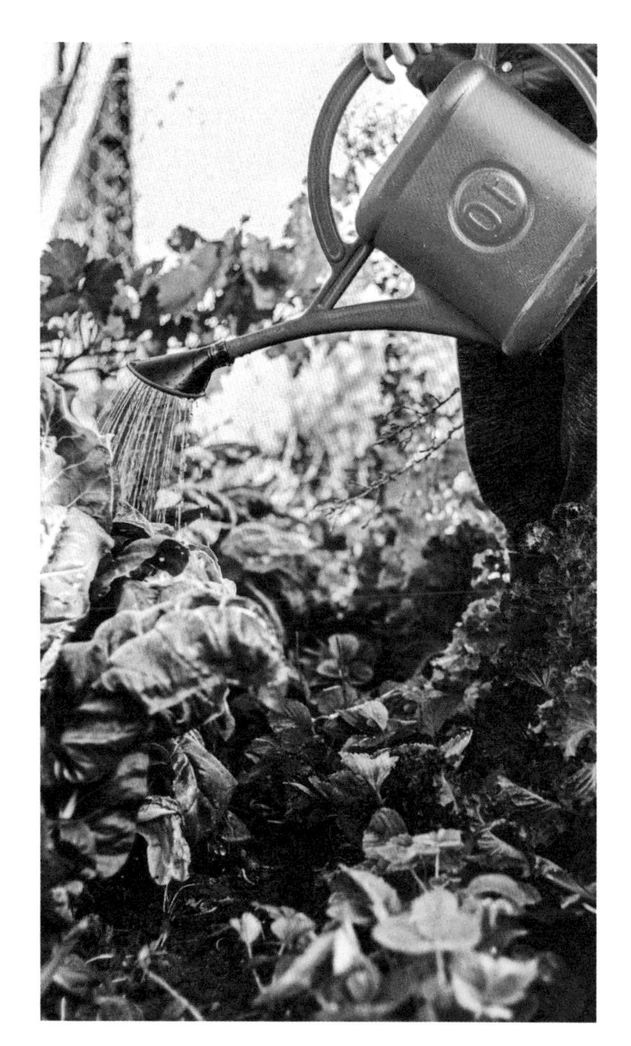

Keep plants well watered during periods of dry weather to avoid any losses.

Autumn

The poet John Keats referred to autumn as the 'Season of mists and mellow fruitfulness', and it is indeed the time for harvesting and spectacular autumn displays as the leaves start to change colour. It is also the time in the gardening calendar for collecting leaves to make lovely leafmould compost. Alternatively, create leaf piles in the garden for hibernating wildlife.

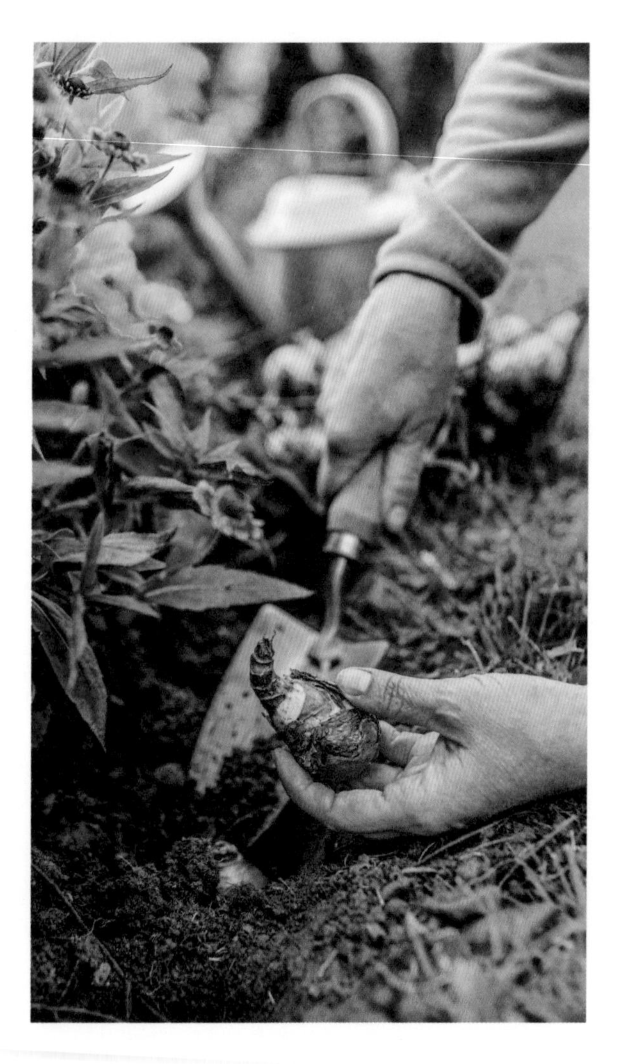

* Rake falling leaves off the lawn to prevent them killing the grass. Add them to the compost heap or make some leafmould.
* If possible, go and visit a public garden famous for its autumn colour as it is such a spectacular time of year.
* Listen to the weather forecast and be ready with some horticultural fleece to cover up tender plants or extend the growing season.
* Bring tender plants grown in pots inside to provide protection from the cold.
* Plant spring-flowering bulbs.
* You can cut back herbaceous perennials now, but remember that wildlife will benefit if you wait until early spring.
* Continue cutting the lawn, and after the final cut, carry out autumn maintenance such as scarifying and aeration.
* Autumn is one of the best times for planting trees and shrubs because the soil is still warm from summer.
* Prune hedges.

The best time to plant spring-flowering bulbs is the previous autumn.

Winter

It might all look quiet in the garden, but there are plenty of jobs to be done. Garden compost, also known as the engine house of the garden, will benefit from being turned over, speeding up its decomposition. Keep an eye out for wildlife and supply birdseed and fresh water (particularly if the water freezes) to help them survive the cold months.

* Start planning the new growing season. Now is the time to sit down, browse through those seed catalogues and get ordering.
* Now is also the ideal time to give the shed a thorough tidy. And the greenhouse, if you are lucky enough to have one.
* While the plants are dormant, take hardwood cuttings of trees, shrubs and roses.
* Prune fruit trees and bushes, including apples, pears, gooseberries, blueberries and blackcurrants. Do not prune stone fruits such as plums, apricots and peaches until the sap is rising.
* Check tree stakes and replace any that have started to rot.
* Check tree ties and make sure they are not too tight around the trunks.

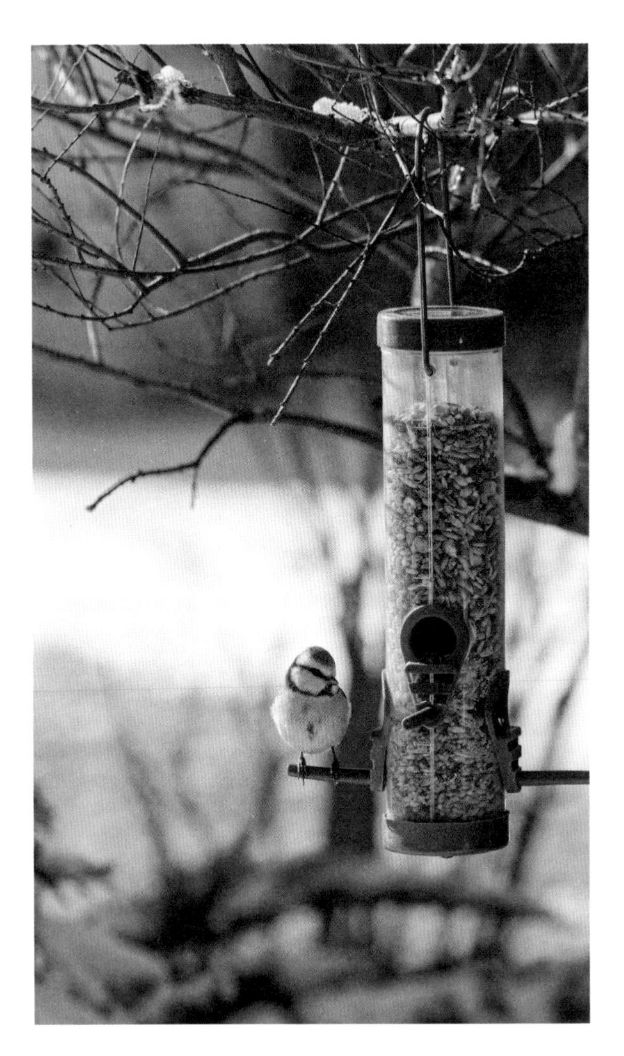

Keep birdfeeders topped up during winter to stop birds going hungry.

CHAPTER 2

HOW DOES YOUR GARDEN GROW?

Whether you are looking at a blank canvas or an established garden, contemplating the horticultural stamp you might wish to put on your outside space is always an exciting time. This chapter will help you plan and plot your gardening dreams and set you on the path to turning them into reality. There are so many different styles and themes of garden you could create. Whether you wish to conjure up a taste of the Mediterranean with a dry garden full of herbs and drought-tolerant plants or a lush subtropical border, or are inspired by the beautiful gardens of Japan, there is a type of garden to suit everybody's budget and taste.

However, although you might have a preferred style or function for your garden in mind, it is worth assessing the space fully first. For example, you need to check issues such as how much sun it receives and whether the soil is clay or sandy. Is it exposed to the wind, requiring windbreaks, or will slightly tender plants be hit by frost? Once you have assessed your garden, you are ready to get started. This chapter will guide you through the essentials of what your garden needs to flourish.

Designing your dream garden

Planning a garden is one of the most exciting aspects of moving into a new home. It is a space that you can personalize to suit your needs, taste and lifestyle. Before starting, though, it is worth considering the type of garden you would like. While there are no hard-and-fast rules when designing an outdoor space, an understanding of the different types of garden that are open to you can be helpful.

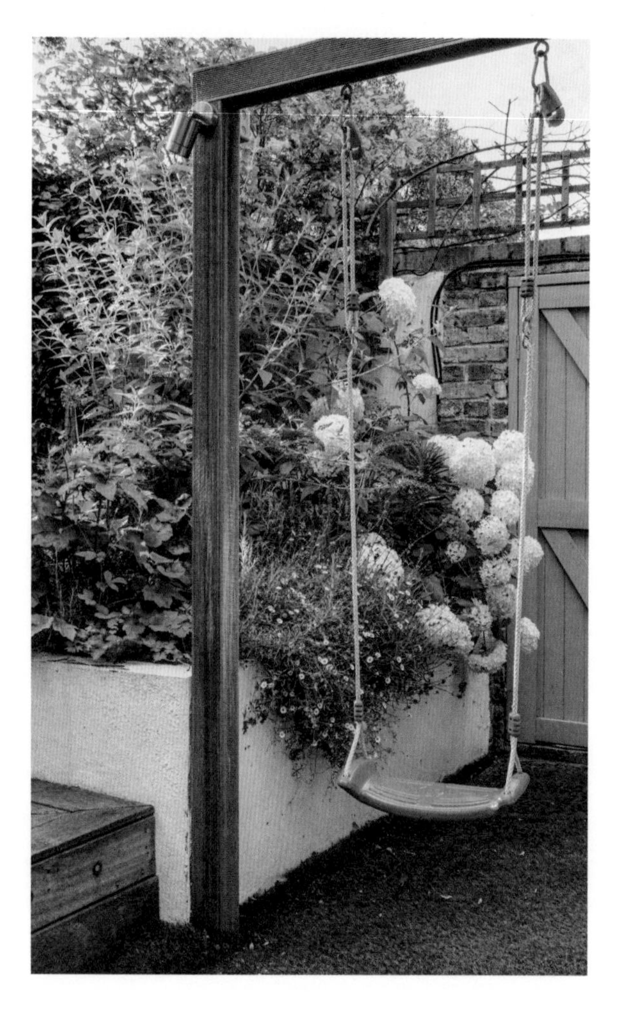

FAMILY GARDENS

A few features will make a family garden enjoyable for everyone, irrespective of age. Creating an interesting, beautiful space will encourage children outside. The mental well-being of both adults and children can benefit from 'green therapy'. Consider the following factors for a family garden:

* Size – open areas give children space to play.
* Material – lawns provide a soft playing surface.
* Robust plants – choose large, tough plants that can withstand children playing among them or kicking balls into them.
* Entertaining – seating areas where the family can sit and enjoy the garden together.
* Safety – ensure the space is secure, so children can't accidently run out onto the road, and keep ponds fenced off if small children use the garden.
* Edible plants– growing food is a great way to entice children outdoors. Try sweet-tasting crops such as sugar snaps, strawberries and raspberries.

Swings are great fun for young children, and can be tucked away so they do not take up much space.

PET-FRIENDLY GARDENS

It's not just humans who love an outside space. Most pets enjoy being out in the garden too, but there are some considerations to bear in mind:

* Provide some shade and shelter for pets from the midday sun, such as trees and shrubs or pergolas and other structures.
* Ensure the garden is secure, so dogs can't escape.
* Dogs can damage a lawn by burning patches with their wee (mainly female dogs). Some will dig up lawns, too. Consider alternative materials such as patios or decking if this is likely to be a problem.
* If the garden is large enough, then consider a 'sacrificial' area of the garden, where dogs can 'do their business' and play without damaging the remainder of the garden.
* Fence off ponds, so wildlife remains undisturbed.

BALCONY GARDENS

Although space is limited on a balcony, and large trees and shrubs are out of the question, there are still lots of opportunities for growing summer bedding, herbaceous perennials, succulents and many other plants in pots and containers. Most fruit and vegetable crops can also be grown in pots. Just make sure the balcony isn't too exposed to wind, in which case a windbreak may be necessary. With a balcony, you might be restricted by the amount of sunlight it receives, but plenty of plants can still be grown in these conditions. Try hanging baskets on the wall and trailing or climbing plants around railings and the sides of the balcony.

URBAN/COURTYARD GARDENS

Gardens tend to be smaller in urban areas, so if you have a good-sized plot, then you are lucky. But there are lots of ways to take advantage of the vertical spaces in small plots, as they are usually surrounded by walls and fences where you can grow climbers or trailing plants. You can also use the back wall of the house, which is perfect for hanging baskets.

Containers and raised beds provide a perfect solution if you want to grow plants in soilless urban environments such as patios and courtyards. Please note that in urban gardens, it is worth seeking out plants suitable for shade as nearby buildings can block out some of the light.

Small courtyards can be made to feel cosy, intimate and relaxing if they are surrounded by lots of greenery.

A garden just for you

Although gardens are loosely classified as formal or informal, you can incorporate numerous styles in an outdoor space. Formal gardens tend to be more rigid and some may see them as an attempt to curb or control nature, whereas informal gardens go with the natural flow. There are many variations of the two styles, with most gardens being a blend of formal and informal features. Gardens also tend to evolve with time and are very much a reflection of their owner's personality. Take a look at the key differences here and see what appeals to you.

FORMAL GARDENS

* Incorporate balanced and proportional shapes in planting and garden features.
* Usually contain straight planting lines, repeated patterns and lots of structure.
* Use evergreen hedging such as box and yew.
* Topiary is frequently a feature.
* Ponds and water features are often symmetrical.
* Fine manicured lawns, often with patterned stripes.
* Linear tree avenues in larger gardens.
* Single-bed planting themes, such as a rose bed.
* Very often a contrast of foliage and their textures as opposed to bright flowers.
* Straight rows in vegetable gardens.

INFORMAL GARDENS

Informal gardens include potagers (see page 32), cottage gardens and wildlife gardens. Many gardens have informal features, whether intentional or not, such as:

* Less structure than in formal gardens.
* Irregular beds with a mixture of different plants.
* Loose, flowing planting schemes.
* Lots of colour – often brighter than you find in formal gardens.
* Winding, curving paths with little symmetry.
* Wildlife ponds and irregular water features.
* Long grass and wildflower meadows, or patches of wildflowers in smaller gardens.
* Potagers and mixed planting in kitchen gardens.

Opposite: *This garden combines straight, formal lines and informal planting.* ***Right:*** *A typical cottage garden with a meandering path and loose, informal planting.*

COTTAGE GARDENS

Cottage gardens are usually considered a type of informal garden, with lots of 'relaxed' mixed planting. Very often, there are rustic features such as pergolas, arbours and stone walls, all made from traditional materials. Old brick paths, winding pathways and traditional cottage garden plants are used to create a nostalgic, bucolic atmosphere. Plants often include rambling roses trained on walls and fences, as well as self-sown perennials and annuals such as hollyhocks, verbascum, delphiniums, foxgloves, lupins, borage and cornflowers.

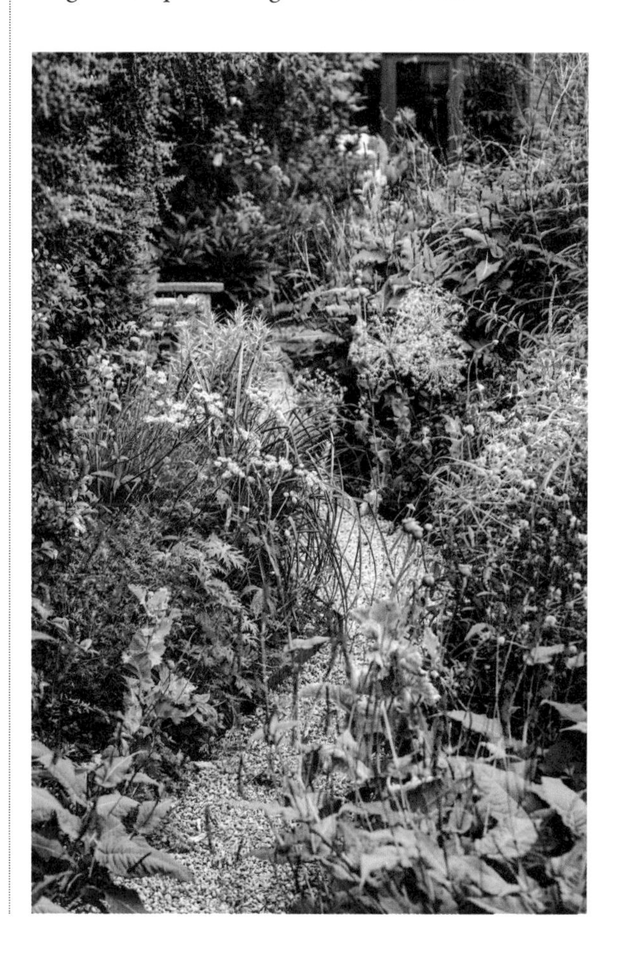

Grow your own food

Many people start gardening because they want to grow their own food. Not only does this mean they can enjoy a greater variety of mouthwatering fresh produce than is found in the supermarket, but growing your own is better for the environment as it reduces air miles. Growing fruit and vegetables can also help you save money and you can be sure that no artificial fertilizers or chemicals have been used.

A kitchen garden can look just as beautiful as any ornamental one. Many kitchen gardens produce colourful flowers/blossom, berries and fruits. The leaves of vegetables such as kale, lettuce, cabbages, asparagus and artichokes are just as eye-catching as ornamental foliage plants, while the structure of many trained fruit trees can be one of the most beautiful features in any garden.

ALLOTMENTS/COMMUNITY GARDENS

If you don't have space outside where you live to grow your own, you could consider renting an allotment. Rental prices can be very reasonable, and there is usually plenty of room to grow a significant

POTAGER PERFECTION

The term potager comes from the French word *potage*, which means 'soup', but is generally used to describe an ornamental or attractive kitchen garden that looks beautiful as well as being edible. This usually involves combining fruit, vegetables and herbs that have contrasting textures and flowers.

amount of food. Most sites will also allow you to put up a shed or greenhouse. Not only is it fun to have space to grow your own food, but it is a lovely place to meet like-minded gardeners and become involved with the local community. It is also useful for learning and exchanging tips with your allotment neighbours, and even for swapping seeds.

Some plots don't allow you to grow fruit trees, so it is worth checking with the allotment committee first. However, due to a rise in the popularity of growing your own food, you may need to join a waiting list for a plot. Contact your local council for lists of allotments in your area. Bear in mind that allotments can be time-consuming, so if you aren't sure you are going to be able to maintain a full-sized plot, you could consider renting a half-sized one, or even sharing one with somebody else.

DESIGNING WITH FRUIT AND VEG

* Use foliage-based edible plants to create a tapestry of textures, such as the ferny foliage of asparagus and the glaucous leaves of Savoy cabbages.
* Create structure with upright features such as fruit trees trained as espaliers, cordons or stepovers.
* Edge garden paths with scented herbs such as lavender and santolina.
* Provide evergreen structure by planting herbs like rosemary, sage, thyme and bay.
* Bright berries such as redcurrants, blackcurrants and pink currants or red gooseberries can look just as colourful as many flowers.
* Instead of laying a traditional lawn, consider using the aromatic camomile plant instead.
* If you don't have soil in your garden, use raised beds to create a simple kitchen garden.

***Opposite:** Raised beds can be used to grow vegetables in small gardens. **Right:** Most vegetables can be grown successfully in containers and look beautiful as well as being edible.*

EDIBLE BEAUTY

Don't forget that many flowers are edible too. Grow a few nasturtiums, geraniums or pansies for a colourful and tasty display.

The joys of sun and shade

When assessing a garden you need to work out the areas that will receive sunlight and those that will be in shade. In the northern hemisphere the sun rises in the east and sets in the west. A south-facing garden receives the most sunlight, while north-facing gardens get the least. In the southern hemisphere these light levels are the other way round. A garden with an eastern aspect receives cooler morning light and west-facing gardens get warmer evening sun. The warmest, hottest part of a garden will be facing southwest in summer. Even if your garden is very sunny or shady, there are lots of beautiful plants that will thrive there.

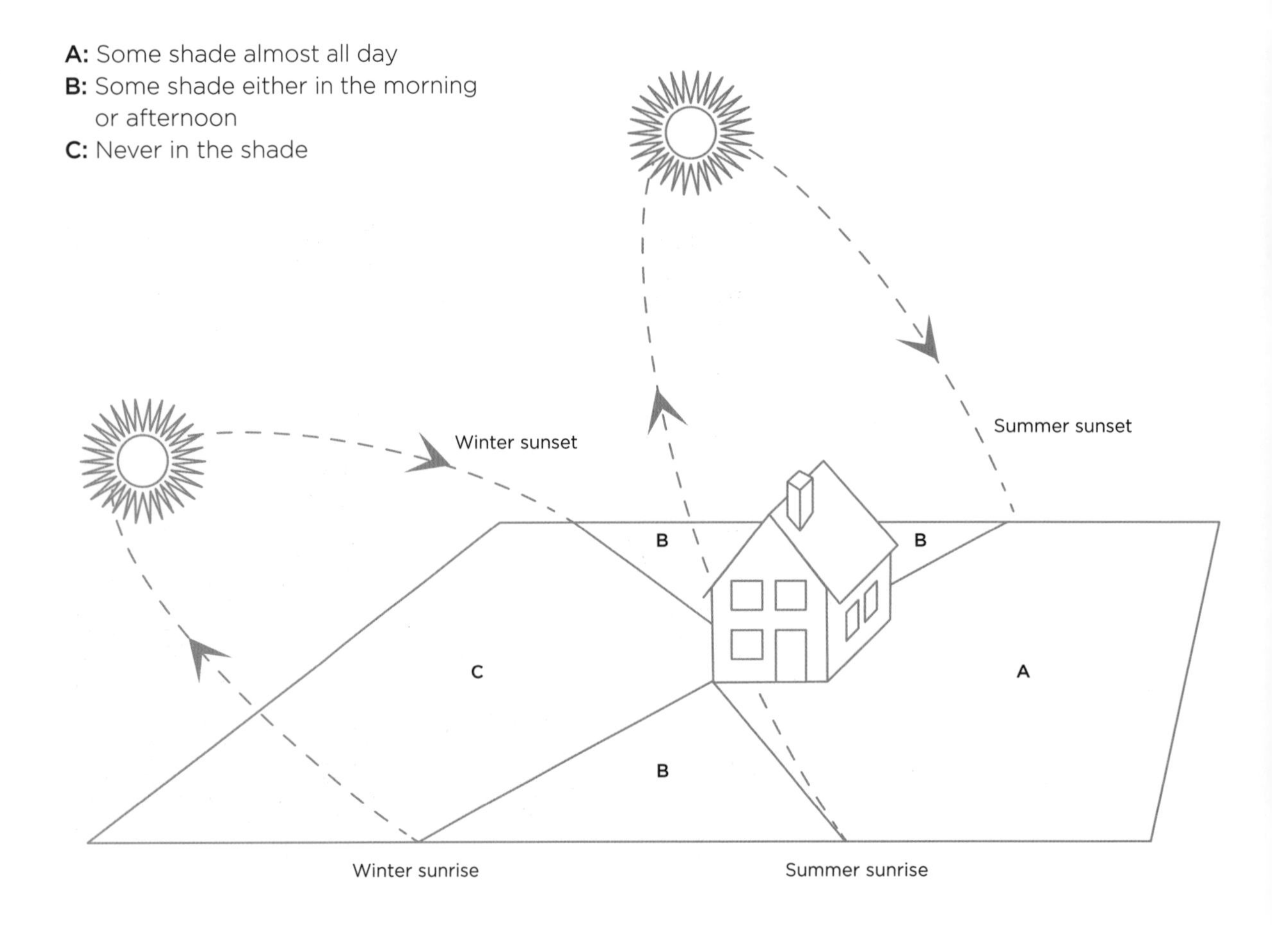

The direction in which a garden faces, or its aspect, is only part of the story with regard to how much light it receives. Nearby buildings, structures like fences and pergolas, and large trees and tall hedges all block out light, casting heavy shade even in the most southerly of gardens. This is often the case in courtyard gardens surrounded by buildings. You can do little about nearby houses, but trees and hedges can be pruned to reveal more light (speak nicely to your neighbour if their tree is blocking the sun).

To assess light levels, check at different times of day, as the sun traverses the sky in an arc, which means the light is constantly changing. The sun is also far lower in winter than in summer, which affects light levels too. Don't despair if you have a north-facing or very shady garden, as there are lots of plants for these areas, as well as for dappled, partial or light shade. These gardens are also a more comfortable temperature in summer and require less watering.

Choose plants that will tolerate shade if you are planting beneath a tree canopy.

GROWING BENEATH SHADE

The shade cast by deciduous and evergreen trees differs. Whereas evergreen shade is all year round, deciduous trees only provide shade later in the season once their leaves appear. Some plants such as bluebells take advantage of this, flowering early in natural woodlands to ensure they receive light before the tree canopy fully emerges. In the garden, try growing late-winter and spring-flowering bulbs like winter aconites, grape hyacinths, hyacinths, snowdrops and crocuses to beat the emergence of leaves on deciduous trees.

Enjoy the three climates

One of the biggest factors that determine the types of plants you can grow in your garden is the location. Most of us realize that the closer we live to the equator, the warmer the weather, allowing more tender or tropical plants to be grown. However, local conditions are far more complex than that, and there will be places further south with harsher, colder weather than some places in the north due to streams of warm winds.

MACROCLIMATE

This is the overall climate of a region or country. In large countries this would probably cover the entire state or country. For example in the USA, the macroclimate of Florida is much warmer than the macroclimate of Alaska, while in England the north is generally colder than the south. Knowing the overall macroclimate of your region is useful because it will guide you as to what plants you can grow. In the USA, the country is divided into climate zones, from 1 to 13, to inform gardeners and farmers which areas are the warmest and coldest. Being aware of the macroclimate of your region is essential for giving you a rough indication of what you will and won't be able to grow successfully in your garden.

MESOCLIMATE

This refers to localized weather conditions. It is equivalent to the difference between two towns situated a few miles apart. For example, one town might be several degrees warmer since it is at the top of a hill, while the other is lower down in a frost pocket. Factors that affect a mesoclimate include the elevation, gradient and aspect. If you want to know what plants you can grow, look at nearby gardens. They will have a similar mesoclimate. On the other hand, gardens in the next town, or at the other end of yours, might have some localized differences.

MICROCLIMATE

By far the most subtle of the climate types, the microclimate refers to the tiny differences in temperature in a garden. For example, it might be a couple of degrees warmer near the house than a few metres away. Or perhaps the temperature is milder near the pond than by a north-facing wall. It could even be the contrast between the shady side of a rock in a rockery and the other side in sunlight – a shade-loving plant would thrive in one, but perish in the other. The microclimate could be the difference between a plant surviving a frost or having a warm enough environment to flower. So, it is crucial to recognize where the warmer and colder areas are in your own garden. The good news is that you can manipulate a microclimate to a degree. For instance, shade can be created by growing a tree or erecting a shed, while sunlight can be increased by lowering a hedge or removing a branch that is casting shade.

Opposite: *Most types of fruit tree prefer to grow on warm, south- or southwest-facing walls.* ***Below:*** *Slate can be used as a mulch on the surface of containers.*

To subtly change the microclimate in your garden, use some white pebbles as a mulch under plants to reflect more light. Or, if you are growing a plant in a frost pocket, place some slate or another dark material underneath it, as this will absorb warmth in the day and might maintain the temperature enough during the night to help the plant survive.

TIPS ON KNOWING YOUR GARDEN

It is important to understand the conditions in different parts of your garden. Various features and objects will affect light levels and temperature. Select the right plants for these areas, and if they are tender, look for the warmest and most sheltered spots. Key areas of the garden to consider include:

- Side of house - can create a wind tunnel.
- Greenhouse/cold frame - ideal if you want to grow tender plants.
- Existing beds and borders - other plants can provide protection from the cold.
- Containers - can be susceptible to frosts since their roots are more exposed.
- Raised beds - provide better drainage, meaning the soil can warm up faster.
- Patios - can take longer to warm up due to the cold surface temperature.

Tip: Mulch the surface of the soil in winter to protect tender herbaceous perennials that have died back underground. The extra layer of insulation should help them reappear the following spring.

Frost and wind

No matter what the size of garden, various meteorological factors will determine whether a plant will thrive or struggle there. These include the aspect of the garden, the level of wind exposure and the amount of frost it receives, as well as the general climatic and localized conditions of the region. If your garden is exposed to wind or susceptible to frost, seek out plants that thrive in these conditions and appreciate the beauty of a frosty garden in winter.

TIPS ON FROST

Ways to protect your garden from frost include:

* Waiting as long as possible before planting young seedlings.
* Hardening off seedlings in a porch or cold frame for a few days before planting outside.
* Covering over vulnerable plants with fleeces or cloches if frost is predicted.

Frost can damage or even kill plants, so choose hardy types if your garden is prone to very cold weather and frost.

FROST

Frost can be a real killer when it comes to plants surviving in a garden. The most vulnerable time for plants is spring when seedlings are emerging from the ground and buds breaking from their dormancy. Cold sharp frosts in spring can destroy them, especially if plants have been lured out early due to unseasonably warm weather in the previous weeks.

Some gardens are more prone to frosts than others. While some of this is purely down to regional weather conditions, a garden may also have frost pockets, which can be better or worse depending on certain features. As warm air generally rises, areas of the garden in dips or valleys will usually take the brunt of the cold frost as it is exchanged with the rising warmer air. So, if your garden is at the bottom of a slope or hill, it will be more vulnerable. Sometimes frost will drift away if there is even lower ground to move to, but trees, hedges, walls, fences and buildings may stop the colder air moving away. Close proximity to areas of water such as rivers, lakes and even ponds can raise the temperatures slightly.

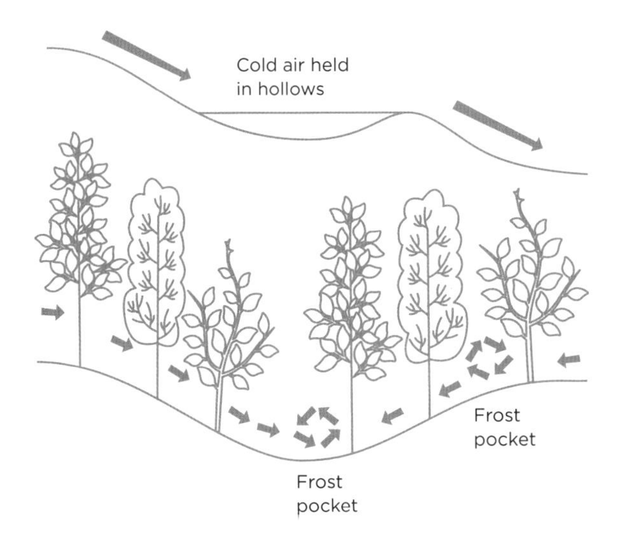

WIND

A strong or cold wind can quickly decimate a vulnerable plant. It is worth assessing a potential garden before planting to check where the prevailing wind comes from and whether the site is completely exposed or has some protection. You may wish to provide some hedges as windbreaks.

Some plants are more susceptible to wind damage than others, so check before buying. For example, the fine foliage of Japanese maples will be shredded by a harsh wind and so these should be avoided in an exposed garden. Conversely, plants like hawthorns, blackthorns and other hedging plants are fully hardy and can withstand the worst of the weather.

Plants can also suffer 'wind rock' when blown back and forth, which destroys their root systems. This is why plants like roses are lightly pruned in autumn to reduce their 'sail' when battered by winter winds. The wind in coastal regions can also be laden with salt which causes yet more damage. In these areas, choose plants that can tolerate a salty wind.

PROTECTING PLANTS FROM WIND

Windbreaks are the most effective way of protecting plants from wind damage. Hedges are the best solution, as they slowly filter the wind and reduce the speed and impact of the damage. Walls and fences may initially seem to provide protection, but they very often cause more damage, as the wind hits the top of the wall and then rebounds downwards, causing even faster eddies on the other side where the plants needing protection are growing. You can use man-made filter fences designed to slow down the wind, but these can look unsightly.

STEP-BY-STEP TECHNIQUE

GET TO KNOW YOUR SOIL

Knowing what type of garden soil you have is key as this will dictate whether a plant thrives or struggles. A plant grown in the wrong soil will be sickly and may even perish. Before planting anything in the ground, it is worth testing the texture of the soil to see if it is sand, clay or silt, as this will determine if it will be free-draining and fertile. You can also test the acidity of the soil, which again will influence the plants you can grow successfully.

Soil is usually divided into three categories – clay, sand and silt – depending on the size of the soil particles. Clay soil has the smallest particles, and so drains poorly, but has good water and nutrient retention. Sandy soil is the opposite, with a gritty texture and large particles that allow for good drainage, but does not hold onto nutrients well. Something in between clay and sand is silt. You can do a textural analysis test (see opposite) to see whether a soil is clay, sand or silt. Loam is the ideal soil type, being a good balance of the three.

You can change or 'improve' all three soil textures by adding organic matter. This opens up the spaces between the tiny particles in clay soils, which improves drainage. Added to sandy or silty soils, it binds the large soil particles together, helping them to absorb water and hold nutrients for longer. You may think adding grit to a clay soil would improve the drainage, but it can have the opposite effect, binding the tiny, sticky particles and making it set like rock.

Soil can also be tested for acidity. Some plants prefer a slightly acidic soil, whereas others like neutral or alkaline conditions. Soil acidity is measured with a pH soil testing kit (available online or from garden stores). These are easy to use and give fairly reliable readings. However, if you are investing a lot of time and money in your garden, you can send soil samples to a soil-testing laboratory for more accurate results. A pH reading of 7 is neutral, whereas anything lower is considered acidic and higher is alkaline. The ideal soil would be somewhere between 6.5 and 7.5. Plants that prefer slightly acidic soil (pH 5 to 6.5) include rhododendrons, camellias, magnolias, blueberries and some heathers. Those that thrive in alkaline soil (pH over 7) include lilac, lavender, cotinus, lily of the valley, honeysuckle and verbascum.

Lime is often used to raise soil pH, following the application rate given on the packet. Wood ash is a natural alternative, but not as long-lasting. Apply about a shovel load to every square metre.

YOU WILL NEED

* Soil sample for testing
* Deep saucer
* Watering can

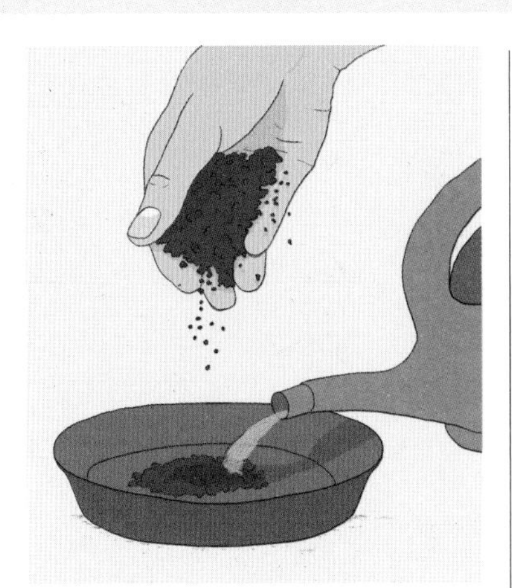

1. Dig up a handful of soil from the area of garden you wish to test and place it in a saucer. Add a little water to make the soil slightly damp, then stir until you have a moist paste.

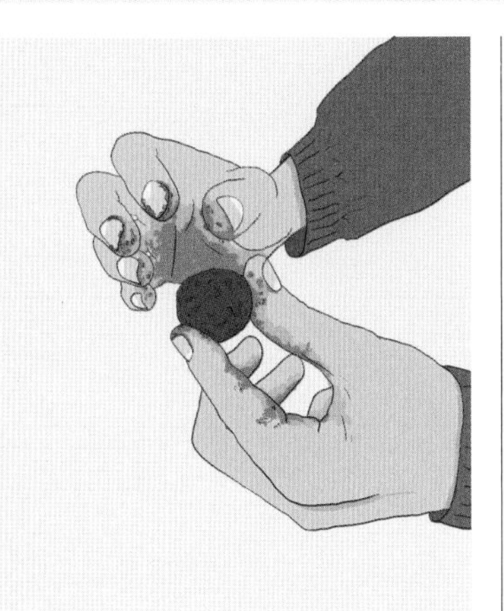

2. Mould the soil sample into a ball – about the size of a table tennis ball – and leave to dry out for a few minutes.

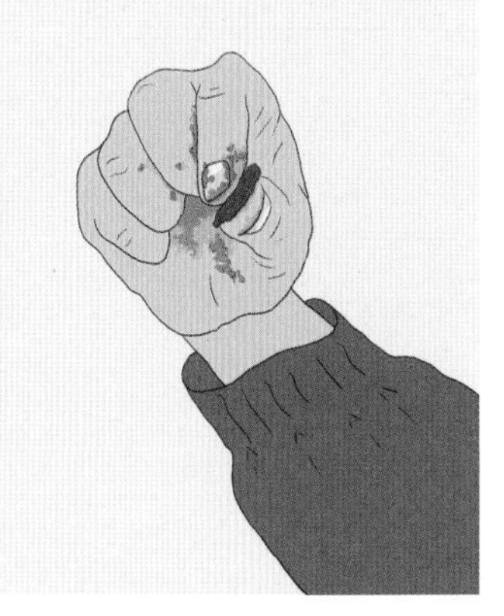

3. Press the ball lightly between your forefinger and thumb. If it crumbles immediately, almost to the touch, then the sample is a sand-based soil.

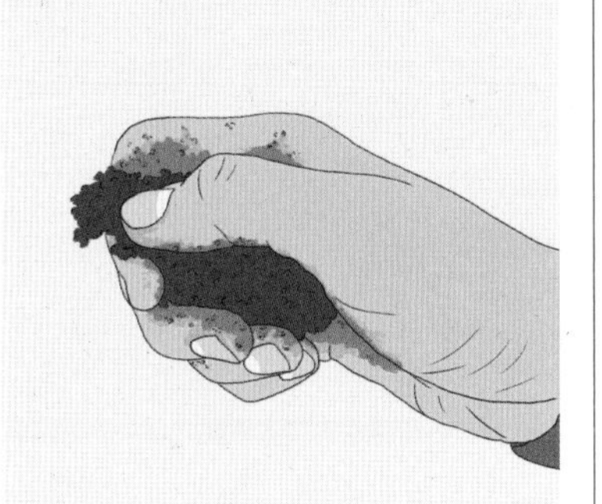

4. Next, try to roll the ball out into a ribbon or worm shape. If the ball crumbles, then the sample is a silt-based soil.

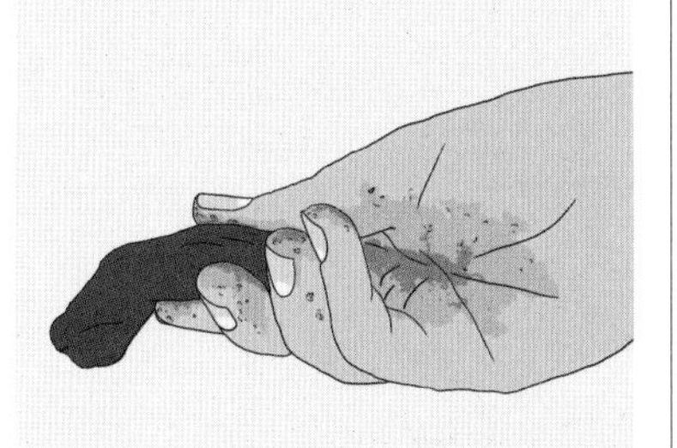

5. If the soil still holds its form when rolled into a ribbon or worm shape, then the sample is a clay-based soil.

ERICACEOUS PLANTS

Plants that prefer acidic soil are often referred to as 'ericaceous'. This word is derived from the genus name for a group of heathers, *Erica*, which like acidic conditions. If you want to grow 'ericaceous' plants, but have alkaline soil, you might want to consider growing them in containers, using peat-free, ericaceous potting compost. However, some heathers, such as *Erica carnea* and *E.* x *darleyensis*, can be grown in neutral or alkaline soils.

CHAPTER 3

GARDEN DESIGN

This chapter explores how to make the most of your outside space using clever tricks of the trade to create a perfect garden. We begin by looking at the garden as a three-dimensional space and at the concept of perspective, as it is amazing how placing plants or objects in the foreground, background or in a row can alter the way a garden is viewed. A careful positioning of key features such as paths, patios, seating areas, raised beds, sheds and even compost heaps can be used to make the space feel more inviting and comfortable too.

This chapter also explains how to create decorative beds and borders and use focal points successfully, and examines the key role that colour and texture play in the mood of a garden, being able to excite or soothe, depending on what colour palette you choose.

There are suggestions for how to create a hidden nook if you crave a peaceful seating area in the garden. Also included is guidance on how to create height because, let's face it, not all of us have lots of horizontal space at our disposal. Finally, there is a step-by-step explanation of how to create a garden design plan, so you can pull all these tips together.

Your garden as a 3-D space

When creating a garden, remember that it is a three-dimensional space, with a length, width and height. So, it is worth considering these as well as the garden's perspective, or how it looks when viewed from different angles. You can use a few basic design tricks to alter the perspective of a garden. Wide gardens can be made to feel longer and thinner, for example, and narrow gardens wider. Even the smallest of spaces can feel much bigger if they are cleverly designed.

Most people view their garden from the back of the house or when entering it from the back door. So, this is a good starting point when determining how to design the shape and sightlines of your garden and what features you would like to include, such as paths and patios, specimen trees or other structures like arches, arbours and pergolas. However, you also need to think about how the garden looks from other angles. For example, try viewing it from a bedroom or study overlooking the garden where you spend a lot of time reading or working. Not only do such viewpoints provide a lovely bird's-eye view, but you can also design shapes that look attractive when viewed from above. The reflections in ponds, for instance, can be admired more easily from upstairs.

Also consider how the garden looks when viewed from the seating areas or even the angle from an arbour or summerhouse. And don't forget that your garden will look different as the seasons change, so bear that in mind when selecting plants. You could include a deciduous tree such as rowan (*Sorbus aucuparia*) or crab apple (*Malus sylvestris*) that has spring blossom, autumn colour and also berries.

THE LONG AND SHORT OF IT

Perspective is how a garden looks when you stand or sit and view it from different positions. Luckily, you can manipulate the perspective to change how the garden appears, like a magician using sleight of hand.

If a garden is long and narrow, you can make it feel wider by placing features across its breadth. For example, a low hedge or path leading from once side to the other will draw the eye outwards to the perimeter of the garden, instead of to the end, making the space feel broader. Or a wide garden can be made to look longer by creating pathways and rows of plants leading up through the space.

To exaggerate the length of a garden, try tapering a path as it leads towards the far end or place repeating features such as standard roses or upright trees along the length of the space, with slightly shorter versions closer to the house and taller ones towards the end in ever-increasing sizes. Simply take the opposite approach if you want to foreshorten the perspective because the garden looks too long, using taller plants at the front and shorter ones in ever-decreasing sizes towards the back.

A garden can be made to appear larger if part of it is obscured, creating a sense of intrigue. Here the garden seems to continue around the corner, inviting visitors to explore.

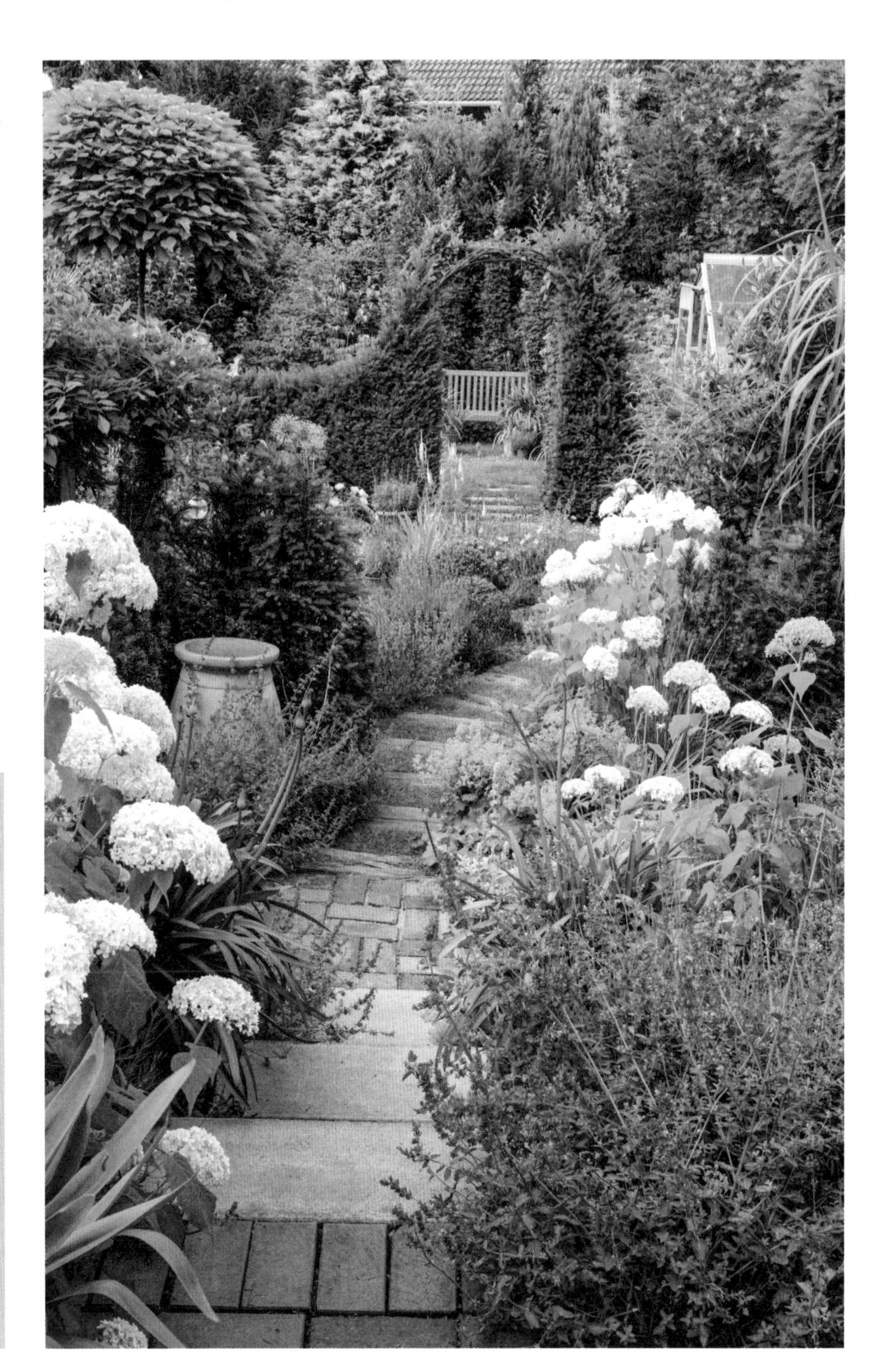

COLOUR TRICKS

You can use colour in the garden to alter perception of its size. If you use hot or warm colours, such as red, pink and orange, in the border, they will feel closer to the house than they really are. Conversely, cooler colours like white, blue and green will feel further away.

Follow the path...

Paths are practical features, enabling you to move from one garden area to another, but there is far more to them than just functionality. They can also be a key part of a design by visually linking different parts of the garden. You can use a path to create a journey from one area of interest to another and to add exciting patterns and shapes.

Long, sinewy, curvy or twisting paths can be used to extend your journey through a garden. This is a useful technique in a small plot, as it makes the space feel bigger. You can exaggerate the feeling of more space by creating a path that leads out of sight. Even if the destination is just a hidden compost heap, this not only creates a sense of mystery, but also makes the garden feel as if it extends elsewhere and is therefore much larger than it really is.

Straight lines, on the other hand, give the design a structured backbone. Lots of great gardens are organized around a straight axis, bisecting the space at key points. Try running a path across the garden to create a sense of width and draw the eye outwards, or up the length of the garden towards a focal point.

PATH MATERIALS

The materials used for a path can bring further interest to plants and other features. The choice of material can also influence the ambience of a space.

WOOD CHIPS Paths made from wood chips are ideal for informal gardens, especially beneath a tree canopy or between bulbs in woodland areas in larger gardens. The material is also cheap, and local tree surgeons may be happy to give you a trailer of wood chips. If not, bags can bought from garden centres or ordered online. Wood chip paths are easy to construct. Just level the ground where the path is to run and spread the chips to a depth of about 6cm (2¼in). The path will need topping up every year or two, as the chips will slowly decompose. Edging the path with branches on each side will prevent the wood chips spreading onto beds and borders.

GRAVEL Suitable for formal and informal settings, gravel comes in different sizes and colours, the most popular being pea shingle. It is fairly cheap to buy, compared with paving and stone. To make a path, spread the gravel on a membrane or landscape fabric to prevent it being absorbed into the soil beneath. It is advisable to edge a gravel path, perhaps with brick or wood, to stop the gravel migrating elsewhere.

GRASS A verdant grass path is soft to walk on and pleasing to the eye. It is also quite easy and cheap to build, either by sowing grass seed or laying turf, but will need mowing regularly. Choose a hardwearing grass like rye that can cope with the level of footfall.

STONE AND BRICK Athough expensive, stone and brick paths are the most durable, meaning they are low-maintenance. Some types of stone, like York stone, can be costly, but there are cheaper options. Recycled bricks give a cottage-garden feel, whereas newer bricks and pavers are very contemporary.

Opposite: *Gravel paths are easy to lay and make a space feel informal.* ***Right:*** *Wood is a warm, natural material and can be used to good effect in both modern and traditional gardens.*

Raised beds

Raised beds are often used for growing vegetables and herbs, although many other plants can be grown in them too. They provide a much more comfortable height for gardening than if you are growing directly in the ground, as there is no need for bending over and straining the back. Raised beds are ideal for people with mobility issues or just those who like to be more comfortable when working.

A raised bed is simply an elevated area of ground or soil for growing plants, which is usually contained within a wooden frame. If you decide to grow plants in this way, there are so many benefits as follows:

* The soil or compost in raised beds will not become compacted because it is not walked on.
* Soil or compost warms up faster than in the open garden since the bed is raised off the ground.
* More comfortable for working.
* No need to edge raised beds, unlike those in lawns, which need constant work to prevent grass encroaching.
* Raised beds have better drainage.
* Can provide a design feature, offering structure to a garden.
* Are a good solution if your garden has poor soil or there are problems with pests and diseases.

Raised beds can be filled with topsoil, general-purpose potting compost or homemade garden compost. This means you can choose a soil suitable for the plants you wish to grow. For example, for growing herbs you can add lots of horticultural grit to the compost to improve the drainage. Alternatively, if you want to grow cranberries or blueberries, then use peat-free ericaceous compost and mix with rotted pine needles (to lower the pH).

If your garden has been suffering from an infestation of a particularly pernicious perennial weed such as bindweed or ground elder, or the soil seems to be harbouring a disease such as club root, then building a raised bed away from these areas may provide a solution for growing in fresh new soil.

Raised beds are also usually more productive than if you are gardening directly in the ground because the soil warms up faster and has better drainage, which means it does not stay wet and cold for long. They can be built on hard surfaces such as patios or concrete, but will drain much better if they are placed directly over soil or on a lawn.

BUILDING A RAISED BED

Some raised beds are literally just one timber's width high, or about 20cm (8in). However, if you have mobility issues or a poor back, then you may want a higher bed. The height of a table is probably the most comfortable position for the majority of people. Just bear in mind that the higher the bed, the more garden compost you will need to fill it.

An ideal size for a raised bed is no wider than 1.5m (5ft). This should enable you to reach into the bed from all sides to maintain the plants. You can buy beds in kit form and construct them on site, but they can easily be made from scratch too:

* A cheaper alternative to a kit is to build your own raised bed by screwing pressure-treated lengths of timber to four corner posts for a rectangular bed.
* Raised beds can also be constructed from bricks or breeze blocks, although this requires a certain amount of skill to mortar the material together.
* For smaller areas, lots of repurposed materials can be used to make a raised bed, which is then filled with your choice of soil or compost. This includes piles of rubber tyres, large dumpy bags (made of polypropelene) or wooden pallets screwed together and lined with a permeable fabric.

Opposite: *Raised beds can be made from a range of materials, including concrete.* ***Below:*** *Characterful wooden fruit crates can be repurposed into a collection of small raised beds.*

Keyhole gardening

A keyhole garden is a variation of a traditional raised bed. It is in the shape of a keyhole when viewed from above and has a compost heap in the centre. This sustainable gardening system reduces the need for watering or feeding with fertilizers as in the open garden. Keyhole gardens are cheap to make and require minimal DIY skills. You end up with a fertile soil that is perfect for both vegetables and ornamental plants. A keyhole garden is also a great talking point in the garden.

Keyhole gardens are often made from rocks, but other materials such as wood, or in this case bricks, can also be used.

A keyhole garden is usually round with a pie-shaped 'slice' or walkway cut from it. This access point means that you can easily reach the centre of the compost heap. The heap is the heart of this sustainable system, which gradually leaches nutrients into the surrounding soil in the raised bed, reducing the need to use fertilizer. The moisture from the heap also reduces the need to water.

The idea for keyhole gardening originated in Lesotho, in South Africa, where local people working on poor or infertile soil would build keyhole gardens using materials found for free in the surrounding landscape, usually rocks and stones. The compost heap in the centre of the bed would be regularly topped up with organic material and this would leach into the soil, thus increasing the fertility and reducing the need to water.

Traditionally, the heap would have been made from a permeable material such as reed or straw which would allow the nutrients from it to leach out slowly. These days, keyhole beds can be made from any material, including bricks or timber, but the usual material is stone because it is easy to stack and build into the keyhole shape. You can also adjust the size of the bed to suit the dimensions of your garden.

HOW TO BUILD A KEYHOLE GARDEN

1. Mark a circle with a diameter of 3m (10ft) and then cut out a triangular segment, in the shape of a pie slice, from the outside to the centre.
2. Push three or four upright wooden posts inside the area to create a circular compost heap in the centre with a diameter of about 50cm (20in). Wrap a 60-cm (2-ft) high length of chicken wire around the posts to make the heap. Use wire clippers to cut a 20 x 20cm (8 x 8in) 'flap' in the bottom of the wire for emptying the compost if necessary.
3. Use rocks or stones to create the outside retaining wall to a height of 50cm (20in). They can just be stacked on top of each other, although will be stronger if mortared with cement. Also stack rocks or stones on either side of the walkway leading to the central compost bin to a height of 50cm (20in).
4. Fill the outer bed with organic material such as garden compost and soil. The surface of this material should be higher at the centre and lower near the retaining wall to allow nutrients to gravitate outwards and downwards.
5. Fill the compost heap with compostable material and keep adding organic waste (see pages 100–1). When the compost is ready, spread it on the surface of the soil.
6. Plant with young vegetable plants and grow as usual, but hopefully with less watering or feeding required.

Decorative beds and borders

One of the most important considerations when designing a garden is the shape of the beds and borders. Most small to medium-sized gardens have long, narrow, rectangular borders that frame the outside edges of a courtyard or lawn. However, there are lots of other exciting shapes you can use to bring your garden alive.

ADD A CURVE

Instead of a straight border, try creating a sweeping curve. To ensure this approach works well, you need to be bold and exaggerate the line. A gentle bend in the border will either just go unnoticed or look as if your straight lines are crooked. So, consider bringing a curve right across half the garden, starting at the back and bringing it down into something much narrower towards the house. You then have a border with lots of exciting depth and a lovely wide corner at the back of the garden to add plants with height.

ADD DEPTH

Make the borders in your garden nice and deep. If possible, the borders can cover almost half the area. With deep borders you will feel as if you are in among the flowers when sitting outside. Big and bold borders will completely transform the experience of being in your garden.

ISLAND BEDS

Flower borders do not have to be pushed up against the sides of the garden as if something has forced them to one side. Instead, create island beds that you can walk around and explore. These will make the space feel more dynamic. Try laying a length of garden hose on the lawn or patio to create the design before cutting out the bed to work out what shape you prefer and what will work best in the space.

Focal points

A garden usually benefits from having one or more focal points. A focal point will draw the eye towards a purposefully positioned object or feature and help to unify the surrounding landscape. Whether you are walking towards or just looking at the focal point, it will give the eye something to rest on, thereby creating meaning and giving context to an otherwise empty space.

POSITIONING A FOCAL POINT

Focal points can be used to pull a garden design together. They draw the eye in certain directions, which helps with the flow of the space and how it is perceived. For example, if the garden has an unsightly shed or compost heap, an interesting focal point on the other side, or even just past it, will draw attention away from the ugliness and direct the view towards a more attractive feature.

One of the most effective places to position a focal point is at the end of a path. If a path just ends in a dead end, the walk can feel pointless. You can also site a focal point where two or more paths converge, at the end of a border, as a feature on a lawn, or in the centre of an island bed.

IDEAS FOR FOCAL POINTS

A focal point can be anything, as long as it stands out and is strategically placed to draw the eye. Statues, for example, have been used for centuries as focal points. But a statue doesn't have to be large and grand – it can also be modest, small and just enough to catch your attention. Other ideas for focal points include:

∗ Sundial ∗ Garden pond or water fountain ∗ Plant in a pot or a cluster of plants ∗ Impressive specimen plant ∗ Specimen lawn tree – perhaps weeping or fastigiate in habit, or with good autumn colour ∗ Bench or chair ∗ Wall- or fence-mounted picture or water fountain ∗ Free-standing piece of sculpture or art ∗ Bird table or bird bath

Opposite: Putting curves into a path adds interest to an otherwise linear design. Right: A feature at the end of a path draws the eye.

Enjoying colour and texture

Colour in the garden is one of the key factors that influence our mood. Texture is important too. This is crucial to remember if you are trying to create a specific ambience or atmosphere. Of course, colour is not just provided by flowers. The materials used to create garden features like paths, walls, fences and water features, for example, also add colour and texture. By carefully planning planting schemes you can create a garden that either excites or soothes you.

THE COLOUR WHEEL

When designing a garden, use a colour wheel to work out which colours complement each other and which ones clash. A colour wheel is based on three primary colours (red, yellow and blue) – they sit next to the secondary colours (orange, green and violet) and the tertiary colours (red-orange, yellow-orange; yellow-green, blue-green; and blue-violet, red-violet). To create a strong contrast, try juxtaposing two complementary colours opposite each other on the wheel, such as, yellow and violet. For a subtle effect, use colours next to each other.

Planting groups are always best in threes, or other odd numbers. So, try using a trio of colours, one from each third of the colour wheel and evenly spaced, to create an exciting colour combination.

Don't forget that fruit and berries also provide a range of hues. The foliage of evergreen shrubs or even lawns can be useful, providing a verdant, yet neutral backdrop to show off brighter colours.

The table opposite offers guidance on selecting colours to create different moods, whether you opt for a calming palette or a vibrant one. If you have room, try using both palettes, starting with calming colours and moving on to vibrant ones, before gently restoring the tranquil mood again. Play around with colours to see how they affect your mood.

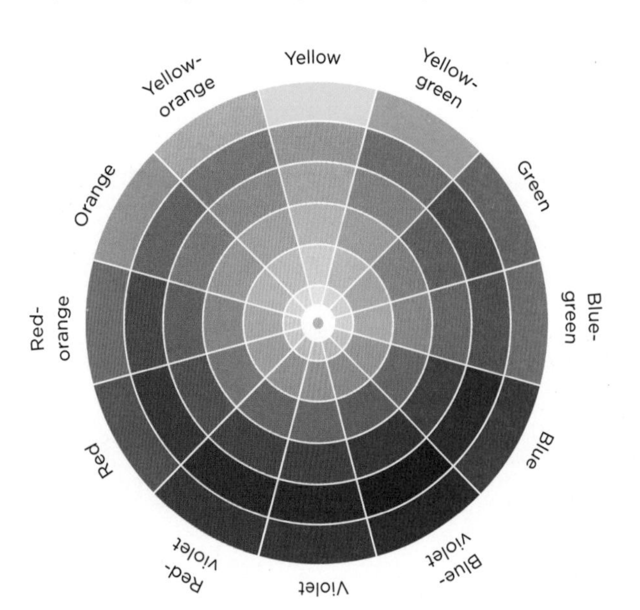

Using a colour wheel when selecting plants can help you visualize which colours will clash with or complement each other.

CREATING A PLANTING SCHEME

You can draw on the power of colour to manipulate the mood of a garden, whether you are looking for an upbeat atmosphere using hot colours or a soothing one with pale colours. Consider the effect of the seasons on the colour scheme as well as the impact of texture.

Tranquillity Pastel or muted colours generally have a relaxing, soothing effect on the garden. Use soft versions of white, cream, greens, blues and mauves to evoke serenity and tranquillity. Avoid clashing colours and plant in blocks that transition gently and gradually through the soft hues.

Vibrancy Use hot colours to create exciting flower borders with a buzz. Colours can include reds, oranges, yellows and pinks. The brighter, the better. Don't be scared to jumble the colours up to create some liveliness.

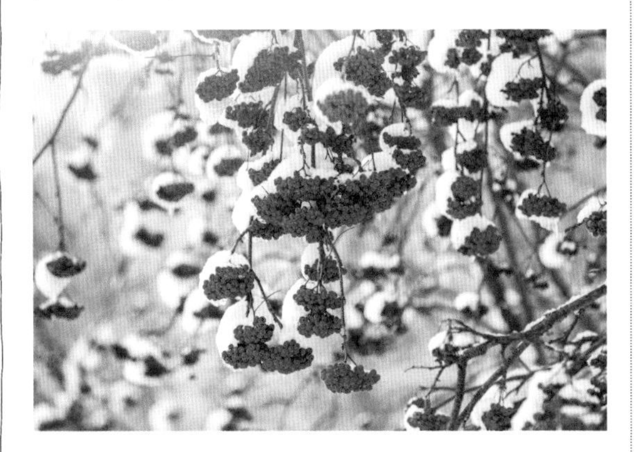

Seasonality Consider the seasons in a colour plan. Plants with autumn foliage and berries come into their own later in the year, while others work their magic in spring, then return to insignificance. Anticipating which colours appear when involves planning, and it may take a few seasons to see how the plants and landscaping work together through the year.

Texture This can also be used to striking effect in a border. Whether it is spiky cacti, the plumes of ornamental grasses or the feathery fronds of ferns, plants with different textures can be used to create a rich tapestry and knit planting schemes together.

A garden for relaxation

Gardening is not just hard physical graft. It is also about taking time out to relax and enjoy the surrounding space. One of the best ways to do this is to create an inviting seating area. This might be anything from a wooden bench to a soft hammock swinging from a tree. It could include tables and chairs for alfresco dining or a reclining sunlounger. Garden sofas and beanbags are also available made from hardwearing outdoor fabric, so they can withstand the weather.

SEATING AREAS

Position benches so you can enjoy the best views of the garden. Even in a small garden or courtyard, it is far more pleasant to be looking out over a flowerbed or containers full of flowers, or even at a focal point. Alternatively, benches can be positioned for watching wildlife such as birds on feeders, ensuring they are far enough away not to disturb them.

You should also consider whether you want to sit in sun or shade, and position the seating area accordingly. If the garden is large enough, you could strategically place some areas to catch the early morning sun for enjoying breakfast or a coffee, and another facing south or southwest for evening relaxing and entertainment. For alfresco dining, it can make life a lot easier if the seating area is near the house, so that plates, cutlery, food and drink can be easily moved outside and back indoors again.

OVERHEAD COVER

A pergola or arbour above a seating area is a great way to create shade from the midday sun in summer. You can also train climbing plants up the posts and along the top. Planting evening-scented flowers, such as evening primrose (*Oenothera biennis*), tobacco plant (*Nicotiana sylvestris*) or perhaps night-scented phlox (*Zaluzianskya ovata*), can enhance the magical experience of sitting outside on a warm summer's evening.

HIDDEN NOOKS

Screening off a seating area can create a delightful hidden nook. If there is a little corner somewhere in your garden, then try planting hedging around it to create a sense of seclusion. Alternatively, make a living willow arbour by inserting young shoots (known as withies), spaced at intervals of 10cm (4in), in the ground around the seat. As they grow, the withies can be woven and pulled together at the top to form a little canopy.

For instant screening, fences and trellis can be erected. If you already have an established hedge, or thicket of bamboo, carve out a seating area by pruning a gap with loppers or a saw. This feature will need regular maintenance to stop the plant regrowing and encroaching on the seating area.

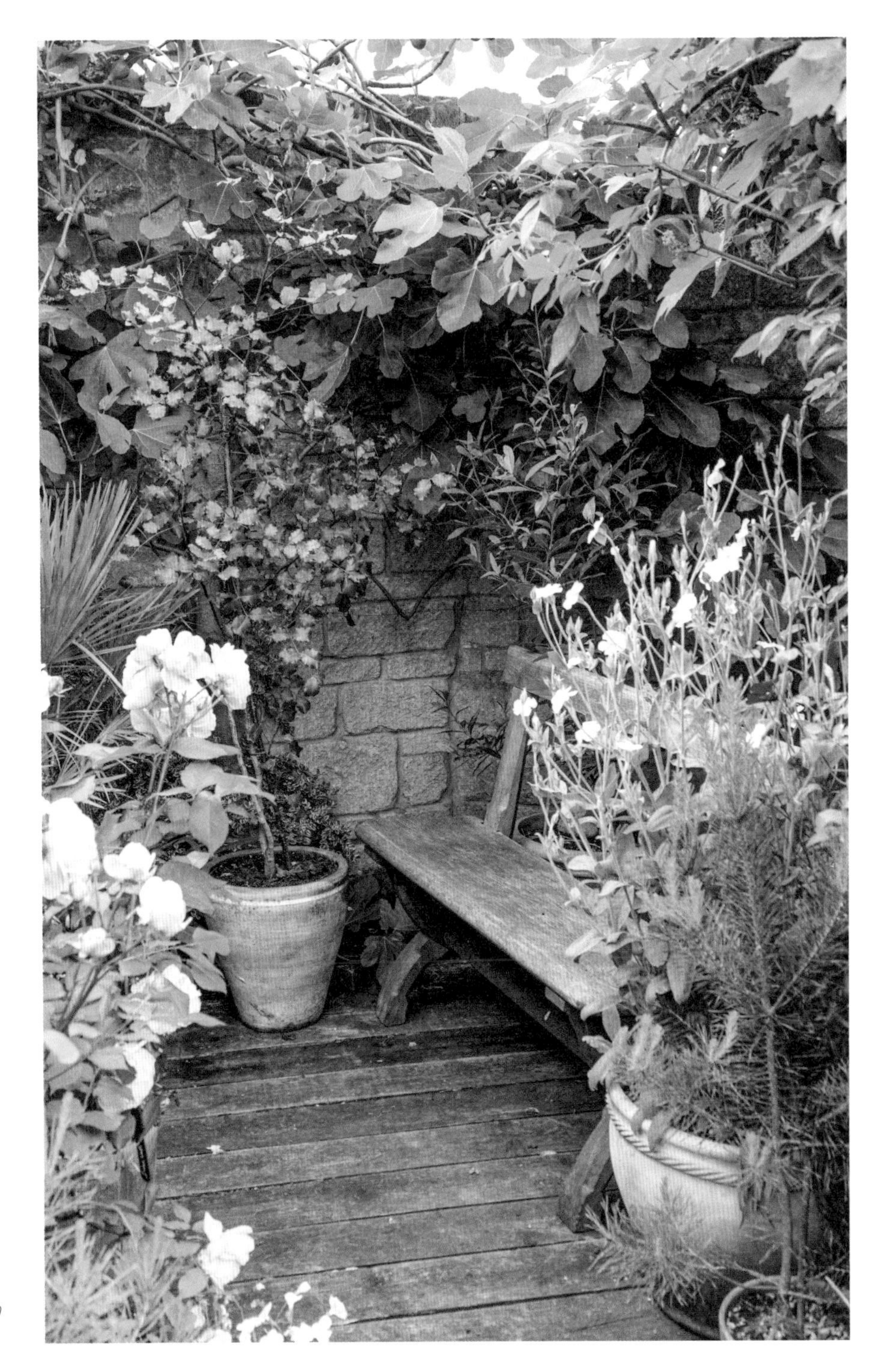

A peaceful nook can be created simply by surrounding a bench with some attractive plants.

Make the most of the vertical

One of the key stages when creating a garden is to add some height. Without it, a space can feel flat and uninspiring. Vertical elements will lift the eyes upwards and make a garden feel larger and more dynamic. Not only is adding height good design practice, it can also be a practical solution to creating more planting space. This is particularly useful in small gardens where the ground surface area is limited.

Look at the perimeter of the garden, including fences, walls and even the back of the house. These spaces can be utilized for growing plants. You can either grow climbers directly on them, or fix planting modules to the walls and grow individual plants in the pockets. Planting modules for walls are available in a range of sizes and some have the advantage of being self-watering.

Planting a tree or shrub is one of the more obvious ways to add height. Choose a tree with a 'fastigiate', or columnar, shape if horizontal space is at a premium, as these trees are much narrower and take up less space. Alternatively, pleached hedging is useful for growing plants in parts of the garden that would otherwise be empty. The plants in a pleached hedge are trained as single bare trunks to a height of about 1.5m (5ft) and then the canopy is trained horizontally outwards.

It is not only trees and shrubs that can add height. Many tall herbaceous plants can also be grown for dramatic effect. Plants such as sunflowers, delphiniums and hollyhocks can be used at the back of a flowerbed and fill a vertical space nicely.

Repeat the perennials regularly down the length of the border to punctuate the design. Occasionally, drift taller plants towards the front to create further interest.

Climbing plants can be trained up wigwams. Place these strategically at regular intervals in a border for maximum effect.

Archways, arbours and pergolas are also suitable structures for growing plants upwards and adding height to the garden. Archways also provide extra space for training plants up and along. In addition, they are useful for enticing visitors to move from one area of the garden to another and for framing a view.

If you are going to walk through an archway regularly, then it is best to avoid thorny plants such as rambling roses, but they are ideal for grapevines and kiwi plants, or scented plants like chocolate vine (*Akebia quinata*), star jasmine (*Trachelospermum jasminoides*) or climbing honeysuckles (*Lonicera*).

Opposite: *Rustic trellis can add height and interest to an otherwise featureless corner.* ***Left:*** *Archways trained with plants provide extra growing space and make attractive features in their own right.*

The hardworking garden

For most of us, designing a garden is not just about creating a beautiful space as it usually needs to be functional too. We have to think about incorporating paths, patios and storage areas for tools, bikes and other materials, perhaps in a shed or lockable boxes. Compost heaps, greenhouses, vegetable patches, bins, washing lines and parking may also need to be considered. With careful planning, these features do not have to encroach on the beauty of the garden.

DECORATE THE SHED

For anything larger than a courtyard garden, sheds are essential for storing tools and other paraphernalia. These structures can be beautiful as well as practical, so they do not necessarily have to be tucked away in a corner. Consider painting them in a colour that enhances the planting schemes of the garden. They can be turned into beautiful features, with ornate gables, thatched or tiled roofs, pretty porches and lots of other attractive elements.

If you're short of space, you can grow plants up the side of a shed. Rambling roses, *Wisteria sinensis* or *Clematis montana* can quickly transform a dull shed into an object of beauty. For autumn colour, consider covering the shed with Virginia creeper (*Parthenocissus quinquefolia*), which turns a striking crimson red just as the weather becomes colder.

Right: *Link practical spaces in the garden such as sheds and bins with hard paths for easy access.* ***Opposite left:*** *Make sure a compost bin is easy to reach from the kitchen or garden.* ***Opposite right:*** *Rotating composters are designed to turn over compost easily and speed up decomposition.*

BUILD A COMPOST HEAP

Composting is essential for most gardens because the material produced by a compost heap can be used to feed and nourish the soil. Composting also provides an environmentally sustainable way of recycling any garden material and fruit and vegetable clippings from the kitchen. In most gardens, compost heaps are hidden around the back somewhere out of sight. If the heap literally consists of a few wooden pallets nailed together with some nails, then that is possibly the best place for it. However, there are many modern compost bins that look chic and contemporary and can be used as garden features in their own right. You can also purchase rotating drums in bright, attractive colours and these can take pride of place on the patio.

OTHER PRACTICAL CONSIDERATIONS

If you are going to have an unsightly compost heap tucked away somewhere, it is worth trying to keep it close to the house, to save you having to walk too far with kitchen waste. It's also worth laying a hard path, made of bricks or patio slabs, leading directly to the compost heap, so wheelbarrows of garden waste can easily be pushed along it.

SCREENING

If you need to hide unattractive features in your garden, then the quickest solution is a fence panel. Alternatively, try installing some trellis and growing an evergreen climber on it. Evergreen hedging is also a good solution, but takes a few years to become established, unless the initial plants are large.

STEP-BY-STEP TECHNIQUE

MAKE A GARDEN PLAN

Planning a garden is always exciting, but it will save time in the long run if you make a plan first before sticking a spade in the ground. If you have inherited a garden, and have the time, it is worth observing it for a full year before starting, as you may have plants that only reveal themselves at certain times. It is also better to wait and think about how you will use the space, as things may change in the first few months.

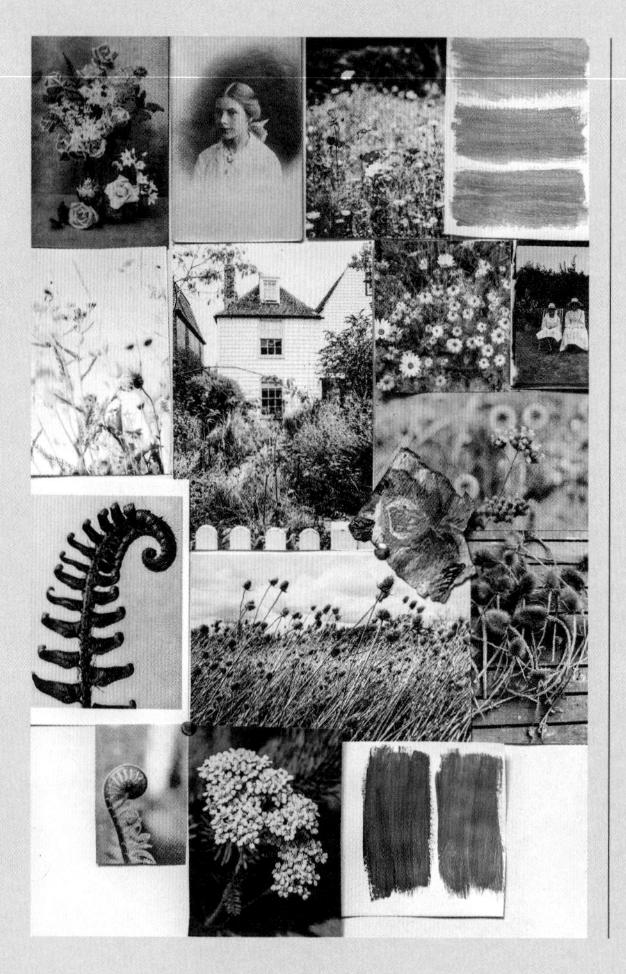

A completely empty garden is usually the easiest space to take on, as you have a blank canvas and no alterations need to be made before you start. A garden is also easier to plan when it is all laid bare before you. However, in existing gardens, there could well be particular features you wish to retain and some beautiful specimen plants that would definitely be worth keeping.

YOU WILL NEED

* Notepad and pen
* Large piece of paper
* pH soil testing kit
* Pinboard and pictures for a mood board
* Tape measure
* Hard-landscaping materials
* Selection of suitable plants

Creating a mood board can help you decide on an overall design and theme for your garden.

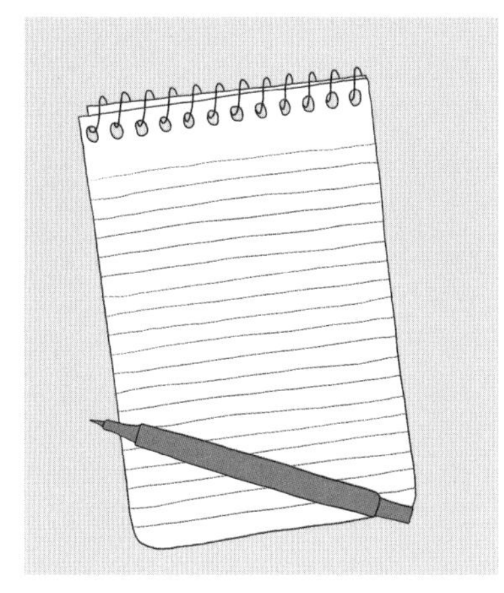

1. Make a list of all the essential features the garden will need, such as washing lines, a shed, a bin area, compost heaps, bike storage and water butts, as well as where you would like paths and seating areas.

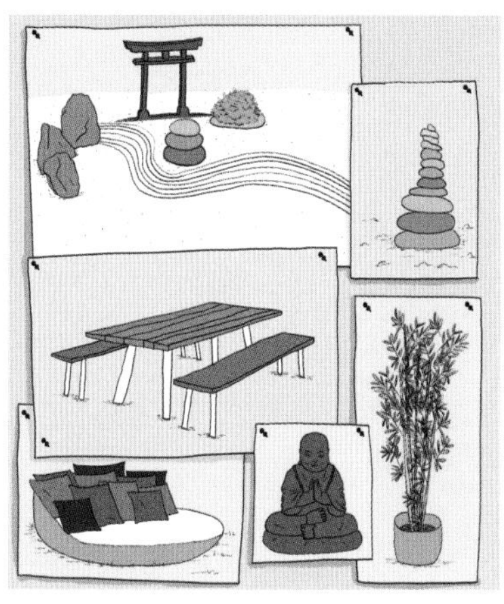

2. Decide on the style of garden you would prefer, whether this is formal, modern or low-maintenance or perhaps a cottage or kitchen garden. Creating a mood board can help you keep track of all your design ideas.

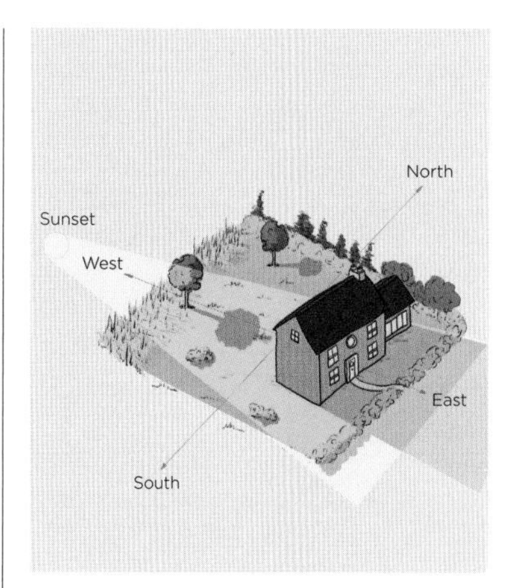

3. Next assess the areas of sunlight and shade (see page 34). Make sure you check the light levels at different times of the day. Research plants suitable for the aspect of the garden, then add them to your list.

4. Roughly sketch the design of the hard landscaping – patios, decking, paths and raised beds, for example – on a large piece of paper. Once you know where the bare bones of the garden will be, you can start designing the planting.

5. After you have established the garden plan, it is worth doing all the hard landscaping first before you start purchasing any plants.

6. When the hard landscaping is complete you can begin on the planting. Place all the plants in their pots in position to check they look right before planting.

Dahl
Pam How

CHAPTER 4

RIGHT PLANT, RIGHT PLACE

One of the most enthralling and fascinating aspects of choosing plants for a garden is that there is a plant for every type of location. Whether your garden is in sun or shade, there is an embarrassment of riches for both types. In fact, one of the dilemmas when it comes to picking plants is that there are so many to choose from, it is hard to know where to start.

In this chapter, we suggest the types of plants you can choose if your garden is baked in the sun all day long. It also provides inspiration and advice if your garden is in the shade. After all, there are almost as many gorgeous shade-dwelling plants as there are sun-lovers.

Fortunately, gardening is not just for one season. There are beautiful plants for every day of the year. Becoming a good gardener is about understanding the seasons and knowing what will flower when. This helps you plan your garden displays and succession of flowers throughout the seasons. So this chapter has suggestions for an array of colours and textures, as well as flowers for all four seasons. Never again will you need to suffer from a dearth of interest in the garden in a particular month. You can enjoy a plethora of interesting and striking flora, foliage and fruit 365 days a year.

Plants for sun

Many plants thrive in a hot, sunny garden, and they usually originate from dry, arid areas like deserts, the Mediterranean, South Africa or the North American prairies. There are lots of suitable types, including cacti and succulents, herbs and many silver-leaved plants that will bask in the sun and require little maintenance. Sun-loving, subtropical plants and bedding plants have more exuberant foliage and flowers, and so require a more fertile, moist soil to keep them looking lush.

MULCH MAGIC

Mulching beds and borders with gravel will help to reduce water evaporation, while gradually improving drainage, as it slowly washes down and works its way into the soil.

LEAVES DESIGNED FOR HEAT

One of the best indicators that a plant will thrive in hot conditions is its leaves. Anything with narrow, silvery, spiky or scented foliage is probably going to enjoy the heat. Classic examples include lavender, rosemary, salvias, agapanthus, alliums and cistus.

HOT BORDER PLANTS TO TRY

LAMB'S EAR (*STACHYS BYZANTINA*) has hairy leaves, which are another indication that a plant can thrive in a warm, sunny garden. With its soft, fluffy, silvery foliage and pinkish-purple flower spikes, lamb's ears are ideal at the front of a border.

BLACK-EYED SUSAN (*RUDBECKIA*) prefers a richer, more fertile soil than many sun-lovers, but adores a sunny spot. Flowers are red, orange, yellow and gold, or a combination of these, and have dark centres.

***AEONIUM* 'ZWARTKOP'** is an impressive succulent with reddish-purple foliage. It is ideal for a container on a sunny patio, or as a feature in a gravel bed.

GO TROPICAL

Many tropical plants with their large, lush leaves, such as cannas, palms, strelitzias and banana palms, also love the sun. Their architectural foliage will bring instant drama to a border. Add some bamboos to provide upright structure, and brightly colourful flowers like dahlias, salvias and echinaceas in the foreground. Plants with strap-like leaves, such as agaves, yuccas, agapanthus, cordylines and phormiums, are also suitable for a tropical look.

BEDDING PLANTS

Many bedding plants are tender and come from warm climates, meaning they are sun-lovers. But they need regular watering if grown in a container or hanging basket. Reliable bedding plants include zinnias, petunias, marigolds, geraniums and coleus.

DID YOU KNOW? Sunflowers originate from South America and they love hot, sunny conditions – so much so, in fact, that their flowerheads follow the path of the sun as it moves across the sky.

Opposite: *Many Mediterranean herbs and plants with silvery foliage prefer warm, sunny positions.* ***Right:*** *Aeonium succulents are perfect for dry, arid conditions.*

Maximize shade

Many gardens, particularly in urban areas, have areas of shade where they are surrounded by other buildings. Neighbouring trees can cause similar issues. Thankfully, such a scenario should not be regarded as a problem, as there are lots of plants suitable for shady spots, so do not despair if your garden is not a suntrap.

There are two extremes when it comes to shady gardens, one being moist and the other dry, although most fall somewhere in between. The range of plants suitable for either group includes everything from climbers to herbaceous perennials as well as trees and shrubs. Try to pick bright flowers and foliage for a shady spot as dark colours can add to the dimness.

There are some beautiful foliage and textural plants suitable for these conditions. The good news about shade is that you will rarely have to water the plants, except perhaps during periods of extreme drought.

DRY SHADE REMEDY

If your garden is in dry shade, try incorporating some organic matter such as peat-free, general-purpose compost into the soil because this will help retain some of the moisture.

There are lots of plants to choose from for shady conditions. Below are a few suggestions:

HART'S TONGUE FERN (*ASPLENUM SCOLOPENDRIUM*) thrives in damp, shady nooks and crannies. It has shiny, upright, green fronds, and will bring the magic of a woodland to any garden.

PERIWINKLE (*VINCA MINOR*) is possibly one of the most versatile plants available, thriving in sun, shade, moist or dry conditions, but it is happiest in moist, well-drained soil. It is ideal for providing ground cover on awkward banks. This subshrub has attractive spring flowers in blue, white or pink. There are variegated forms, too.

HOSTAS are familiar to most gardeners and have large, impressive leaves. They are herbaceous perennials and ideal for a shady border. Just watch out for slugs and snails.

JAPANESE MAPLE (*ACER PALMATUM*) is a small to medium-sized tree with dramatic, colourful foliage and spectacular autumn colour – there are numerous cultivars to choose from. It prefers sheltered, dappled shade in moist but well-drained soil.

TREE FERN (*DICKSONIA ANTARCTICA*) gives any garden the wow factor. Originating from Australia, these ferns have fibrous trunks and dramatic fronds. Ideal for a partially shady spot under a tree.

Opposite: *Hostas have attractive, patterned foliage and arching flower spikes. They thrive in shady conditions.* ***Right:*** *Periwinkle (*Vinca minor*) makes a useful ground-cover plant under a tree canopy.*

CLIMBERS

Many climbers are suitable for shade because they climb and scramble up trees in the wild, so are used to growing under a dense canopy. Climbers suitable for the shade include most ivies – do not forget there are also ivies with beautiful, variegated or coloured foliage such as *Hedera helix* 'Buttercup', *H. helix* 'Midas Touch' and *H. helix* 'Silver Queen'. Other shade-loving climbers include the lovely, fragrant honeysuckle, *Lonicera periclymenum* 'Serotina', climbing hydrangea (*Hydrangea petiolaris*) and Chinese Virginia creeper (*Parthenocissus henryana*), which has reddish foliage in autumn.

OTHER PLANTS TO CONSIDER

Foxglove (*Digitalis purpurea*)
Japanese spurge (*Pachysandra terminalis*)
Lady fern (*Athyrium filix-femina*)
Mahonia × *media* 'Charity'
Primrose (*Primula vulgaris*)
Willow gentian (*Gentiana asclepiadea*)

Winter planting

It may come as a surprise to discover that winter is one of the most exciting times of the year in the garden. Once many trees and shrubs are denuded of foliage and herbaceous perennials have died back, it is time for the winter plants to take centre stage. There are beautiful tree trunks, colourful winter stems, bulbs popping up on lawns and flowers with intoxicating fragrances.

TREES

There are trees with beautiful tree trunks suitable for a small garden that really make a statement, whether planted on their own or in a cluster of three or five. One of the most popular is the silver birch. There are a number of impressive ones, but *Betula utilis* var. *jacquemontii* is considered one of the best. It has a brilliant white trunk that really stands out against the green background of a lawn. Other popular choices are some of the ornamental cherry trees, with the Tibetan cherry (*Prunus serrula*) having a spectacular, deep red trunk, and the Himalayan cherries, *P. himalaica* and *P. rufa*, both with chocolate-coloured trunks.

Snake-bark maples, with their stripey trunks, are also impressive. Some of the most popular species include *Acer davidii, A. grosseri* and *A. capillipes*. For more tree-trunk drama in the winter garden, try the paperbark maple (*Acer griseum*) with its colourful peeling bark.

The white stems of birch trees can be used to striking effect in winter gardens.

SHRUBS WITH COLOURFUL STEMS

From a distance, a shrub border filled with the brightly coloured stems of dogwood (*Cornus*) can almost look as if the garden is on fire. Some of the brightest are *C. sanguinea* 'Midwinter Fire' and 'Winter Beauty' with yellow, orange and red stems. Willow (*Salix*) is just as pleasing, with bare winter stems in a range of colours, including white, black and purple. For the best colour, cut back winter stems to near ground level in late winter each year.

SCENTED SHRUBS

If you venture outside during winter, it is possible to become entranced with the most intoxicating fragrances from winter-flowering shrubs. Some of the best include Christmas box (*Sarcococca hookeriana* var. *humilis*), *Daphne bholua* 'Jacqueline Postill' and wintersweet (*Chimonanthus praecox*).

BULBS

Whether planted in the lawn, at the foot of trees or scattered among flowerbeds, bulbs can really pack a punch in winter displays. Snowdrops (*Galanthus nivalis*) are often known as harbingers of spring, but they will rear their white, nodding heads from mid-winter onwards. Other bulbs worth growing are winter aconite (*Eranthis hyemalis*), which has yellow flowers that are bright enough to cheer the dullest of winter days, and hardy *Cyclamen coum* with its pretty, heart-shaped leaves and vivid flowers in a range of colours, including white, pink and purple.

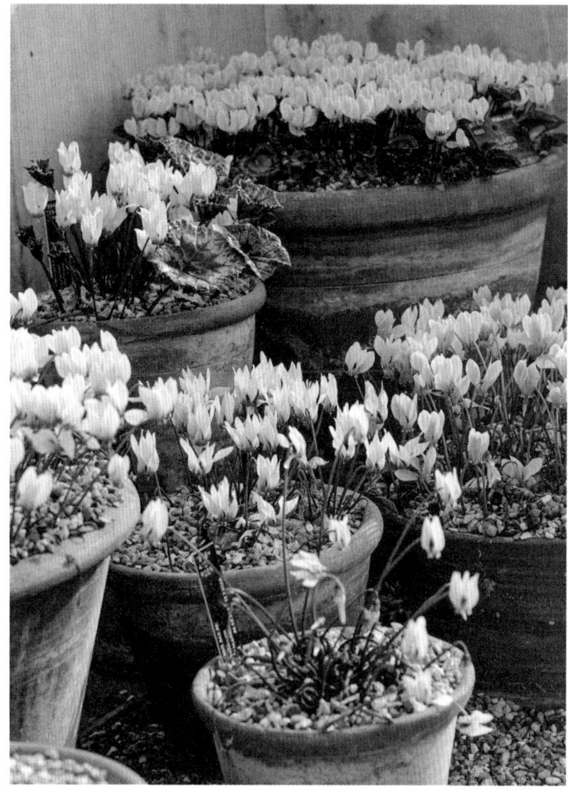

Top right: *The bare stems of dogwoods in winter come in a range of colours, including orange, yellow and red.*
Bottom right: *Cyclamen are a popular and colourful winter-flowering bulb.*

Spring planting

This is the season when the garden erupts in colour. It is hard to say which plants have the greatest impact: the bright, show-stopping spring bulbs or the spring-flowering shrubs. Either way, you are guaranteed a spectacular display. Most bulbs and shrubs can be grown in containers and if these are placed near the house, their vibrant spectacle can be enjoyed from indoors.

FLOWERING TREES

The most impressive displays of spring blossom are probably provided by varieties of ornamental cherry (*Prunus*). Ranging in colour from bright pink to purest white, the blossom can look like delicate clouds floating in the blue spring sky. Many of the best varieties come from Japan, where the beauty of the spring blossom is celebrated in a series of festivals and events called *Hanami*.

Another group of trees with impressive blossom are the crab apples. Varieties such as *Malus × zumi* 'Golden Hornet' and *M.* 'John Downie' are two of the most popular.

FLOWERING SHRUBS

Spring-flowering woodland shrubs can also be relied on to provide a wow factor in the spring garden. They include rhododendrons and azaleas, camellias, magnolias, enkianthus, pieris and many more, and they are guaranteed to create a riot of bright colour – in some cases, wildly brash and loud colours. The good news is that you do not need to have a woodland to enjoy these shrubs, as there are small and compact versions of most of them. Alternatively, you can grow the shrubs in containers. Many of these plants do require an acidic soil, though, so it may be necessary to grow them in ericaceous compost if the pH of their existing soil is above 6.5.

If you do not have particularly acidic soil, then other spring-flowering shrubs that can bring a pop of colour to the spring garden include the purple elder, *Sambucus nigra* 'Black Beauty', the mock orange, *Philadelphus* 'Virginal', *Weigela* 'Bristol Ruby' and *Forsythia × intermedia* 'Spectabilis'.

BULBS

For many people, the highlight of spring is the stunning displays provided by spring bulbs. There are hundreds of bulbs to choose from, but the following are among the most popular:

* *Crocus*
* Daffodils (*Narcissus*)
* English bluebells (*Hyacinthoides non-scripta*)
* Hyacinths (*Hyacinthus*)
* Snake's head fritillaries (*Fritillaria meleagris*)
* Tulips (*Tulipa*)

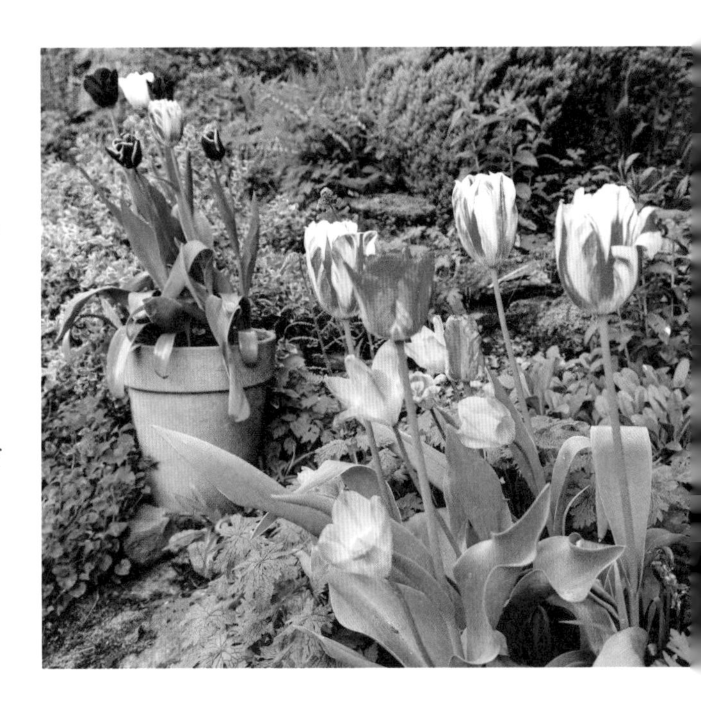

Opposite: *Mock orange (Philadelphus) is a spring-flowering shrub with a sweet scent.* ***Right:*** *Tulips are quintessential spring bulbs whether in containers or in open ground.*

Summer planting

Summer is the highlight of the gardening year when we can really enjoy our outside spaces. Many plants are in flower and the air is heavy with fragrance, climbers scramble over supports, and bees buzz soporifically. Just bear in mind that summer is a season of two halves: early summer is very much an extension of spring and then the garden transitions to another range of exciting plants as the summer season progresses.

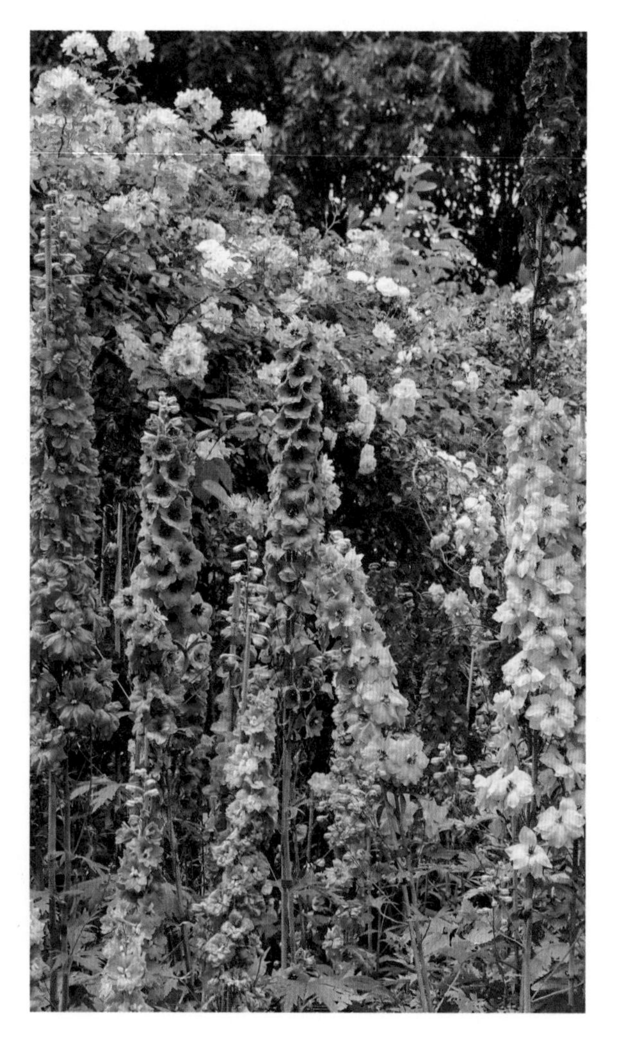

BEDDING PLANTS

For those of you who like an instant effect, then brightly coloured bedding plants are the go-to flowers for summer. They are usually either annuals or tender exotics, meaning they will only last one year, before succumbing to frosts.

There is a plethora of bedding plants available in a range of colours and they are suitable for containers and hanging baskets. They can also be used to create patterns in borders and flowerbeds. Some of the most popular summer bedding plants include busy lizzies, begonias, lobelia, petunias, gazanias, pansies and marigolds, but there are many, many more.

You can colour-coordinate planting schemes or create patterns, or mix things up completely with lots of vibrant, exuberant and clashing colours.

Bedding plants can be grown from seed, but this usually requires a warm greenhouse and a long growing season, which is not practical for most people. The easiest way to grow them is to buy trays of bedding from the garden centre in late spring and plant when all risk of frosts is over.

The tall, stately flower spikes of delphiniums in summer are perfect for the back of the border.

HARDY ANNUALS

These are plants that flower for one year and then die. They are hardier than bedding plants, so can usually be sown in early spring. There are lots of exciting plants to choose from, including sunflowers, sweet peas, annual poppies, nasturtiums, love-in-a-mist (*Nigella damascena*) and the poached egg plant (*Limnanthes douglasii*).

HERBACEOUS PERENNIALS

You truly are spoiled for choice when it comes to this group of plants. Some of the most popular include phlox, delphiniums with their tall flower spikes, and penstemons which have masses of flowers. With such a wide choice, pick those that suit your colour scheme and growing conditions. Consider their height and architectural qualities, too. Deadheading the flowers may extend their season into autumn.

CLIMBERS

Surround yourself with flowers by training climbers on trellis and wigwams as well as walls, fences and into trees. Climbing and rambling roses are a good choice, but you can also try clematis, passionflowers and the chocolate vine (*Akebia quinata*), which will all put on a spectacular floral display.

SHRUBS

Roses are the obvious summer choice, but others worth considering include fuchsias, cistus, hebes, ceanothus, lavender and buddleias. The options are, in fact, endless for summer shrubs for the garden.

Climbing and rambling roses can be trained up trellis – their colour and scent are a real asset in the garden.

SMALL TREES

After the striking blossom of spring, there are fewer trees flowering at this time of year, but some highlights include the Chinese dogwood, *Cornus kousa* var. *chinensis*, with its showy, white bracts in mid-summer, the long racemes of white flowers of *Styrax hemsleyanus* and evergreen *Magnolia grandiflora*, which has large, white flowers and a heavenly, lemon-and-vanilla scent.

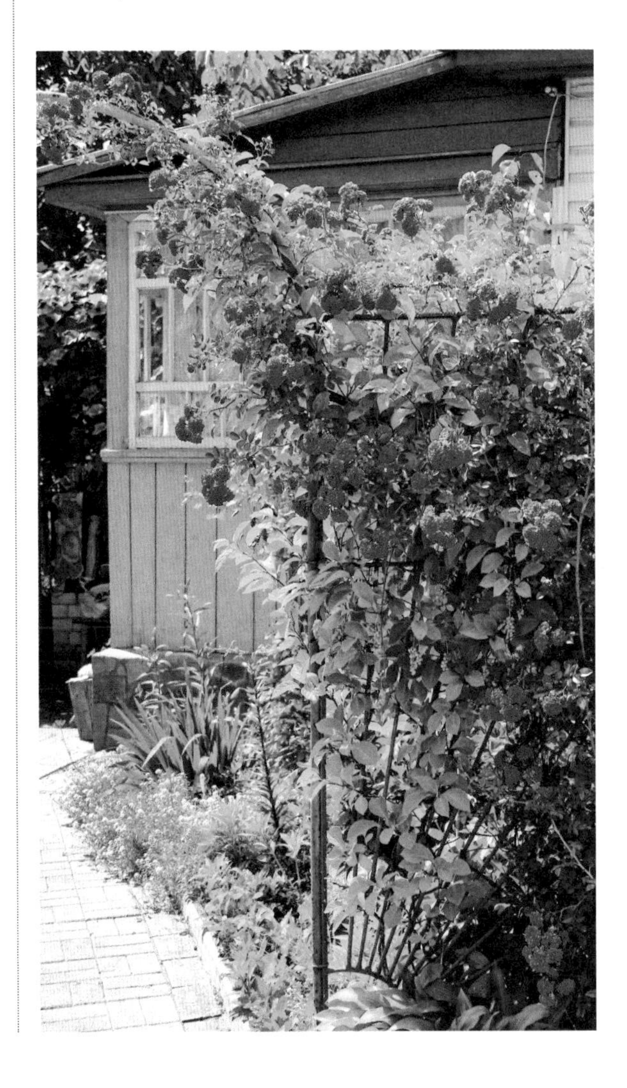

Autumn planting

Autumn is often a kaleidoscope of colour as plants reach their zenith in terms of flowers, fruit and foliage. The colour of autumn foliage takes centre stage at this time of year, as so many trees and shrubs put on a final display before dropping their leaves and going into winter dormancy. But there are bulbs, climbers, herbaceous perennials and berries to enjoy at this time too.

AUTUMN FOLIAGE: TREES AND SHRUBS

Shrubs with good autumn colour include *Cotinus* 'Grace', with its vibrant copper hues, and the stag's horn sumach (*Rhus typhina*). There are colourful Japanese maples too, but two of the most popular are *Acer palmatum* 'Sango-kaku', with crimson-red and yellow leaves, and *A. palmatum* 'Bloodgood'.

For larger gardens, some of the best trees are *Liquidambar styraciflua* and *Nyssa sylvatica*. The katsura tree (*Cercidiphyllum japonicum*) not only has spectacular autumn colour, but the leaves also give off the scent of burned sugar or candyfloss.

BERRIES

Berries abound in autumn. Rowan (*Sorbus aucuparia*) produces bright orange bunches and holly (*Ilex*) also starts to put on a display, which extends into winter. There are other shrubs with red, yellow and orange berries, including *Pyracantha coccinea*, *Cotoneaster conspicuus* and *Berberis darwinii*, but perhaps the best of all is *Callicarpa bodinieri* with purple berries.

Left: *Bees adore the end-of-season flowers of ice plants (*Hylotelephium spectabile*).* ***Opposite:*** *Deciduous trees adorned with red, gold, orange and yellow autumn leaves.*

CLIMBERS

Virginia creeper (*Parthenocissus quinquefolia*) is the pick of the crop in autumn, with its impressive displays of crimson foliage scrambling over walls, fences and up the sides of houses. There are also a few grapevines such as *Vitis vinifera* 'Purpurea' that are worth growing. These not only have colourful leaves, but will also produce a few grapes, which could be squeezed and made into a wine.

HERBACEOUS PERENNIALS

Late-flowering herbaceous perennials come into their own, with dahlias, chrysanthemums and asters all spilling over from summer into autumn with their impressive blooms. The ice plant (*Hylotelephium spectabile*) is another lovely herbaceous perennial, with succulent foliage and reddish pink flower florets. To add a hot sizzle to an autumnal border, you could do worse than *Hesperantha coccinea* 'Major' with its red-hot flower stem poking above ground when others are thinking of retreating below.

BULBS

Closer to the ground there are some impressive bulbs for the front of a flowerbed or perhaps at the base of a feature tree. Among the highlights are the nerines with their exotic, trumpet-like, pinkish flowers. Other choices include naked ladies (*Colchicum autumnale*) and winter-flowering crocus like the saffron crocus (*Crocus sativus*). There is also bright and colourful *Cyclamen hederifolium* which has pink-purple and sometimes purple flowers.

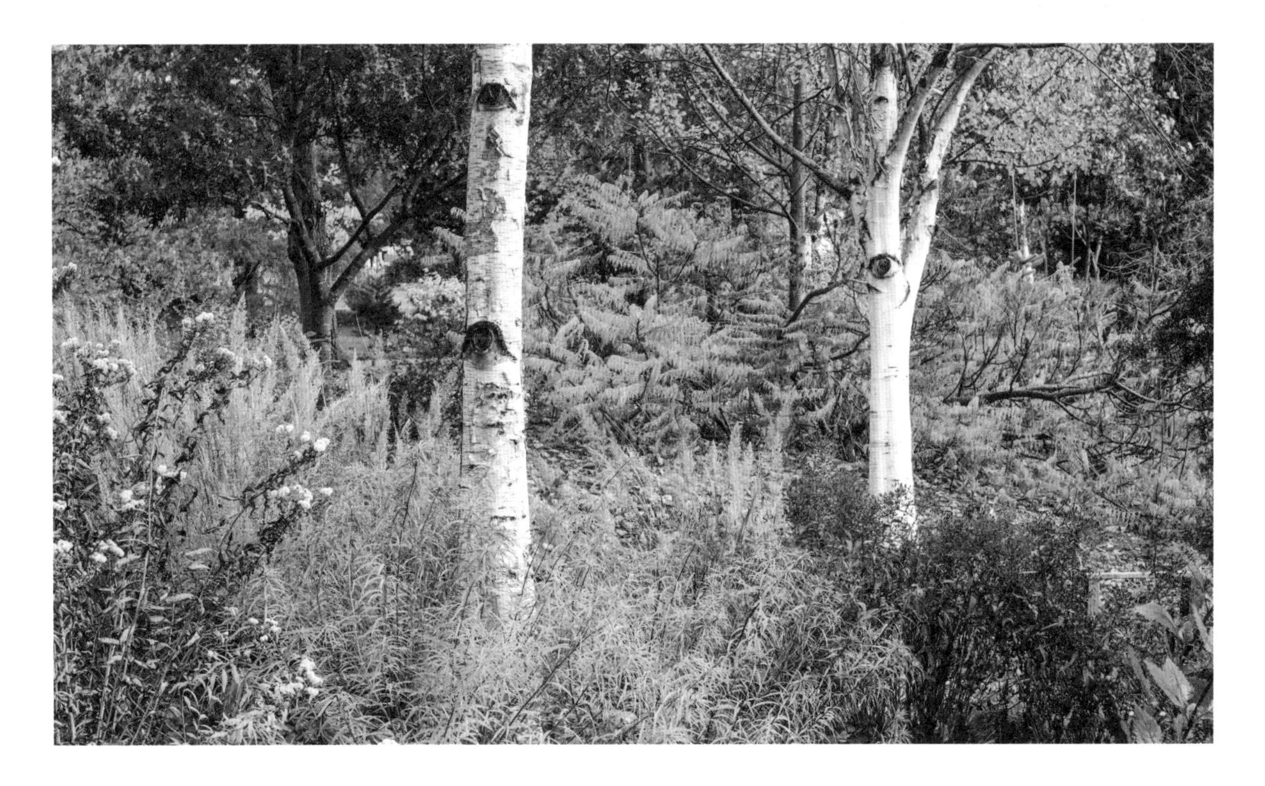

How to choose plants

Regard a visit to the garden centre as a chance to receive good advice, place plants side by side to try out colour combinations, and discover new plants. You should always check whether the plants you like will suit the conditions in your garden, but there are also other things to consider before buying. Many people find new plants die a few weeks later, perhaps because they were planted in the wrong place or had a defect, but this is easily avoided if you know what to look for.

Before purchasing, always check over the plant carefully. If possible, remove the plant from its pot and inspect the roots to see if it is root-bound. If it is, then it could struggle to establish properly as the roots may continue to circle around and around after planting, eventually strangling the plant. It also means the plant has been languishing in the pot for a long time and is probably weak and starved of nutrients, and will also be susceptible to pests and diseases as it does not have a strong immune system.

* Do not select summer bedding plants late into the summer as they will only last a few more weeks.
* Avoid plants that look nutrient-deficient – keep an eye out for yellow leaves or stunted growth.
* Look for bargains. Overcrowded herbaceous perennials can be split to produce more plants.
* In trays of vegetable seedlings, there may be more than one in each module. These are free plants, so are worth getting.

Check plants over carefully before purchasing to make sure they are healthy and disease-free.

INVASIVE PLANTS

Some plants are listed by the government as invasive and yet they can still be purchased easily. Always check the label and research plants online first. For example, *Cotoneaster horizontalis* is an attractive plant, but it can cause real problems, particularly if grown near a waterway, due to its spreading habit. Some bamboos can also be invasive and become a nuisance, so think carefully before purchasing.

CLIMBER DAMAGE

If you are buying a climber to scramble up the sides of the house, check how it grows because it may damage the building. Climbers grow in two main ways. Some send out tendrils, which are a type of suction pad, or aerial roots and use these to grip onto a surface and self-climb, while others need the support of a trellis or other structure and regular tying in. If you choose a climber from the first group, just be aware that they may damage brickwork and mortar joints if they get too much of a grip. The climbers that cause most damage to buildings are ivies and Virginia creeper (*Parthenocissus henryana*), but there are others.

POLLINATION

Check to see whether trees need another pollinator to produce fruit or berries. This is often the case with some fruit trees, but it can also affect ornamental plants such as junipers and hollies, where only a female pollinated by a nearby male will produce any fruit or berries.

CYCLE OF LIFE

Check whether the plant is an annual, biennial or perennial. Annuals only live for one year and then die, so will need replacing or propagating each year. Biennials live for just two years, and perennials live for a number of years.

LOOK FOR LOCAL

If there are unusual local plant varieties, then it is worth acquiring them for your garden. They should be well suited to the local climate and soil. If they are rare, planting them in your garden will help ensure their continuation. This is particularly true of local apple or other fruit varieties, but there are local ornamental plants too. Look out for plants named after areas near you. So, if you live in South Devon, England, then plants such as *Vinca* 'Dartington Star' (which is now called *Vinca major* var. *oxyloba*), the Dittisham plum (*Prunus domestica* 'Dittisham Ploughman') and the heritage apple *Malus domestica* 'Upton Pyne', would be local, for example.

TIPS ON CHOOSING PLANTS

- What is the eventual height and spread of the plant?
- Does it need something to climb up or on?
- Does it prefer light or shade?
- What soil or potting compost does the plant require?
- Is it an annual, biennial or perennial?
- Does it have a fast or slow growth habit?
- Will it sprawl and spread?
- Is it evergreen or deciduous?

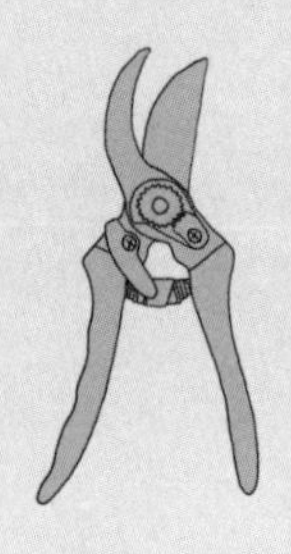

STEP-BY-STEP TECHNIQUE

ENCOURAGE WILDLIFE

Sharing your outdoor space with wildlife is one of the great joys of having a garden. There are many things you can do to encourage wildlife, including installing a birdfeeder or bird table, creating wood piles, sowing wildflowers, and growing a variety of plants that flower at different times. Grow plants in a range of sizes too, as creatures forage at different heights.

The best thing you can do to encourage wildlife is to sow some wildflowers to attract insects like butterflies, moths and bees. Suggestions include:

* Bird's-foot trefoil (*Lotus corniculatus*)
* Common knapweed (*Centaurea nigra*)
* Cornflower (*Centaurea cyanus*)
* Corn marigold (*Glebionis segetum*)
* Foxglove (*Digitalis purpurea*)
* Ox-eye daisy (*Leucanthemum vulgare*)
* Viper's bugloss (*Echium vulgare*)

You can attract other wildlife like birds, toads and hedgehogs with a few simple additions to the garden.

YOU WILL NEED

* Logs or sticks and fallen leaves
* Birdfeeder or bird table and bird and bat boxes
* Evergreen shrubs
* Water source, such as a pond, bird bath or saucer

Sowing or planting lots of wildflowers will attract the local wildlife to your garden.

Create a log pile in a shady part of the garden. Stack the logs in a heap and it will attract toads and perhaps even a slowworm. If you do not have any logs, a pile of leaves in a quiet corner will attract invertebrates and a hedgehog might make its home there.

Place a birdfeeder, bird table and/or bird box in the garden. This will entice a variety of birds to feed and nest. There are bird boxes for birds of different sizes, so try to pick those you think will suit the birds that frequent the area. A bat box will also attract bats.

Plant some evergreen shrubs, as they are particularly useful for creating nesting opportunities in spring. They also provide cover for the rest of the year, so that creatures feel safe in the garden.

Add a water feature such as a garden pond as this will attract wildlife for drinking, feeding and bathing. In smaller gardens, a bird bath or saucer filled with water will suffice.

GROW BERRIES

Birds are attracted to berries in the garden. Try blackberry (*Rubus fruticosus*), elder (*Sambucus nigra*), which is shown below, Guelder rose (*Viburnum opulus*), holly (*Ilex*) and rowan (*Sorbus aucuparia*). Ivy is a brilliant source of berries later in the year, but its late-autumn flowers are also vital for bees as they forage for nectar when few plants are around.

TIP ON INSECT-FRIENDLY FLOWERS

Pick plants to provide flowers throughout the year, as they will be a valuable supply of nectar for bees and other insects to forage on. Avoid those with double flowers since bees struggle to extract nectar from the restricted entrance to the blooms.

*Elderflower (*Sambucus nigra*)*

CHAPTER 5

HOW TO PLANT AND ESTABLISH A GARDEN

As with many things in life, to thrive and do well plants need to be given the best possible start. This chapter guides you through a variety of techniques, including how to plant trees, shrubs, herbaceous plants and bulbs. Getting the process of planting right is critical for a plant to grow successfully. Adjusting to its new environment is the most perilous time of a plant's life, so making sure this is done correctly is important.

Not only is planting correctly crucial for a garden to look good, so too is arranging the plants in a practical yet appealing way, so they can be displayed to full effect. Creating a border, or even planting a container, needs to take into account all the plants' seasons of interest, as well as their height, spread and colour, among other factors. In this chapter, there is advice on how to arrange plants to show off their best attributes.

For something a little more on the wild side, there are clear instructions for creating a small wildflower meadow, so local wildlife can enjoy the flowers and seedheads as much as yourself.

Planning and planting

The process of arranging plants in a border so that they look good is a real art. There are lots of factors to take into account, such as colour schemes, height differences, seasonality of interest, and so on. However, there are a few basic rules which, if followed, will make your beds and borders look beautiful and colourful.

TIP ON BORDERS

In long borders, you might like to repeat plants in a scheme, as this can create a rhythm to the plant patterns.

Left: *An informal or natural planting scheme takes planning and skill to ensure it does not look contrived.*
Opposite: *If possible, avoid buying plastic pots and instead look for those made from alternative materials such as coir or cardboard.*

PLANTING IN THREES

When putting a group of plants together, most designers like to plant in groups or clusters of three. For larger planting areas, odd numbers are used such as groupings of five or seven. Even numbers such as two and four tend to look contrived and are not so pleasing to the eye.

MIX IT UP

Flowers borders do not have to consist only of herbaceous perennials and annuals. Shrubs can be included too. These are often referred to as mixed borders. Shrubs can be used to punctuate or accentuate the design, if placed throughout the planting scheme. Evergreen foliage will provide year-round interest, while the structure of branches from taller shrubs, whether evergreen or deciduous, will provide a permanent backbone to any design.

POSITIONING PLANTS

Arrange the plants on the flowerbed to ensure you are happy with their positioning. As a general rule of thumb, shorter plants should be at the front and taller ones towards the back, but you can occasionally bring some of the taller ones forward to create a bit of variation among borders. However, with island beds the planting is usually slightly different, with lower ones around the edges and taller ones in the centre.

HOW TO PLANT

Squeeze the plants out of their pots. Gently tease some of the roots out that have started to spiral around the rootball. Dig individual planting holes with a trowel or small spade and drop in the plant. The hole should be the same depth as the rootball and twice the diameter.

Herbaceous perennials will benefit from having a layer of mulch placed around their roots after planting. A good choice of mulch would be well-rotted manure or garden compost. One quick technique for mulching around lots of plants after planting if they are in a single flowerbed, is to cut back the foliage on young plants and then cover each one with the flowerpot they were removed from. This stops their leaves getting smothered with the organic matter. Then mulch the entire flowerbed and remove the pots afterwards.

AVOID PLASTIC POTS

To avoid buying plastic pots, it is possible to purchase plants in containers made from coir. This material is a natural by-product of the coconut industry. The pots are planted directly into the soil and eventually break down naturally. This means you don't have to dispose of or recycle plastic pots afterwards.

The beauty of bulbs

Bulb is used as a generic term for swollen underground storage organs, including 'true' bulbs as well as corms, rhizomes, tubers and tuberous roots. This group of plants provides a wonderful array of colours in the garden. With careful planning you can have interest all year round, with various bulbs appearing in almost every month. They are also ideal for displays in containers. Over the winter, hyacinths can be forced on indoors, so their aroma can be enjoyed from the comfort of a warm house without having to venture outdoors.

Bulbs are a great investment, as most are perennials, and so once planted they should put on a spectacular floral display for years to come. Try the following:

* Winter – snowdrops, winter aconites
* Spring – daffodils, bluebells, hyacinths, spring crocus, snake's head fritillaries and tulips
* Summer – lilies, dahlias, agapanthus, cannas, gladioli, montbretia, ginger lilies
* Autumn – autumn crocus, colchicums, nerines and autumn cyclamens

WHERE TO PLANT

Bulbs are an incredibly versatile feature of planting schemes and can be planted in a variety of different areas of the garden, including:

LAWNS To give the impression that bulbs have 'naturalized' in the lawn, scatter them over the area and then plant them where they fall.

UNDER TREES Plant bulbs under tree canopies. Their bright colours can accentuate trees that have distinctive and beautiful trunks such as silver birch (*Betula pendula*) and ornamental cherries like *Prunus serrulata* and *P. maackii*.

FLOWER BORDERS Bulbs are a fantastic way of brightening up flower borders. Smaller bulbs are usually planted at the front of the border and larger ones at the back.

Tulips, which are 'true' bulbs, bring a splash of bright colour to the springtime garden.

CONTAINERS Planting bulbs in containers is an ideal way to brighten up a porch or patio. When they've finished flowering, if there is room, simply tuck them out of the way somewhere until next year, and bring out another container full of the next season's display of bulbs.

HOW TO PLANT

There are various techniques for planting bulbs. The simplest method is to use a trowel to plant individual bulbs where you want them. To do this, simply dig a hole, insert the bulb to the correct depth (see box, right) and then cover with soil.

There are also specific bulb planters available, which make digging holes deep enough for bulbs easier. These are essentially long, narrow trowels which are pushed into the ground to make a hole, and the bulb is then popped in. The advantage of using a bulb planter is that it causes less disturbance to the immediate area of a lawn or flowerbed. Some bulb planters have a long handle and a mechanism that releases a bulb into each hole, which saves on the back-breaking work of bending down to plant each bulb in turn. If you are planting lots of bulbs, then dig a trench or hole, add the bulbs in an upright position and then backfill with soil.

CHECK THE GROWING CONDITIONS

Different types of bulbs have different growing requirements, so always check their light/shade requirements first, as well as whether they prefer moist conditions or light, well-drained soil. Add horticultural grit if they require well-drained soil.

HOW DEEP?

Generally, a bulb should be planted to a depth that is two or three times its height.

WHICH WAY UP?

Do make sure bulbs are planted the right way up. In most cases, they are the shape of a lightbulb, but upside down. The flatter 'root plate' should be at the bottom and the thinner tip pointing upwards. Tubers, rhizomes and corms are closely related to bulbs, but have a different shape. Usually, there are emerging, swollen buds on the surface, which should face upwards, and a system of roots underneath that should be facing down.

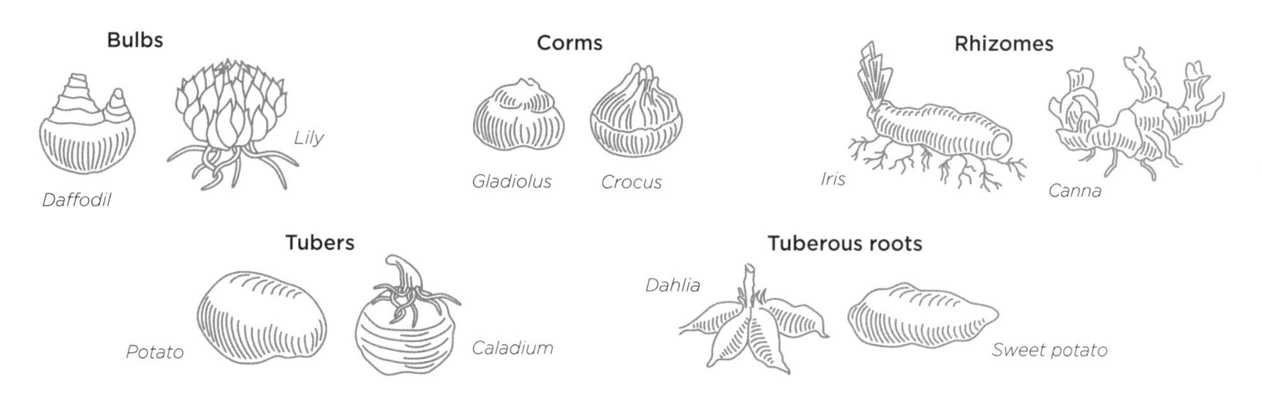

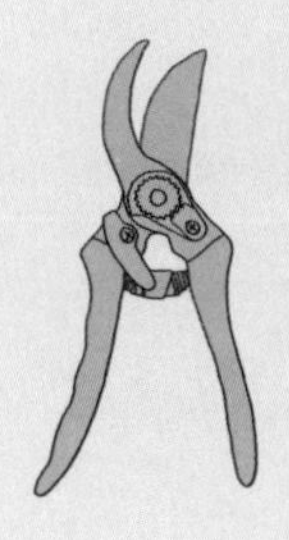

STEP-BY-STEP TECHNIQUE

PLANT A TREE OR SHRUB

Trees and shrubs bring so much to a garden, including height, structure, colour and seasonal interest, as well as attracting birds and other wildlife. Planting a tree or shrub may seem simple, but a poorly planted specimen is the most common reason for trees and shrubs to fail within the first few years, as they are usually planted too deep, which makes the trunk or stem rot.

If you follow a few simple planting rules, a tree should live for years, probably even outliving you. Trees can be expensive, and although a wonderful investment, it is tragic if they die prematurely because they were not planted correctly at the start.

Before buying a tree or shrub, check its growing requirements to ensure you have a suitable space in your garden. You need to assess its ultimate size and width; its preferred soil conditions; and the weather conditions that it will tolerate (for example, wind-tolerance and sun/shade preferences).

PLANTING TIMES

Trees and shrubs are often sold in containers. They can be planted all year round, but it is best to avoid extreme weather conditions such as frozen ground or drought. If you are planting in the summer, the plants will need regular watering in their first year.

The optimum time for planting most trees and shrubs is autumn, as the soil is still warm from the summer, allowing the plants to establish themselves before starting to grow in spring. Spring is also a good time for planting, particularly if the trees or shrubs are slightly tender and might suffer during their first winter. The step sequence opposite shows how to plant a tree. The same process applies to shrubs, although these will not need staking.

YOU WILL NEED

* Spade
* Stick or bamboo cane for checking planting levels
* Peat-free potting compost (optional)
* Tree stake and lump hammer (for a tree)
* Tree tie or pair of tights (for a tree)

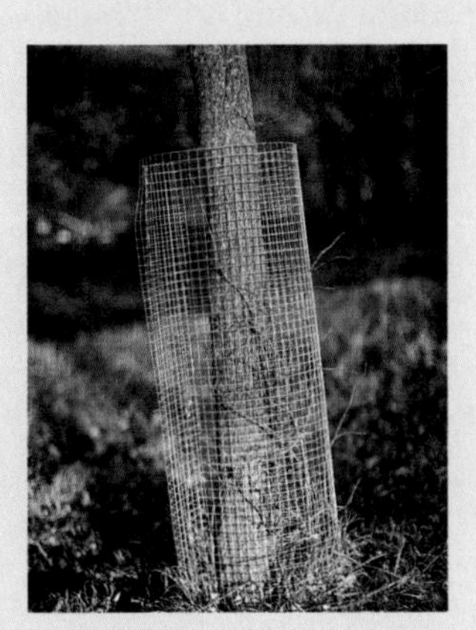

TREE DEFENCE

Use special guards to protect trees against rabbits gnawing the trunks as well as when cutting close with lawn mowers and string trimmers.

1. Remove the tree from its pot and measure the depth and width of the rootball. You may need to scape off any loose compost from the top to reveal the top of the root system and the bottom of the trunk.

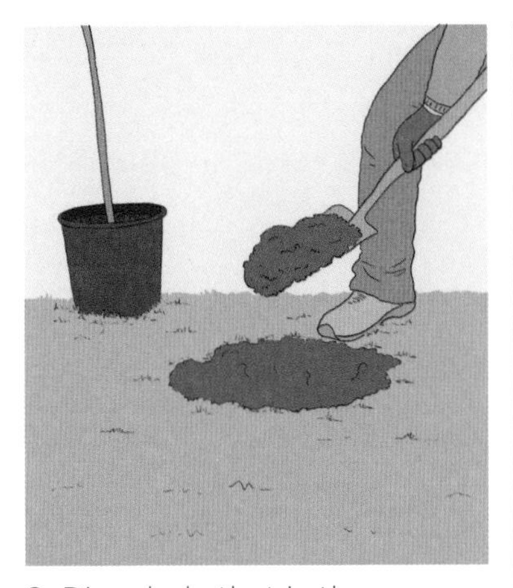

2. Dig a hole that is the same depth as the rootball and at least twice the diameter. Avoid digging over the bottom of the hole unless it is very compacted, as this can cause the tree to sink after planting.

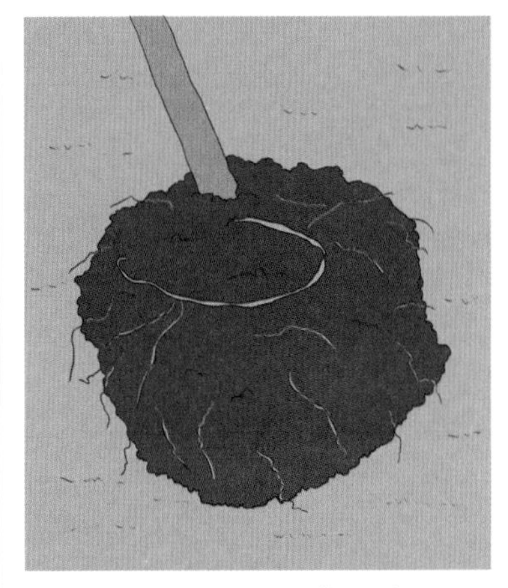

3. Check the rootball and loosen roots that are growing tightly around each other. Otherwise, they will continue to wrap around, causing the plant to strangle itself, rather than growing outwards.

4. Put the tree in the hole. Place a stick or bamboo cane across the top of the hole to ensure the rootball is level with the surface. If not, it may be necessary to adjust the depth of the planting hole.

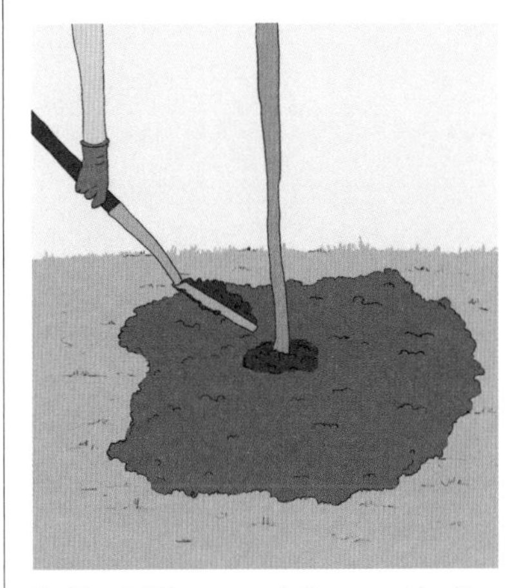

5. Backfill around the rootball using the spoil from the hole, firming it in as you go. If the soil is poor quality, you may need to add some compost to the soil.

6. The tree may need staking for the first couple of years. Use a lump hammer to drive a stake into the ground at an angle of 45 degrees, taking care not to damage the rootball. Tie the tree to the stake with a tree tie or a soft, flexible material like a pair of tights.

STEP-BY-STEP TECHNIQUE

SOW A WILDFLOWER MEADOW

Converting an established lawn into a wildflower meadow will not only reward you with a spectacular display of flowers, but the local wildlife will thank you for it too. Furthermore, you won't have to mow the grass every week or two because wildflower meadows only need to be cut once a year in autumn. If you wish, you can also turn a new area of garden into a beautiful wildflower meadow.

Perennial wildflowers prefer a low-fertility soil, or the surrounding, more vigorous, grass will out-compete and smother them. A lawn converted to a wildflower meadow can take a year or two to establish, but it is well worth the wait. You can sow a wildflower seed mix or plant wildflower plugs directly in the grass. Plugs may be more expensive, but will be easier to become established. Some suggestions for perennial wildflowers include:

* Field scabious (*Knautia arvensis*)
* Forget-me-not (*Myosotis arvensis*)
* Hedge woundwort (*Stachys sylvatica*)
* Knapweed (*Centaurea nigra*)
* Lady's bedstraw (*Galium verum*)
* Ox-eye daisy (*Leucanthemum vulgare*)
* Meadowsweet (*Filipendula ulmaria*)
* Yarrow (*Achillea millefolium*)

Cut established meadows once a year in autumn as soon as the flower seed has ripened. Shake the seedheads to ensure seed continues to spread. Remove cuttings, or they will break down and fertilize the soil, allowing the grass to compete with the seeds.

YOU WILL NEED

* Lawn mower
* Landscape or garden rake
* Garden fork or three-pronged cultivator
* Wildflower seed (available online)
* Spring-tine rake
* Watering can or garden hose with a fine rose
* Netting or old CDs or strips of foil, canes and string, to protect seeds from birds (optional)

AN ALTERNATIVE TECHNIQUE

Another way to sow perennial wildflowers is to cut the established grass short, remove the clippings, then sprinkle a layer of sand, 3cm (1¼in) deep, over the grass. Sow the seed mix into the sand, which will thrive in the nutrient-poor soil.

TIP ON TIMING

If the grass is very fertile, postpone sowing a wildflower mix for a year. Instead, sow the semi-parasitic yellow rattle (*Rhinanthus minor*) in the grass in autumn, to reduce the soil's fertility.

1. Perennial wildflowers prefer a low-fertility soil. Cut the grass extremely short and remove all the clippings.

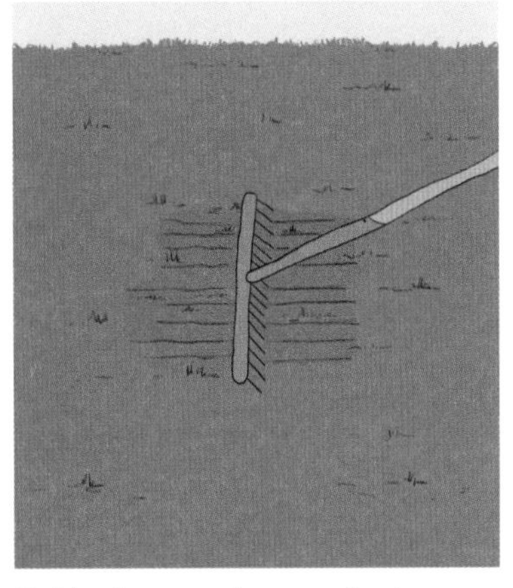

2. Next, use a large rake to 'scarify', or scratch away, the grass in places, leaving 50cm (20in)-square bare patches in the lawn every 20cm (8in), for sowing seed. This should be enough for the wildflowers to establish in the lawn.

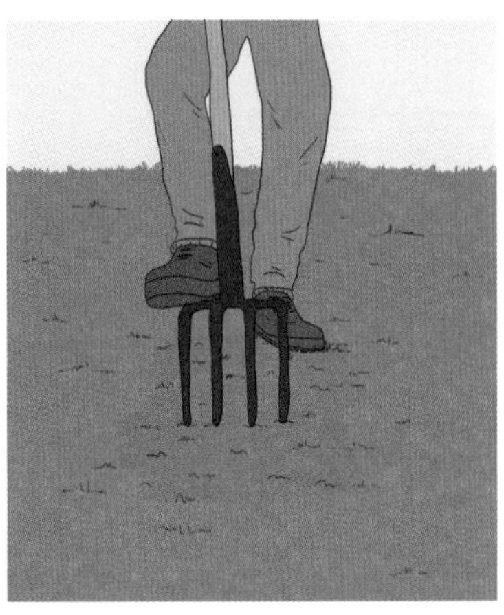

3. Break up the soil in these bare patches using a fork or three-pronged cultivator, then rake it level.

4. Following the recommended sowing rates on the seed packet, sow half the seed mix in one direction and the other half at an angle of 90 degrees to this, to ensure an even coverage of seed.

5. Rake the seed into the soil with a spring-tine rake. If it will be dry, water with a watering can or garden hose fitted with a fine rose, to avoid disturbing the seed. You can protect the patches from birds by covering with netting or garden canes strung with CDs or foil strips.

6. As the season progresses, continue to cut the grass around the patches of wildflowers short, to give them time to get established.

CHAPTER 6

PLANT MAINTENANCE

Caring for and maintaining plants as they grow is important if they are to flourish and look their best. In this chapter, there is advice on the things you need to do to achieve this, including how to weed effectively, so they do not take over the garden. Although it is important weeds do not ruin all your hard work by smothering and competing with your chosen plants, which you have nurtured, bear in mind that some are beneficial for wildlife.

There is guidance on how to mulch a flowerbed or around a tree to retain moisture and suppress weeds. Some of the growing techniques you may have heard of, such as 'pinching out' or 'pricking out', are also explained here. Another key aspect to keeping plants alive is ensuring that they are watered and fed, so there are some handy tips on the best ways to do this.

There is guidance on pruning trees and hedges to ensure they put on healthy fresh growth each year. And if you have ever wondered how to trim a hedge and keep it straight, then this is the chapter for you. Finally, if you are keen to learn how to garden without having to dig, there is information on how to grow crops using the no-dig technique.

When to weed

It can be very satisfying and therapeutic working your way through a border or vegetable bed removing the weeds. For some it is as enjoyable as popping bubble wrap. Whether we love it or loathe it, weeding is an important aspect of gardening. Although gardeners are far more tolerant of weeds now than in the past, due to their benefits for wildlife, there are still times when it is necessary to keep control of the weeds.

There is no clear definition of what a weed is. They are just unwanted plants that are growing in the wrong place. They may be invasive bamboos spreading through a garden, a vigorous patch of stinging nettles, Spanish bluebells smothering native English ones in the UK, or simply moss on the driveway. They can even be trees, shrubs and climbers, such as a large, spreading *Rhododendron ponticum* smothering out local, indigenous plants or an ivy strangling a specimen tree.

WHY DO WE WEED?

Weeds are born survivors and, if allowed to, will often out-compete existing garden plants. If weeds are not controlled, they can quickly take over a garden. They have various methods of spreading, floating in the air like a dandelion seedhead, for example, or sending down pernicious roots, as is the case with ground elder, bindweed and couch grass. To ensure that your chosen plants can thrive, you will need to remove some weeds, for these reasons:

* Weeds compete for the nutrients in the soil that would otherwise be used by the plants you want to flourish in the garden.
* Weeds will also smother out nearby plants as they outgrow them, reducing the available sunlight.

There are both annual and perennial weeds. Annual weeds tend to spread by seed while perennials usually have an encroaching or underground root system that allows them to move through the soil. Some plants, like the perennial dandelion, use both techniques to colonize as much ground as they can.

Annual weeds have a shallow root system and can often be pulled out by hand. For slightly larger weeds, a hand fork may be used to prise them up. Alternatively, a hoe can be pushed just below the surface of the soil, severing the roots from the remainder of the plant. Ideally, try to remove annual weeds before they have set seed, to prevent them spreading further on warm days. The plants can be left on the surface of the soil after hoeing to desiccate and wither. Annual weeds growing in the cracks of patios can be removed with a scraper or patio knife. They can also be added to the compost heap, as long as there are no seeds in the weed material.

Perennial weeds are trickier to remove than annual weeds. They often have deep, pernicious roots, and if any part of this system remains, even a tiny section, they will continue to spread. The most effective method for removing perennials is to dig them out of the ground using a fork, taking care not to leave any roots, although this is not always easy. Avoid adding perennial weeds to the compost heap immediately after weeding as this will allow them to spread (see page 100).

COVER AS CONTROL

One of the best methods of controlling weeds is to cover over the soil, as weeds will rapidly colonize any bare areas. Ideally, cover the soil with plants. Otherwise, cover with organic materials such as wood chips, garden compost or well-rotted manure.

TYPES OF WEEDS

There are thousands of different weeds, but these are some of the more common ones you may find in your garden.

Chickweed (*Stellaria media*)

Annual weeds

Annual meadow grass (*Poa annua*)
Chickweed (*Stellaria media*)
Fat hen (*Chenopodium album*)
Groundsel (*Senecio vulgaris*)
Hairy bittercress (*Cardamine hirsuta*)
Shepherd's purse (*Capsella bursa-pastoris*)

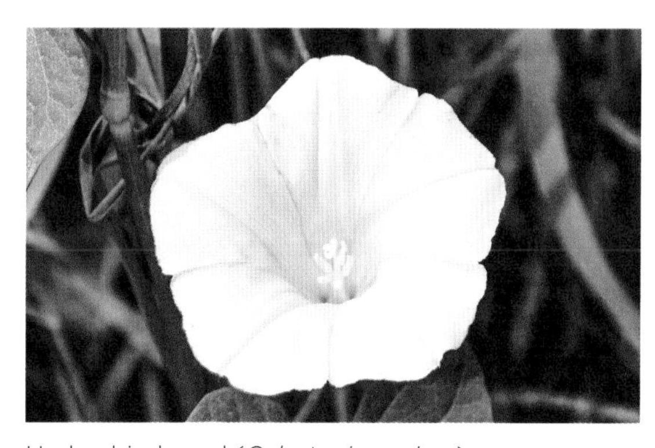

Hedge bindweed (*Calystegia sepium*)

Perennial weeds

Couch grass (*Elymus repens*)
Dandelion (*Taraxacum officinale*)
Field bindweed (*Convolvulus arvensis*)
Ground elder (*Aegopodium podagraria*)
Japanese knotweed (*Reynoutria japonica*)
Perennial nettle (*Urtica dioica*)

The magic of mulch

Mulching is the process of covering up bare soil. There are a number of reasons for doing this. It helps retain moisture in the ground, stopping it either evaporating or draining too quickly into the deeper subsoil. This helps plants withstand drought conditions. Mulching will also soak up moisture during heavy rain, thereby preventing the plants from drowning. A layer of mulch over the soil surface will help suppress weeds and prevent soil erosion on damp or exposed sites.

Mulching can also help keep the soil warmer, making germination occur earlier and providing some protection for plant roots from the cold in winter and the frosts in early spring.

MATERIALS TO USE

Inorganic or non-biodegradable materials can be spread over the surface as a mulch. For example, seashells, pebbles and slate can look attractive, with darker-coloured material absorbing the heat and white mulches reflecting the sunshine back onto plants. Landscaping fabric or even chemical-free carpets and rugs can also be stretched over bare soil.

However, while these techniques will help retain moisture in the ground and suppress weeds, they won't improve the nutrients and condition of the underlying soil. For this reason, an organic or biodegradable material is the best type of mulch to use. Materials include garden compost, decomposed wood chips or well-rotted manure. Do not use

Dark-coloured slate is an inorganic material that can be used over the surface of the soil to suppress weeds.

fresh manure or wood chips as these can burn plant roots as they decompose. Cardboard is also a useful material for restraining weeds. The advantage of using organic materials is that they will improve the condition of the underlying soil. The material will slowly get worked into the root zone of the plants as worms draw them downwards and the rain washes the mulch in. Although a few biodegradable materials, like cardboard, are not rich in nutrients, there will be some goodness for the plants, and the mulch will also help retain nutrients in sandy soil and improve drainage in heavy clay soils.

HOW TO APPLY MULCH

If you are spreading garden compost or well-rotted manure, it should be raked over the flowerbeds at a depth of about 5cm (2in). Take care not to leave the mulch in contact with the base of trees and shrubs as it can rot their stems.

ACIDIC SOIL

If you have plants that love acidic soil, such as rhododendrons, some magnolias, camellias, heathers and blueberries, a few mulching materials will help to maintain the pH levels. These include rotted pine needles or rotted pine wood chips. To an extent, coffee granules, rotted oak leaves and rotted citrus peelings will also help maintain low pH levels.

Bottom left: *Organic materials such as shredded bark can help to retain moisture around the roots of plants.* ***Bottom right:*** *Mulch can be applied to flowerbeds to improve the quality of the soil.*

STEP-BY-STEP TECHNIQUE

MAKE A NO-DIG VEG GARDEN

No-dig gardening is a popular technique for creating a kitchen or vegetable garden without the need to cultivate the soil. Instead, it relies on building up a healthy growing medium through the addition of garden compost and other organic materials that rot down on the surface and are absorbed into the beds.

It is claimed that no-dig gardening results in fewer weeds. This is because organic material placed on top of the soil suppresses them. With traditional gardening, the cultivation of the soil can result in accidently chopping through perennial weeds and uncovering dormant weed seed, which ends up exacerbating the weed problem.

Digging over soil also damages its natural structure and reduces soil biodiversity. No-dig gardening suggests that the soil should not be cultivated, but instead the organic matter placed on top will draw worms up to the root zones of plants, naturally aerating the area, but without causing any damage.

No-dig gardening does take patience, as it may take a year or two to convert beds over from a traditionally dug garden. But the reward should be a bed that is easier to cultivate, with fewer weeds, no digging and more vegetables to harvest and enjoy. No-dig gardening relies on a good composting setup, so if you are considering converting to this system, then do also consider having a compost heap for topping up the vegetable beds.

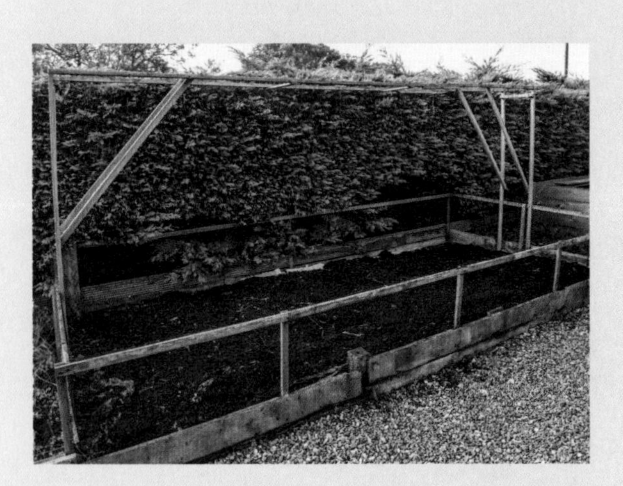

YOU WILL NEED

* Sheets of cardboard
* Garden compost, peat-free general-purpose compost or wood chips mixed with garden soil
* Kitchen fruit/vegetable waste and garden waste
* Trowel
* Your choice of vegetable plants

Covering a bed with cardboard and then garden compost will not only suppress weeds, but also provide a healthy medium for plants to grow in.

1. If you are clearing a bed for the vegetable patch, chop any existing weeds down, including perennial weeds, to near ground level with a string trimmer or hand shears. Leave the material on the surface or add to the compost heap.

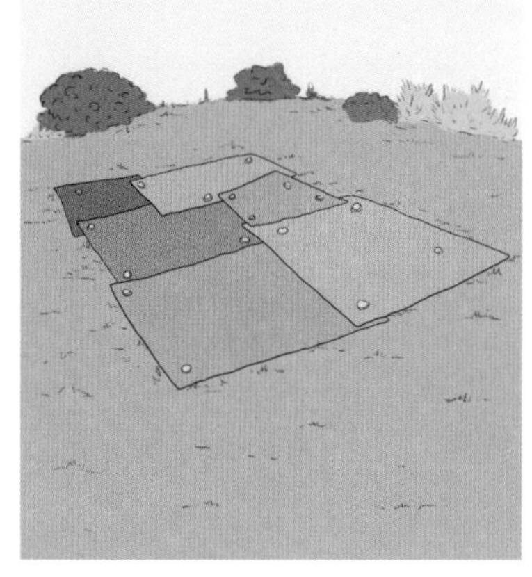

2. Place sheets of cardboard over the entire surface area, leaving no gaps. If there were a lot of perennial weeds, it may be necessary to use two layers.

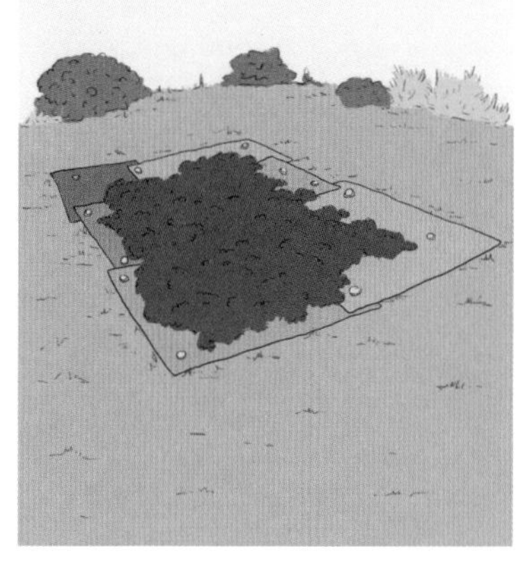

3. Add a layer of compost, 6cm (2¼in) deep, over the cardboard and allow it to start decomposing. If you don't have a compost heap, use a peat-free general-purpose compost or some wood chips mixed with garden soil.

4. Add kitchen and garden waste to the pile and allow to rot down. Once the material has decomposed, add more layers of kitchen/garden waste and also more organic matter.

5. If any weeds appear through the mulch, pull them out by hand. They should be fairly easy to remove as the organic mulch will be loose and the weed roots will probably come out with minimal resistance.

6. After about a year, the organic material on top of the flowerbed should be ready for planting into. Use a trowel to pop vegetable plants into the organic material.

Making garden compost

Often described as the 'engine house' of the garden, a compost heap is a key element in sustainable gardening. Not only is it possible to lose all the waste a garden produces, but fruit and vegetable waste from the kitchen can also be recycled on the heap. Best of all, the compost is a free material that can be added to beds to improve the quality of the soil. It can also be used as a mulch over the surface or dug into the soil.

WATCH OUT FOR WEEDS

Perennial weeds shouldn't be added to the compost heap immediately after they have been dug up, as their roots will quickly spread through the material. Instead, the roots should be dried on a rack in the sunshine for a few weeks to ensure they are no longer active. Another technique is to drown the roots in water until they turn into a brownish sludge, and then add this to the compost heap. A recycled milk carton filled with water is ideal for holding perennial roots to kill them. Also avoid adding annual weeds if they contain seeds.

POSITIONING A COMPOST HEAP

If possible, you should place a compost heap on bare soil, not on a hard surface like a patio. This is because, ideally, worms should be drawn up into the heap where it makes contact with the soil. An area in light shade is the perfect spot for a compost heap because there it will receive more rain than if it is under a dense tree canopy and yet will not dry out too quickly on hot days.

TYPES OF COMPOST HEAP

Closed compost heaps are ideal for small gardens, as they are compact and do not take up too much valuable space. Another benefit is that they are rodent-proof. The most popular types of closed systems are called darlacs, but there are other types too. Some closed systems can even be rotated with a handle, which saves you having to manually turn the material with a fork.

Open composts heaps are better for larger gardens as they can accommodate more material. These heaps do not have a roof and so are open to the elements. A simple yet popular type of open compost heap consists of three pallets nailed together to form the back and two sides.

SECRETS OF COMPOSTING SUCCESS

A compost heap should be turned every few weeks. This draws air into the material and speeds up the process of decomposition. A healthy compost heap should be composed of about 60 percent green, or nitrogen-rich, material and 40 percent carbon-rich material. Keep an eye on the compost heap to check whether it is getting too wet or too dry. If the compost is too slimy, then add some more carbon material. If it is too dry, add more nitrogen material.

Nitrogen materials include grass clippings and herbaceous plant material, as well as fruit and vegetable peelings from the kitchen.

Carbon materials include woody stems, usually left over from pruning, wood chips, shredded paper and cardboard.

In summary, the following are crucial for successful composting:

* Remember to turn the compost regularly.
* Don't let the compost dry out.
* Use a good mix of nitrogen- and carbon-rich composting materials.
* Chop the compost into small pieces before adding it to the heap.

A compost bin can easily be made for free using three old wooden pallets nailed together.

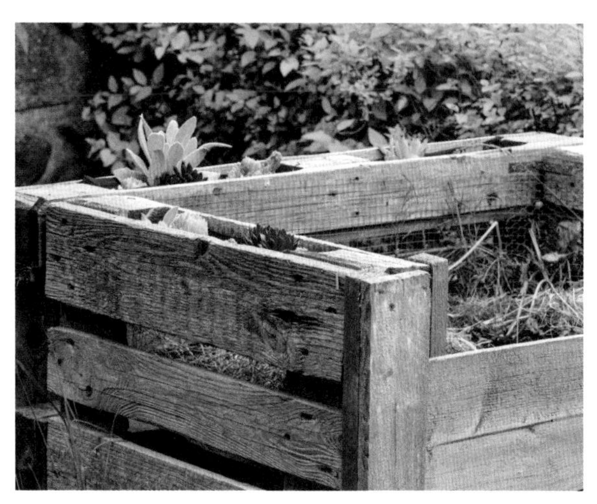

TIPS ON COMPOSTING

Below are some of the materials you can add to a compost heap and others you should always avoid.

Do add

* Herbaceous garden material
* Grass clippings
* Vegetable and fruit waste from the kitchen (citrus peelings can be added, but too many will turn the compost acidic)
* Shredded newspaper and cardboard
* Paper (but avoid shiny, glossy magazines and coloured paper)
* Eggshells (but avoid these if the compost heap isn't rodent-proof)
* Pet bedding from rabbits/hamsters
* Wood chips and shredded branches
* Coffee grounds

Don't add

* Meat/bones
* Egg yolks and whites
* Fish
* Dairy
* Silver foil/wrapping paper
* Glossy magazines and shiny paper
* Pet faeces
* Any material treated with chemicals
* Tea bags are often made from a thin plastic mesh and should not be added to a compost heap (tea leaves and biodegradable tea bags are fine to add)

Watering and feeding

Watering and feeding are critical to a plant's health and survival. Most of the time, plants in the garden will receive enough water through natural rainfall. However, they will be vulnerable in periods of drought, and it may be necessary to keep them alive by occasionally watering them. Plants in containers are more vulnerable because their roots are restricted and cannot seek out moisture or nutrients for themselves, unlike those planted directly in the soil.

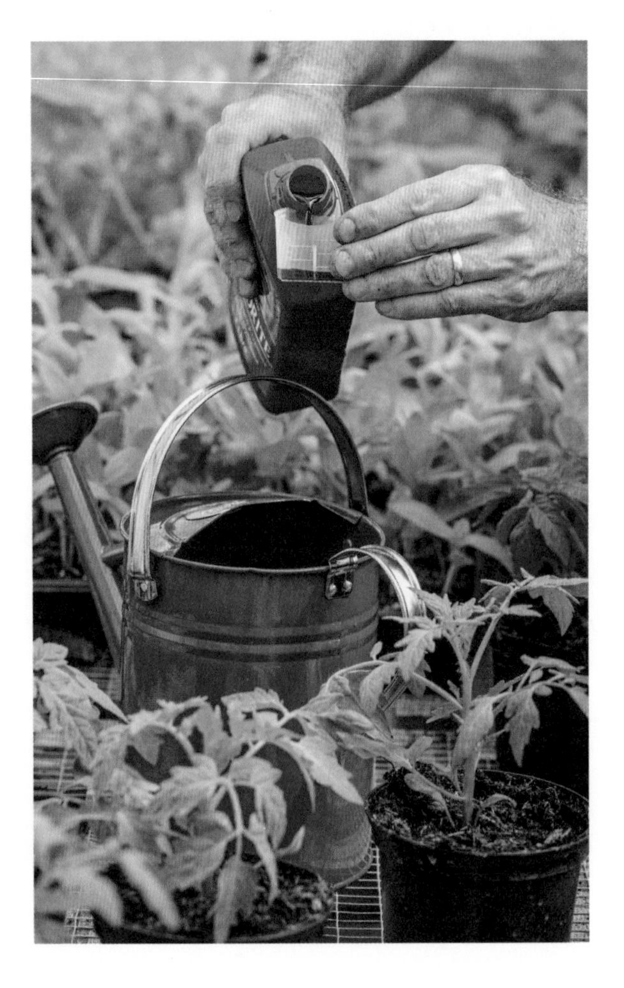

Feed plants every one or two weeks in the growing season to keep them healthy and increase flowering and fruiting.

HOW TO WATER

Target the root area when watering. If plants are in containers, an efficient way of watering them is to place them in saucers and fill these with water. This allows the plant to soak up the moisture through the roots, taking it as and when required. Some signs that a container plant needs watering include:

* The potting compost feels dry (insert your finger into the compost to check).
* The plant is wilting.
* There is less growth than expected.
* The pot feels lighter.
* The pot blows over in the wind.

If possible, collect rainwater in water butts, as this is better for the environment. It will also save money on water bills. Butts can be connected to downpipes on the house, shed and greenhouse.

If you are going away and are unable to find a kindly neighbour to pop in and water your plants, there are a few simple techniques you can try to keep your plants going:

* Move all pots and hanging baskets to the shade.
* Place pots in saucers of water, so they can absorb water when required.
* Give plants a good drink before you go away. It is best to avoid using sprinkler systems as they use a lot of water. They are also not that effective because the water does not always reach the roots.

HOW TO FEED

Plants also benefit from regular feeding during the growing season. They need a nitrogen feed early on in the season, when they are starting to grow, as this will help promote growth and green leafy material. Later in the season, as plants start to flower or fruit, they require more potassium to help them develop their colour, flowering and fruit set. An organic tomato feed is rich in potassium and is ideal for feeding most flowering, fruiting and vegetable plants. Always use organic fertilizers such as seaweed fertilizer, blood, fish and bone, or homemade nettle feeds and comfrey teas (see pages 104–5).

TIP ON FOCUSED WATERING

Create a round pit in the soil, with a radius of about 20cm (8in) from the base of the plant, to produce a reservoir that will retain the liquid when you water. This will stop water running away from the plant and instead allow it to soak into the root area.

In early spring you can apply organic slow-release fertilizers to the soil, which gradually release nutrients through the season. For all feeds, follow directions on the packet, but as a rule of thumb it is mixed with water in a watering can at the recommended rates and watered around the root system, usually every one or two weeks from when the plant starts to flower.

HOW TO SET UP A SEEP HOSE

Although most plants in the open garden are not as vulnerable to drought as container-grown plants, those that have been planted recently may struggle in periods of drought. Setting up a seep hose (a leaky hose) can help reduce the damage caused by a lack of water if you are away or cannot water regularly. Attach the hose to a timer to make an automatic irrigation system, so you can be sure your plants are being regularly watered.

1. Cut some tiny holes in a length of old garden hose, about 10cm (4in) apart.
2. Place a 'closed'-end section at the end of the hose to stop the water coming out when the tap is turned on.
3. Lay the hose just below the surface of the soil, to reduce evaporation, and line up the holes with the plants to ensure water reaches the roots directly.
4. Attach the hose to an outdoor tap with a timer and set this so the water comes on each evening for a few minutes.

STEP-BY-STEP TECHNIQUE

MAKE NETTLE FEED

Making your own liquid fertilizer will save you money when it comes to feeding your plants, as it is completely free. In addition, there is practically no carbon footprint, making it far better for the environment. This liquid feed can be made at home using organic ingredients found in the garden and avoids the use of artificial fertilizers, excess packaging and the impact of distributing them to garden centres or homes.

Stinging nettles (*Urtica dioica*) are rich in nitrogen and iron and can be used as a liquid feed to stimulate and promote a plant's green growth. To use in the garden, add the nettle feed to a watering can at a rate of 1 part nettle feed to 10 parts water. Then apply the diluted liquid to the root area of plants every one or two weeks for the first few months of the growing season, as this is when they require it most.

Once the plant has started to flower, then a liquid comfrey feed can be applied instead. Common comfrey (*Symphytum officinale*) contains lots of potassium, which promotes flowering, fruiting and colour. Comfrey tea is made and applied to plants in the same way as nettle feed.

YOU WILL NEED

* Stinging nettles (about half a black garbage bag)
* Pair of secateurs or scissors
* Two buckets and a heavy brick or stone
* Sieve, recycled plastic bottles with lids
* Watering can

POTASSIUM SOURCE

Another source of potassium for feeding plants is wood ash, which you can get from a bonfire or log burner. Sprinkle the wood ash around the base of plants as they start to produce flower buds.

A natural feed for plants can be made from stinging nettles and is free to make.

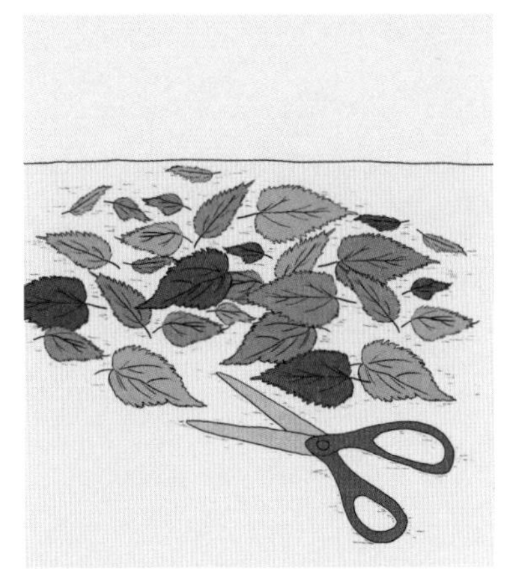

1. Gather up half a garbage bag full of nettles. Chop the nettles into lengths of about 10cm (4in). The smaller the pieces are, the faster the nettles will decompose.

2. Place the nettles in a bucket and fill this with water. Place a brick or stone on the nettles to keep them submerged.

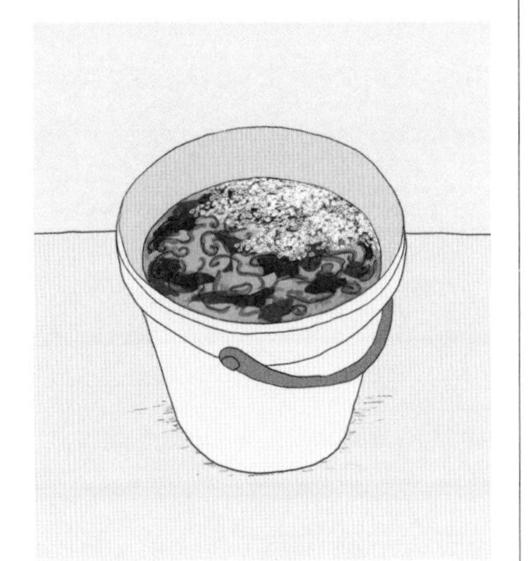

3. Place the bucket somewhere out of the way, such as at the end of the garden. This is because the liquid will start to smell terrible as it decomposes.

4. Use a sieve to strain the liquid into another bucket, then into some recycled plastic bottles for storage. You can keep the liquid in the bucket, but you won't smell it as much in lidded bottles. Mix with water in a watering can (1 part feed to 10 parts water) to apply.

NETTLES AND COMFREY

Stinging nettles grow readily in most gardens, but if you don't have any, they are easily found in the countryside. Always ask permission from the landowner before foraging for them.

Comfrey (below) is harder to find in the countryside than nettles, so it might be worth planting your own patch of comfrey in the garden. The most popular variety for a liquid fertilizer is Boking 14. Plant individual plants at intervals of 75cm (2½ft) in weed-free soil.

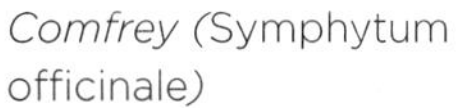

Comfrey (Symphytum officinale)

Caring for growing plants

Various growing techniques are used by gardeners as plants start to get bigger. These allow the plants to grow to their optimum size and reach their full potential, without becoming stunted and nutrient- deficient. Most of these processes are carried out in spring, as the season warms up and plants start to put on growth.

PRICKING OUT

Pricking out plants is removing small seedlings from where they were originally sown – usually a seed tray – and transplanting them individually in larger pots, so they can develop. This is usually a few weeks after sowing and when the plants are about 6cm (2¼in) high, although it depends on the type of plant. Plants are very fragile at this stage, so handle them with care. See page 202 for advice on sowing seed.

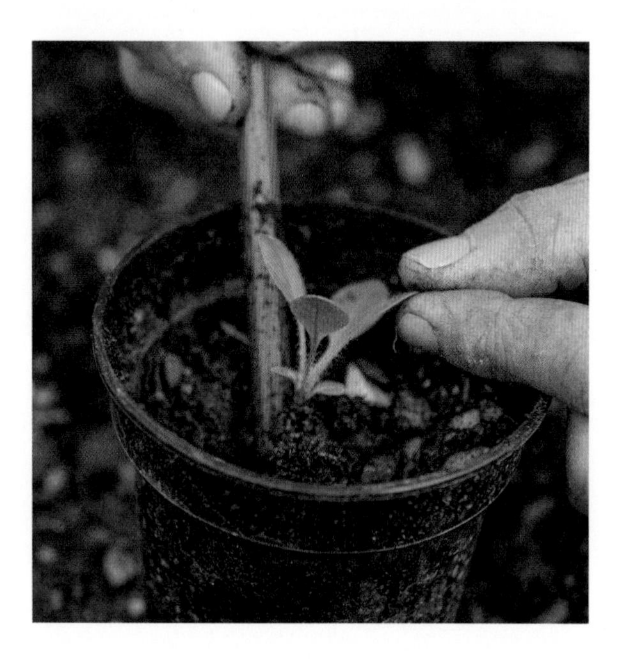

Prepare the pot for the seedling before pricking out to reduce the time it is out of the soil. Fill the new pot with potting compost and make a small planting hole with a dibber or your finger. Use the dibber to gently prise out individual plants, ensuring the root system stays as intact as possible (you can also use a teaspoon, pencil, plant label or popsicle stick). Take care not to damage surrounding seedlings, as at this stage they are often close together.

To prick out, hold the plant by the leaf and not the stem because if the stem is damaged, the plant will probably die, whereas it should survive a bruised or slightly torn leaf. Place the seedling carefully in the hole, cover the roots completely with compost, and very lightly firm in – avoid applying too much pressure and damaging the fragile roots.

THINNING OUT

Once plants reach a certain size in beds, they will need thinning out. This involves removing some of the seedlings to give the remaining ones enough

***Left:** Hold the leaf when pricking out. **Opposite left:** Thin out carrots, so remaining seedlings reach full size. **Opposite right:** Pinch out sublaterals on tomato plants so they channel their energy into ripening fruit.*

space to develop. If plants are not thinned out, they become leggy and fail to reach their full size, as they compete for sunlight, nutrients and water.

Thinning out is usually done on vegetable crops that have been directly sown in the soil. The spacing required between the plants in rows for thinning is generally given on the packets of seeds. Plants that usually require thinning out include carrots, beetroot/beets, radishes, lettuce and cabbages.

PINCHING OUT

This technique is used to encourage a plant to produce more lateral growth, as often more flowers will be produced on these side shoots. Pinching out the plant at a certain height encourages it to focus its energy on producing more laterals, which makes it bushier and therefore more floriferous. Without pinching out, the plant might grow too tall and leggy, and produce fewer flowers.

The height at which a plant is pinched out depends on what it is, but this is usually done in late spring, 15–30cm (6–12in) above ground level, but check the individual growth habit of the plant on the seed packet. To pinch out a plant, simply break off the stem just above a set of leaves by pinching or snapping it between your thumb and index finger.

POTTING ON

When plants outgrow their current pot, they need to be transplanted to a larger one. This process is called 'potting on' and should be done when the plant looks to be outgrowing its existing pot. It is usually in spring a few weeks after pricking out. The new pot should be about double the size of the previous pot and filled with potting compost. A few weeks after potting on, young plants will be ready to go in their final planting position, either in the open garden or transplanted into a container/growing bag.

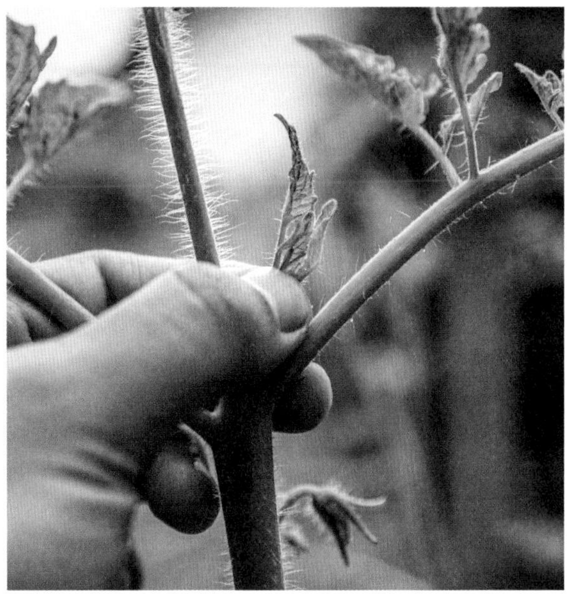

Herbaceous border care

Herbaceous borders are flower borders consisting of non-woody plants. These borders can be as large or small as your garden space will allow. To keep them looking as beautiful as possible, it is necessary to occasionally carry out some maintenance to ensure they are in tip-top condition.

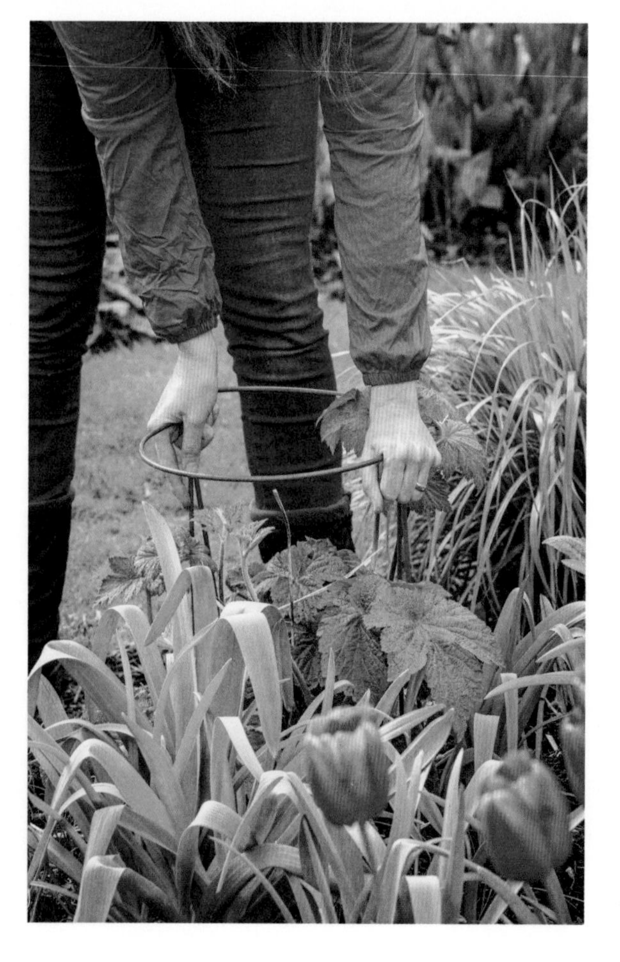

Herbaceous plants will often need supporting in flower borders to prevent them flopping over. To do this, gardeners generally use plant supports to keep the plants upright and looking their best.

Ideally, once the plant is fully grown, the plant support itself should be hidden or unobtrusive. The trick with using plant supports is to get them into position before the plant starts growing in spring, or it gets too big. By doing this, the plant will naturally grow through the support and its foliage will disguise the framework, making the plant look naturally upright and the staking unobtrusive. If this is left too late, it can be very difficult to move the shoots inside the plant support without breaking or damaging them. It is also harder to hide the plant support itself.

There are a range of supports available for staking herbaceous plants in a border. The simplest way to stake a plant is to push three or four equally spaced bamboo canes around the edges of a plant and then

Using supports will keep plants upright and neat, and show off their flowers in the border.

tie string between the canes, about every 20cm (8in) upwards, depending on the height of the plant, so that the shoots can grow up between them.

For plants that have heavy, individual, upright flower stems, such as delphiniums, hollyhocks and dahlias, a single cane can be pushed into the ground near the flower spike. String is then used to tie the flower spike to the cane to keep it upright and prevent its top-heavy weight toppling the plant over.

Twiggy sticks are useful for simply inserting in the ground around plants to prevent them flopping over. One of the most popular materials for these twiggy sticks are natural, pliable branches such as the young stems of hazel and willow. These can be pushed into the ground around the edges of an herbaceous plant, and a structure woven together above it, so that it can grow through the framework. This is certainly one of the more attractive types of staking, and if you have a friend or colleague with a hazel or willow plant in their garden, then the material is free.

Traditional, rusty metal hoops and 'lobster pots' are another choice. They are placed directly over plants and bring a lovely, rustic feel to the borders, reminiscent of a cottage garden.

Purpose-made plant supports can be purchased online and from garden centres. There are many different types to choose from, including those that clip together in a circle or are placed in a row along the front of a border to stop plants from flopping over onto a lawn or pathway.

OTHER JOBS FOR AN HERBACEOUS BORDER

* Deadhead flowers to ensure the plant continues to produce even more blooms.
* Keep the border free of weeds.
* Mulch the bare soil every spring.
* Cut back foliage in late autumn or early spring.
* Leave seedheads at the end of the season for wildlife to enjoy.
* Divide plants that are congested in spring.

THE CHELSEA CHOP

Some herbaceous plants can be cut back by almost half in late spring, using a pair of hand shears. This is called the 'Chelsea Chop' as it is traditionally done at around the same time as the RHS Chelsea Flower Show, in London. As a result, plants become less leggy/straggly. They produce more (but smaller) flowers and the flowering period is extended. More lateral shoots are also produced, which makes plants sturdier and means they need less staking.

Using a pair of shears to trim back an herbaceous perennial in late spring will encourage the plant to flower for a longer period.

Pruning ornamental trees

Ornamental trees don't usually require much pruning during their lifetime, but there are occasions when they will benefit from this. Sometimes a tree will be more aesthetically pleasing if it is pruned – for example, if a tree looks unbalanced or is encroaching into another tree. Occasionally, a branch may also need to be pruned if it has grown across a path or driveway, or is casting unnecessary shade on another area.

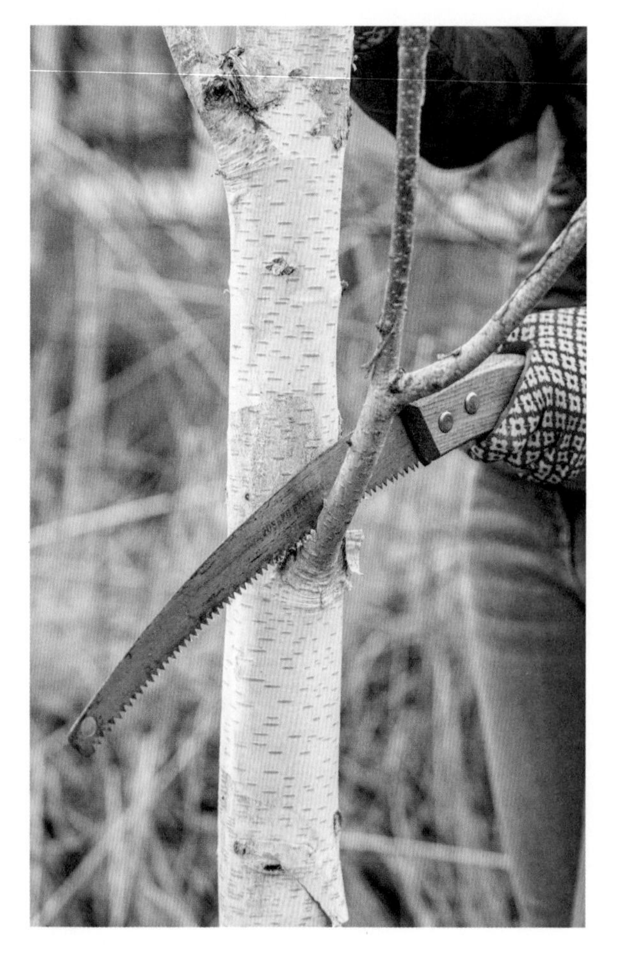

Whereas most fruit trees benefit from an annual prune, ornamental trees are often best left to grow as nature intended. The main reason for pruning would be to remove any dead or diseased branches. If branches are crossing, it is also worth removing one of them, to prevent them rubbing against each other and causing a wound where infection could enter.

TIMING The best time for pruning a tree is usually between late autumn and early spring, before it comes into growth. Pruning at this time also enables you to see the bare shape of the tree. There are exceptions, though, such as ornamental cherry trees, which should only be pruned when actively growing, as they are susceptible to disease when wounds are created in winter. They might bleed sap if pruned in spring, but do not worry too much, as this does little to harm the tree.

Use a pruning saw rather than secateurs when cutting any stem or branch that is thicker than two fingers' width.

TOOLS REQUIRED You will need the following tools for pruning:

* Secateurs for branches smaller than a finger's width.
* Loppers for branches bigger than a finger's width, but smaller than two fingers' width.
* Pruning saw for branches thicker than two fingers.

CROWN LIFTING

Some trees have a beautiful trunk, and it is nice to show this off. You may need to prune away some of the lower branches to reveal the attractive bark. This is called crown lifting. Ideally, crown lifting is carried out annually during a tree's formative years, starting when it is young. This is because the branches that develop each year on the trunk will be young and thin when removed, causing less damage to the tree.

Branches are usually lifted (removed) up to about one-third of the tree's height. Trees with attractive trunks that are suitable for crown lifting include silver birches (such as *Betula utilis* var. *jacquemontii*) and ornamental cherry trees like *Prunus serrula* and *P. rufa*.

REMOVING A BRANCH

If a branch needs removing with a pruning saw, use a three-cut technique to ensure the weight of the branch does not tear the bark and cause long-term damage to the tree. The first two cuts are intended to remove most of the weight from the branch (see right). Always use a professional tree surgeon for branches that are out of reach and avoid climbing up ladders. Large, thick branches will require a chainsaw, which should only be used by a trained operator.

THREE-CUT PRUNING

1. **Cut one** About 25cm (10in) away from the trunk make an undercut, cutting halfway through the branch. This will stop the branch tearing up to the trunk.
2. **Cut two** Make the second cut further along the branch, about an inch away from cut one. Cut until the branch falls away – listen for the satisfying 'snap'.
3. **Cut three** The final cut is on the outside of the branch collar, the slightly swollen area at the base of the branch. Make the cut just outside the collar without leaving a prominent stub, which would rot and could cause infection. The wound should callous over if the collar is left intact.

Use professional tree surgeons for any branches that need pruning and are out of your reach. Do not risk climbing up ladders to prune branches. Large, thick branches will require a chainsaw, which should only be used by a trained operator.

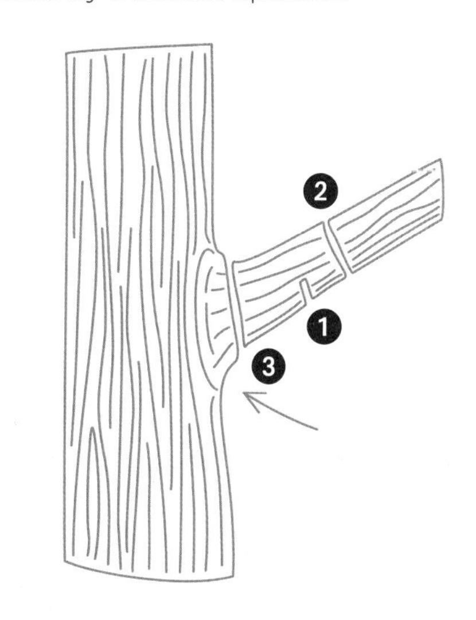

Pruning shrubs and topiary

Shrubs often require more pruning than trees. This is because they tend to have a more sprawling, spreading habit, and therefore become more straggly and congested without regular management. Also, because many shrubs are grown to encourage flowers, regularly removing some of the older growth will encourage a new framework of flowering shoots.

WHEN TO PRUNE

There is a wise saying in gardening circles that the correct time to prune is when you remember. While there is some truth to this, there are also some rules and tips that will encourage better flowering and keep shrubs looking neater. Most shrubs will benefit from a trim once a year.

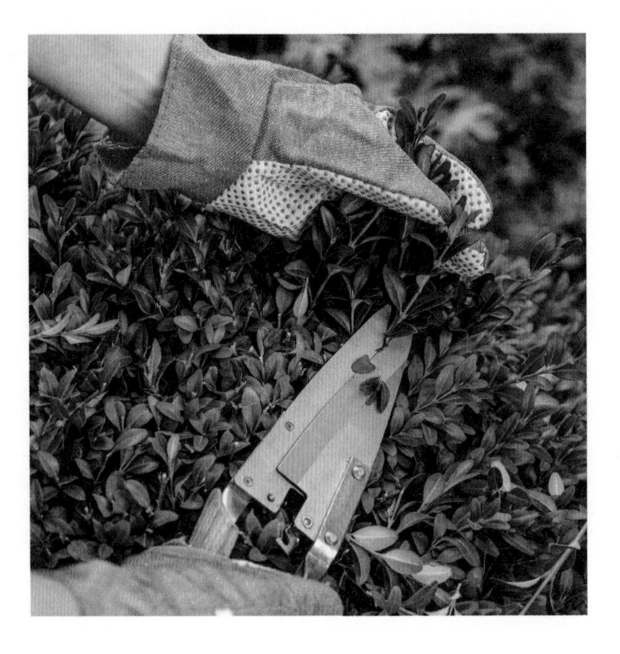

The best time to prune a shrub will depend on when and how they flower, whether this is on the current or previous year's growth.

EARLY-FLOWERING SHRUBS (SPRING AND EARLY SUMMER)

The shrubs in this category usually form most of their flowers on younger branches, which are produced the previous year. Sometimes called renewal pruning, these shrubs should be pruned after they have flowered by removing some of the older flowering shoots and retaining the new ones, which will flower the following year. Look to remove some of the thicker, older stems at the base of the plant with a pair of loppers or secateurs, and use them to trim back some of the other, older shoots which have previously flowered, back to new shoots further down. When pruning, you should be aiming to remove about one-third of the older wood.

Shrubs in this category include *Buddleja alternifolia*,

A small pair of hand shears can be used to accurately shape and trim topiary features in the garden.

Pruning early-flowering shrubs

Chaenomeles, *Deutzia*, *Exochorda*, *Forsythia*, *Kolkwitzia*, mock orange (*Philadelphus*), flowering currant (*Ribes sanguineum*), lilac (*Syringa*) and *Weigela*.

SHRUBS REQUIRING LITTLE OR NO PRUNING

Some plants require hardly any pruning at all, because either because they are slow-growing or they flower freely without much human intervention. These plants are ideal if you are worried about giving pruning a go, or are too busy to prune each year.

Shrubs in this category include *Amelanchier*, rock rose (*Cistus*), *Cornus kousa*, *Chimonanthus*, *Daphne*, *Edgeworthia*, *Enkianthus*, *Fothergilla* and witch hazel (*Hamamelis*).

MID- TO LATE-FLOWERING SHRUBS (MID-SUMMER ONWARDS)

This group of shrubs should be pruned in early spring. They produce their flowers on shoots that grow in the same year, so pruning them early encourages them to send out lots of new shoots to produce flowers later in the summer. Aim to create a framework of mature branches, and then cut back some of the new growth from the previous year to a few buds. Each one of these buds should send out a new flowering shoot in the current year.

Shrubs in this category include butterfly bush (*Buddleja davidii*), Chinese plumbago (*Ceratostigma willmottianum*), *Fuchsia*, *Hydrangea* and *Perovskia*.

REASONS FOR PRUNING

* To keep a plant healthy.
* To shape a shrub.
* To restrict the size of the plant.
* To encourage new growth.
* To make a plant safe – for example, by tackling a heavy, diseased branch that is growing overhead.
* To create a specific effect such as large foliage or striking winter stems.
* To stop biennials flowering/cropping.

Some general pruning tips:

* Keep secateurs sharp because blunt blades can damage plants.
* Always cut near to a bud and do not leave a stub (which is an entry point for disease).
* Take steps to avoid congested canopies as these cast shade and reduce air circulation.
* Remove crossing/rubbing branches.
* Remove any suckers that are growing near the base of a tree.
* Follow the four 'Ds' and remove dead, damaged, diseased and dying branches.
* Always check the timings of when a shrub should be pruned before starting.

STEP-BY-STEP TECHNIQUE

PRUNE A HYBRID TEA ROSE

Roses are pruned each year to keep them vigorous, encourage more flowers and reduce the build-up of pests and diseases. If you're feeling nervous at the prospect of pruning, do not worry; roses are related to the bramble and are as tough as a pair of old gardening boots. They will generally bounce back from most things that life and a pair of secateurs can throw at them.

PRUNING FLORIBUNDA AND HYBRID TEA ROSES

Floribunda roses and Hybrid Teas are two of the most popular types of roses. The main difference is that Floribundas produce flowers in clusters whereas Modern Hybrid Tea shrubs produce large single flowers. They both repeat-flower throughout summer and into mid-autumn. Both types of roses can be pruned in the same way (see opposite). This might look quite harsh, but it does work.

As a general rule, you should hard prune for quality of individual flowers and lightly prune for quantity of blooms. Roses will survive for years without pruning, but they produce more and larger flowers if they are pruned each year.

YOU WILL NEED

* Sharp pair of secateurs
* Loppers or a small pruning saw

Pruning roses helps promote more flowers and it should also mean there is less chance of the plant suffering from fungal diseases like black spot and rust.

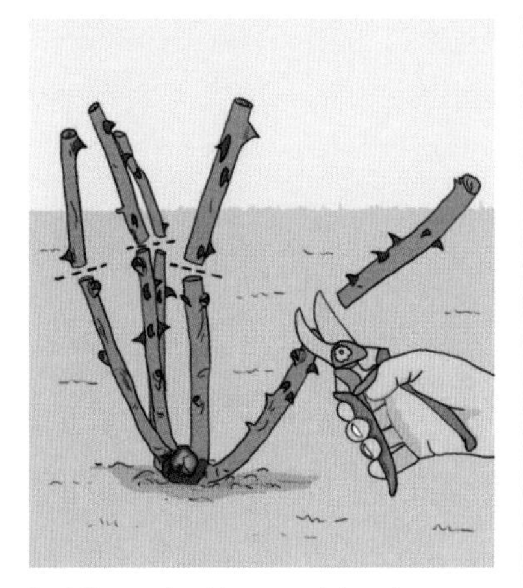

1. After planting, cut back all the shoots to about 15cm (6in), or the length of a pair of secateurs, to just above a healthy bud.

2. The following autumn, after flowering, the new growth can be pruned back by about a third. This reduces the plants' exposure to 'wind rock', whereby the plant can get buffeted by winter winds.

3. In late winter/early spring, use a pair of secateurs to remove dead, diseased or crossing stems. Cut them at the base. For thicker, older stems, use loppers or a small pruning saw or the secateurs.

4. Prune all the remaining healthy stems back to about 15cm (6in) from the ground. Less vigorous shoots can be cut back harder to about 8cm (3in) to encourage stronger growth next season.

DEADHEADING

Deadhead roses after flowering to encourage more flowers. There are two techniques. The second will take longer for new blooms to appear, but it will produce more.

1. Snap back the stem just below the dead flowerhead using pressure between the thumb and fingers.

2. Alternatively, use secateurs to cut back to a healthy bud, about 10cm (4in) further down the stem.

Pruning and training climbers

Climbing plants are useful for adding height to the garden. They can be trained over arches, pergolas and arbours as well as along walls and over fences. Climbers can be annuals, herbaceous perennials or woody shrubs, but there are a few basic rules on how to prune and care for them successfully. The three most popular climbers are featured here: clematis, climbing and rambling roses, and wisteria.

CLEMATIS

Probably one of the most popular types of climber for the garden. There are three different groups, and it is worth knowing the characteristics of each because they are pruned slightly differently.

GROUP 1 Clematis that flower in early to mid-spring, including *C. alpina*, *C. hirrhosa*, *C. macropetala*, *C. napulensis*, *C. montana* and *C. armandii*. These plants only require a quick tidy or light trim after flowering. Just remove any dead shoots and cut back where the plant has outgrown its space. The clematis in this group can be cut back harder, but it is possible that the plant will flower less the following year.

GROUP 2 Large, showy types that flower in early summer, including *C. florida* and *C. patens*, as well as their hybrids such as the popular 'Nelly Moser' and 'Corona'. These produce flowers on old stems and occasionally a second flush of flowers too. They are pruned on a renewal system, whereby about a fifth of the shoots can be pruned back to near ground level to encourage new growth. The remainder are then trimmed back to a pair of healthy buds to retain a framework of a few mature stems.

GROUP 3 Flowering from mid- to late summer, this group includes *Clematis texensis* and hybrids such as *C.* 'Étoile Violette' and *C.* 'Viticella'. Also included

When it comes to pruning a clematis you need to check which one of the three groups it belongs to.

in this group are *C. orientalis* and *C. tangutica* and the popular hybrid 'Bill Mackenzie'. These climbers produce flowers on the growth from earlier that year. Pruning is easy. Simply cut the old stems back to the lowest pair of healthy buds about 15–30cm (6in–1ft) above soil level in late winter or early spring. Alternatively, if you are looking to create a permanent structure – for example, using the clematis to screen something – then they can just be lightly trimmed.

CLIMBING AND RAMBLING ROSES

There are two different types of climbing roses. First, there are rambling roses which tend to have a sprawling, scrambling habit. Then there are climbing roses which have a more upright growth and are usually less vigorous. Ramblers usually flower only once, whereas climbing roses repeat-flower through summer. Despite their differences, they can generally be treated the same when it comes to pruning.

Remove about a third of the old stems at the base, to encourage replacements in early spring. Space out the existing stems equally on the climbing structure or wall they are growing on and prune any side shoots back to a few buds. Roses will produce more flowers if their stems are as horizontal as possible.

WISTERIA

Prune back the new, wispy growth to about 10cm (4in) after flowering to keep the plant neat and tidy. Then in winter you can prune the new growth back harder to a couple of buds. Older, thicker stems can also be removed if the plant is looking congested, to leave a framework of mature, healthy stems.

Pruning clematis

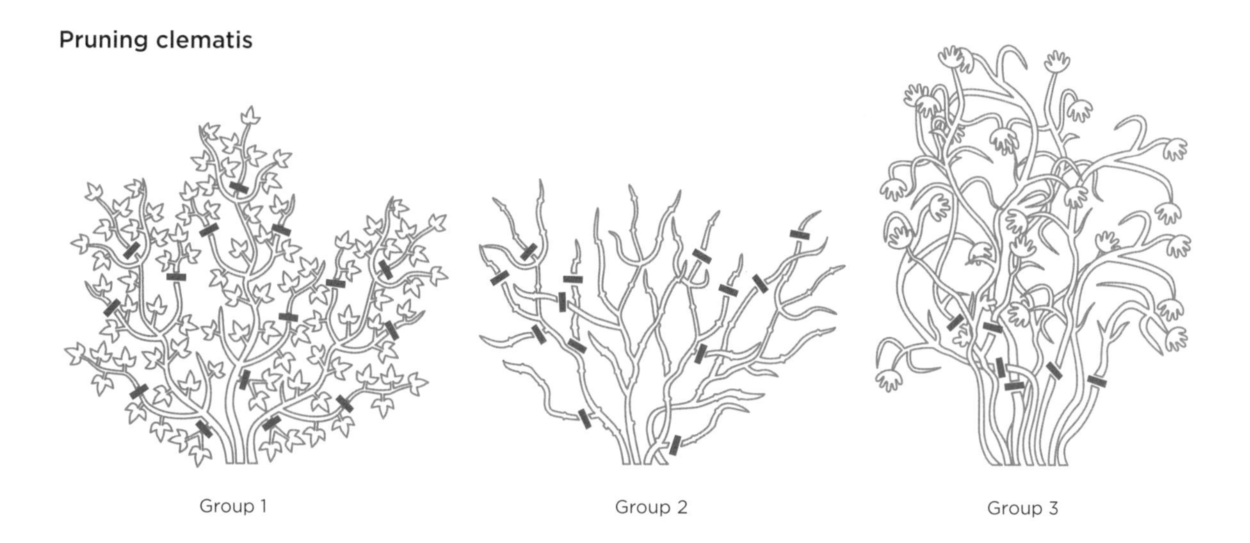

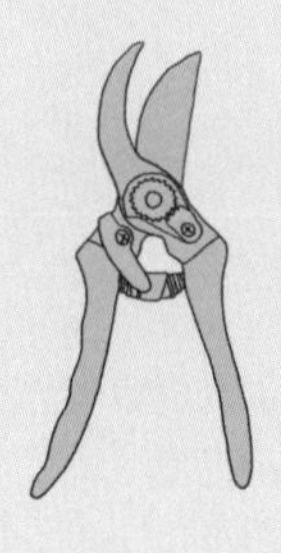

STEP-BY-STEP TECHNIQUE

TRIM A HEDGE

Trimming a hedge is extremely satisfying, and gives a garden definition and structure, as well as making it look well cared for. Avoid the bird-nesting season when planning when to cut a hedge. Times vary depending on country and location, but trimming usually takes place between early spring and late summer. Even outside of this period, always check a hedge to ensure there are no birds nesting.

PRUNING AN ESTABLISHED HEDGE

* Hedges should be pruned once a year.
* Prune deciduous hedges in the dormant season (late autumn to early spring).
* Prune evergreen hedges in early spring.

KEEPING HEDGES LEVEL

If the top of the hedge is not level to begin with, start at the highest end and work your way down. Otherwise, if you start at the lower end, you will find it difficult to get the hedge level.

YOU WILL NEED

* Hand shears or a hedge trimmer
* Ear defenders and a visor or safety goggles (if using a hedge trimmer)
* Two or three stout posts or canes
* String (enough to run the length of the hedge)
* Tape measure
* Stepladder or platform ladder

A well-pruned hedge can act as a beautiful foil or backdrop to plants grown in front of it.

1. Prune back the new growth on the first side of the hedge to the older wood. If using a hedge trimmer, wear ear defenders and a visor or safety goggles; stand sideways to the hedge and cut in an arching movement from bottom to top.

2. Repeat the process on the other side of the hedge, checking with your neighbour first if you need to access their land to do this.

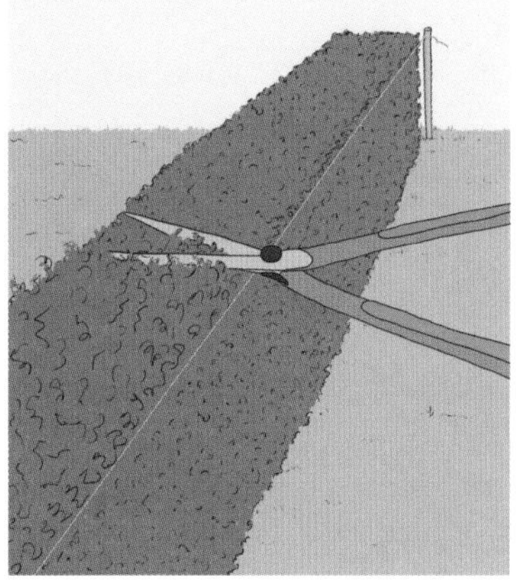

3. To trim the top of the hedge, knock in two posts or canes at each end and stretch a length of string between them at the desired height. Use a tape measure to check the height is the same at each end.

4. For a long hedge it might be necessary to use a supporting post in the middle to prevent the string sagging. Check the height with a tape measure.

5. Standing on a secure, level platform, cut along the hedge holding the hedge trimmer's cutting bar flat against the top to keep it level. Or, if you are using a stepladder, get someone else to hold the base to keep the ladder steady while you work.

6. Once you have finished, rake up the clippings, then shred and add to the compost heap.

Safety Avoid standing on the top few rungs of stepladders. Ideally, use a platform ladder to provide a level platform to work from instead.

NT GARDEN
st 1654

CHAPTER 7

CONTAINER GARDENING

Never let it be said that you do not have space for plants, as they can be grown in the smallest of spaces such as courtyards, balconies, porches and windowsills in pots, windowboxes and hanging baskets. Except for a few extreme locations, there is usually somewhere to squeeze in some plants.

Containers offer a quick and easy solution to brightening up patios and courtyards and also make it easy to ring in the seasonal changes. This chapter provides advice on the basics of gardening in containers, including the best types of potting compost to use and how to water and feed plants.

Like the open garden, a collection of containers can be carefully designed, themed and colour-coordinated to create the look you want, and so there are also suggestions on the types of containers to use to achieve different effects. There is advice on the pros and cons of using stone, metal, plastic or terracotta containers, as well as information on planting and maintenance.

Container know-how

Containers in the form of pots and windowboxes provide the perfect solution for growing plants in small gardens such as courtyards or balconies. They are particularly useful if there are no flowerbeds and any potential soil is of poor quality. They can be used as quick fixes to brighten up even the dullest of corners. Best of all, containers can be replanted frequently with different seasonal plants to provide interest throughout the year.

MOVING POTS AROUND

If the container is heavy, put it on castors/wheels attached to a small wooden platform before filling it with plants. This makes moving it around much easier – and it can be moved to one side to make room for a table and chairs when you are dining alfresco.

Homemade containers can be made from wooden pallets and put on castors for moving around easily.

DESIGNING WITH POTS

When planning a display, plant pots individually or in a group of three, as odd numbers look far better. The pots do not need to be the same size – you could have a large one at the back, and a medium one and small one at the front to each side.

DRAINAGE

Containers need drainage holes, so excess water can flow out of the bottom. To prevent holes clogging up with compost as the water drains through, cover with crocks (bits of old terracotta pot), stones or pebbles. Ideally, raise containers on bricks to improve drainage further. Some have 'feet' for this purpose.

POTTING COMPOST

As a rule, for short-term plants such as bedding, annuals and most vegetables, a general-purpose peat-free potting compost is recommended. For plants in containers for more than a year, then use a soil/loam-based, peat-free potting compost. You can also make your own compost using garden compost mixed with soil in equal proportions. For more on the different potting composts, see page 127.

Containers are also useful for growing acid-loving plants like blueberries, rhododendrons, camellias and some magnolias if your garden has neutral or alkaline soil. These plants should be grown in a peat-free ericaceous compost.

CARING FOR CONTAINERS

* Keep containers free of weeds, as these compete with plants for nutrients.
* Water plants more than those grown in the ground. In summer they may need watering every day.
* Add a moisture-retaining gel or granules to the compost on planting, which will help to retain moisture and release it when needed.
* Deadhead bedding plants and herbaceous perennials to extend the flowering display.
* Feed plants with an organic general-purpose feed once a week when they are in flower.
* Mulch the surface of the compost with well-rotted organic matter, pebbles or slate to retain moisture.

Add a layer of crocks, stones or pebbles to the bottom of containers to stop compost clogging drainage holes.

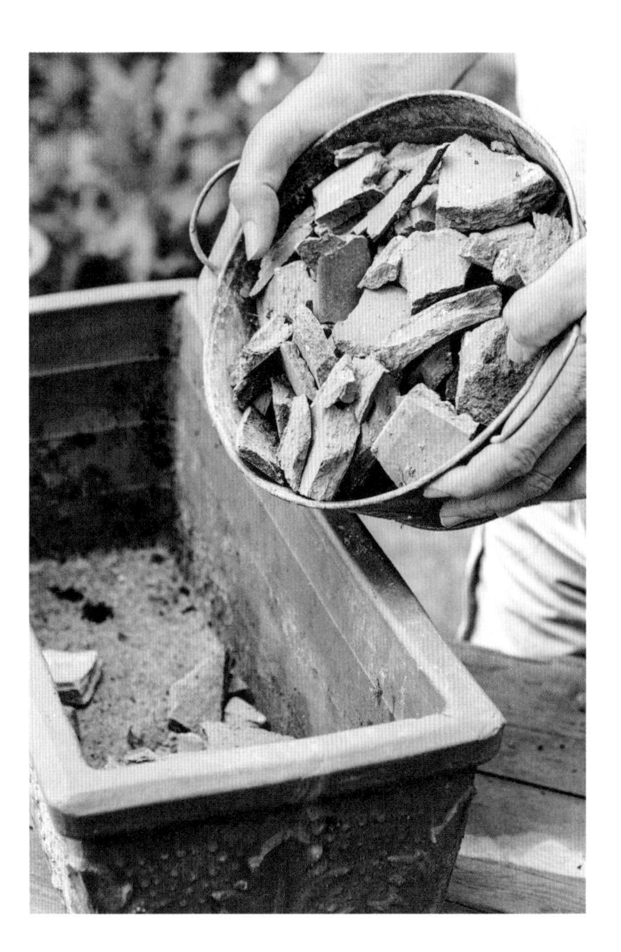

Containers – what's your style?

It's fair to say that there is a container out there to suit every style of garden imaginable, whether you opt for a large terracotta pot, Versailles planter or wooden windowbox. Many plants can be grown in containers provided these are an appropriate size and they are given the right care. They include vegetables, bedding plants, fruit, shrubs and even some trees, although in this case the container will restrict their natural size.

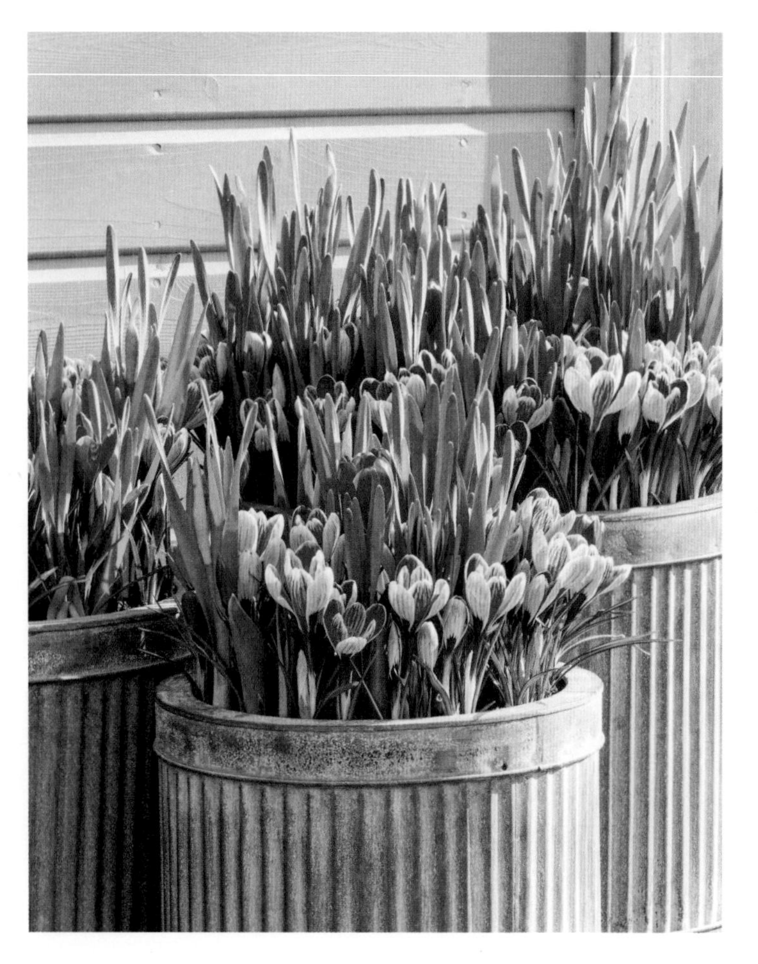

Choose a container that is suitable for the style of your garden. For example, a chic modern container may look incongruous in a cottage garden. Likewise, a beautiful, rustic terracotta pot may look completely out of place in an urban courtyard. Pots and windowboxes are available in different materials, so there will be something that works with your space. There are advantages and disadvantages to each material, so choose appropriately.

TERRACOTTA is a traditional material that brings a rustic or Mediterranean feel to a garden. Terracotta also looks natural and organic. The material is porous, which allows the root zone to breathe more easily. This means that overwatering is not a problem as the container will dry out quite quickly. Terracotta looks darker when the potting compost is moist and lighter when it is dry, making this material a handy indicator as to whether the pot needs watering. In fact, experienced head gardeners have been known to tap terracotta pots with a stick, listening to the pitch of the ringing noise to check if they need more water.

Due to the porosity of the material, terracotta containers regulate temperature better, which means they overheat less in summer and are less prone to winter cold. The disadvantage here is that some are prone to frost damage in colder areas and may crack. Choose containers that are frost-proof, not simply frost-resistant as these can crack when temperatures fall. Since the material is porous, terracotta containers may need watering more than other types. Bear in mind too that it can be quite expensive.

PLASTIC is a lightweight material, meaning plastic containers are easy to move around. They are also cheaper than terracotta or clay containers and they dry out less quickly. But they are not a high-quality product, which may have a detrimental effect on a garden's design. Plastic pots last for years, but how they are produced is not good for the environment – although they can be recycled and reused.

WOOD is a pleasingly natural material, although wooden containers are not as durable as plastic ones and can be heavy to move. To slow down the process of degradation, line the interior with plastic sheeting and treat the exterior with a wood preservative.

__Opposite:__ You can use almost anything as a container if you provide drainage holes. __Right:__ Old wooden barrels make attractive, rustic-style containers for a display of cottage garden plants.

METAL is less commonly used than other materials. Although durable, metal containers can be heavy and become very hot for plant roots if in the sun.

BE CREATIVE

Almost anything can be improvised as a container, so be creative – use sinks, bathtubs, olive oil tins, teapots and even old welly boots. Just make sure there are drainage holes, drilling some in the base if necessary.

Planting containers

Containers provide a quick solution to brightening up parts of the garden and can be used for short-term seasonal displays or long-term enjoyment. If you do not have much ground space, use windowboxes instead of pots. These are perfect for small gardens or apartments that have no garden at all. Due to their long, narrow shape, windowboxes take up little very room perched on a windowsill or hooked onto balcony railings.

PLANTING POTS AND WINDOWBOXES

If you are planting a very large container, then position it first before planting, as it will be very heavy when filled with compost. To plant:

* Make sure there are drainage holes in the bottom of the pot or windowbox. If not, you may need to drill some.
* Put a few crocks or small stones in the bottom of the container to stop the compost leaching out. You can also buy special meshes to line containers.
* Half-fill the container with some peat-free potting compost, to leave room for the plants.
* Arrange the plants in the container to create the effect you want (remember, a windowbox will largely be viewed from one side), then add more compost to cover the rootballs, leaving 1cm (½in) or so at the top to allow for watering.
* Firm the plants in gently and water thoroughly. Put the container or windowbox in position.

SECURING WINDOWBOXES

If you have used a heavy, loam-based potting compost for a windowbox and the windowsill is solid and level, then it should be heavy enough and not need securing. Otherwise, windowboxes are often supplied with brackets and instructions for securing. You can fix the brackets to the wall by

Plants in windowboxes can be changed regularly so there is always a colourful display each season.

drilling holes with a masonry drill bit (if drilling into bricks or cement) and screw the brackets into them. The windowbox then slots into the brackets. Alternatively, screw two vine eyes firmly into the outside of the wall, loop wire around the windowbox on the ledge to hold it in place, and tie both ends to the vine eyes.

TYPES OF POTTING COMPOST

When planting pots, windowboxes or hanging baskets, you need the right potting compost for your choice of plants if they are to thrive. Thankfully, there are lots of composts available which are suitable for most types of plants. In general, you will get what you pay for, with the more expensive ones being of superior quality.

SOILLESS POTTING COMPOST Ideal for short-term displays of annuals and bedding plants, a soilless compost is fine (it is often referred to as general-purpose or multipurpose compost). It is much lighter than soil-based composts, often has a fibrous texture, and can be lumpy and prone to drying out quickly. Ideally, look for peat-free versions. Peat-substitute-based composts make good alternatives. These are made of materials such as coir, wood fibres, green compost and composted bark.

SOIL-BASED POTTING COMPOST For plants that will be in a container for more than one year, such as trees, shrubs and herbaceous perennials, it is better to use a soil- (loam-) based potting compost. These usually contain sterilized loam and other additives like sand and plant nutrients. They are heavier and more stable than general-purpose composts, with a loose, open texture. John Innes is one of the most famous brands of soil-based composts available. Traditional John Innes composts contain peat, however, although some newer recipes such as SylvaGrow are peat-free.

SPECIALISED POTTING COMPOSTS There are various specialist composts available for specific plants, including orchids, bulbs, and cacti and succulents. These are specially formulated with the right amount of drainage material and nutrients to support the types of plants. Ericaceous compost is for acid-loving plants such as camellias, rhododendrons and blueberries.

OTHER POTTING COMPOST INGREDIENTS

Perlite and vermiculite are two common ingredients used in potting and cutting composts. Perlite is expanded volcanic rock and looks a bit like tiny polystyrene balls. It is used to aerate compost mixtures and make them more free-draining. Perlite can be added to cacti and succulent mixes, which require free-draining conditions. Vermiculite, on the other hand, is a mined mineral and can retain moisture up to three or four times its weight, making it suitable for plants such as seedlings that may dry out. Horticultural grit is another material that can be added to the compost to improve drainage.

COMPOST DATES

Just like food, compost can have a Best Before date, so check the label before purchasing, as many of the nutrients may have leeched out or won't be as effective.

Hanging baskets

A hanging basket packed full of bright, beautiful flowers is a sight to behold. They are perfect for brightening up a dreary-looking wall or fence and can also make a front door look more welcoming if suspended from the adjoining house wall. One of the big advantages of growing in hanging baskets is that they hardly take up any space – even the tiniest of courtyard gardens can accommodate a few hanging baskets.

Hanging baskets provide colour throughout the year, with the two main seasons of interest being summer and winter, both of which overlap into spring and autumn. For a winter display, try flowering heathers (*Erica*) and trailing ivies (*Hedera helix*). Winter pansies, primulas (including polyanthus) and cyclamen are also popular. Summer displays might include bedding plants like petunias, pelargoniums, salvias, lobelia and fuchsia. Hanging baskets are also perfect for trailing plants such as ivy and tradescantia, as well as edible plants like strawberries and trailing tomato plants.

PLANTING OPTIONS

Summer baskets can be planted from mid-spring onwards. However, if you are using bedding plants, wait until all risk of frost has passed unless you have a greenhouse to provide protection. Plant winter hanging baskets from mid-autumn onwards. Winter plants are hardy, so there is no need to worry about frosts. For most bedding and seasonal displays, a peat-free general-purpose potting compost is fine. Acid-loving plants like most heathers and a trailing cranberry (*Vaccinium macrocarpon*) require a peat-free ericaceous compost.

BASKET LINERS

The sides and bottom of hanging baskets should be lined before planting to contain the potting compost. The two most popular lining materials are ready-made cardboard liners or a fibrous material, which can be purchased online and from garden centres. Alternatively, you can make your own liner by repurposing some cardboard packaging.

A layer of moss, about 2cm (¾in) thick, can also be used to line the inside of hanging baskets. If you have moss growing in your lawn, then use a spring-tine rake to gather it up. You can sometimes buy moss online, but always check first to be sure it is from a sustainable source.

HOW TO PLANT

First line the basket with moss or a suitable liner. Fill the basket about a third full with potting compost, then start planting the sides, making slits in the liner with scissors or a sharp knife. Push the rootballs of the plants through the slits, so they are resting on top of the layer of compost. Add more compost to cover the rootballs and then plant the top of the basket. Select a prominent plant for the middle and use smaller and trailing plants around the edge. The trailing plants will spill over the sides, making a beautiful feature.

CARING FOR BASKETS

Hanging baskets generally need little maintenance. But remember to:

* Water regularly in summer. If you're going away, place baskets in the shade – a friend may offer to water them, but it will need doing less frequently. Winter displays do not need watering as often, only every couple of weeks or less depending on temperatures. If the basket feels light when you lift it up, then water.
* Add a moisture-retaining gel or granules to the compost when planting to retain moisture and release it when needed.
* Feed once a week with liquid plant food at the rates on the package.
* Deadhead bedding plants regularly to keep them flowering for longer.

Hanging baskets full of summer bedding can add an instant splash of colour to a corner of the garden.

Tabletop gardening

Tabletops are a simple and easy way to grow plants. As the name suggests, this technique involves growing plants on the tops of tables. Gardeners usually grow vegetables in tabletop gardens, but they also make impressive, colourful displays when filled with bedding plants or herbs.

MOBILE GARDENING

If your garden receives limited sunlight, attach castors to the bottom of the table legs. The table can then be pushed easily around the garden to a sunnier location, if necessary, or if you have limited space, moved out of the way for entertaining.

Recycle an old table by removing the top from the legs and turning it upside down for planting.

A range of tabletop gardens can be bought online or from garden stores. Alternatively, you can modify an existing wooden table by attaching 15-cm (6-in) high timber edging around the top to create a frame, or, if the table has a cavity underneath, removing the top, turning it over and reattaching the legs (as opposite). The top is then filled with potting compost.

THE BENEFITS OF TABLETOP GARDENING

* The plants are at a comfortable height, which is ideal for people who have back problems or difficulty bending down to ground level.
* Tabletops provide a place to grow plants and vegetables in outside spaces where there is no suitable soil for growing, such as on a patio.
* Tabletops usually only need about a 15–20cm (6–8in) depth of potting compost to grow plants, which is deep enough for most vegetables. This means filling a tabletop is easy, requiring far less compost than a raised bed at the same height. They are also much lighter to move around.

SUITABLE CROPS TO GROW

Shallow-rooting vegetables are the most suitable crops for tabletop gardening. Try lettuce, radish, cut-and-come-again salad leaves, beetroot/beets, turnips, onions, garlic, chives and globe carrots.

AFTER HARVESTING

Once the plants have finished cropping, remove the plants and old compost. Add the waste to a compost heap if you have one. Replenish the tabletop with fresh potting compost the following year, ready for sowing or planting more crops.

HOW TO MAKE A TABLETOP GARDEN

1. Build three wooden pallets of the same size using old pieces of timber.
2. Put two of the pallets on their side edges to act as the table legs. Lay the top pallet on top to form the tabletop.
3. Screw the three pallets together.
4. Line the underneath of the top pallet with old compost bags or landscaping fabric to stop the compost falling out.
5. Fill the void inside the top pallet with peat-free general-purpose compost.
6. Either sow vegetable seeds directly into the compost or plant seedlings, herbs or perhaps strawberry plants.

CHAPTER 8

FRUIT AND VEG TO TRY

Many of us start gardening because we want to grow our own vegetables, herbs and fruit. The rewards for doing so include delicious food and the satisfaction of having nurtured a plant from plot to plate, or as some people like to call it from welly to belly.

If you want to grow a few different crops in your garden, then this will need some basic planning. You will have to order seeds, clear an area for sowing, and if you have limited space, then the crops should be chosen carefully to ensure you grow the ones you really like. This chapter will help you plan your kitchen garden space and there are suggestions for the best vegetables to grow in a variety of locations. Even if your garden is in shade, do not despair as there are delicious crops to suit different aspects.

The chapter also provides a quick guide to the various groups of vegetables and fruit, so you can make informed decisions when picking the ones you wish to grow. Finally, there is information on growing herbs, so you can use them in the kitchen to help flavour all those vegetables you are growing in your new kitchen garden.

Plan your kitchen garden

There are many rewards to growing your own – fruit, vegetables and herbs taste much nicer than anything you can buy, you can try rare or heirloom varieties not in shops, there are fewer air miles, and you can be assured that no pesticides, fungicides or artificial fertilizers have been used.

PLANT SPACING

1 plant per 2 squares (60cm/2ft)	1 plant per 30cm (1ft) square	4 plants per 30cm (1ft) square	9 plants per 30cm (1ft) square	16 plants per 30cm (1ft) square
Courgette/ zucchini	Broccoli	Lettuce	Parsnip	Carrot
Marrow	Cabbage	Strawberry	Beetroot/beets	Peas/ mangetout
Squash	Cauliflower	Broad bean/ fava bean	Spinach	Radish
Pumpkin	Tomato	Dwarf runner bean	Onions, garlic	Coriander
Rhubarb	Kale	Sweet corn	Leeks	Basil

First, you'll need to plan your kitchen garden and there are a number of things to consider here:

* Which crops will grow in sun or shade?
* Is your garden going to be just for growing edible plants or do you want it to look beautiful too?
* Will you grow the crops in raised beds or directly in the open ground?
* Since raising vegetable can be more time-consuming than growing ornamental plant, how much time can you allocate to a kitchen garden?

PICK YOUR FAVOURITES

Unless you are lucky enough to have a huge garden, space will be at a premium, so it is worth making a list of the plants you would like to grow. Perhaps prioritize those that are expensive to buy and the ones you like to eat. For example, maincrop potatoes are cheap to buy, yet take up lots of room. So perhaps choose something else if you do not have much space.

BEAUTIFUL AS WELL AS EDIBLE

There are many attractive vegetable plants to choose from for a kitchen garden, but below are a few suggestions to get you started:

* Rhubarb plants for their large, decorative leaves (but please note that the leaves are toxic and should not be consumed).
* Swiss chard for the brightly coloured stems.
* Asparagus for ferny fronds.
* Lettuces with red and green leaves, as these provide a nice contrast.
* Savoy cabbages with attractive glaucous foliage.

DON'T DESPAIR ABOUT SHADE. . .

Most vegetables, fruit and herbs prefer full sun. However, a few crops will benefit from some shade. Two of the advantages of gardening in the shade include less watering and foliage scorch from the sun. Some salad leaves may also struggle to make luxuriant growth if they are parched by the sun.

Vegetables that can cope with a moderate amount of shade include lettuce and other salad leaves, root vegetables such as beetroot/beets and carrots, leeks and kohlrabi. You can also grow brassicas such as cabbages, kale and purple-sprouting broccoli, along with radishes and broad/fava beans.

. . .OR NORTH-FACING WALLS

Some fruit trees can be trained as fans on north- or east-facing walls, or on fence panels. Very often north- or east-facing walls and fence panels are left bare, without any plants, yet a few fruit trees can be trained on these as decorative 'fans'. Fans are an ornamental way of growing a fruit tree flat against a suitable surface with the branches spread out. Suitable fruits for fan-training in this way include gooseberries, redcurrants and white currants, cooking apples, sour cherries (*Prunus cerasus*) and Williams Bartlett pears.

GROW PERENNIAL CROPS

When planning your kitchen garden, it is worth considering where the perennial vegetables will go first. This is because once they are in the ground, they are harder to move than most other vegetables which are annuals. Perennial crops include asparagus, rhubarb and sea kale (*Crambe maritima*), as well as culinary herbs such as rosemary, thyme and sage.

Apples and pears

Apples and pears are one of the most popular types of fruit to grow, and it is not surprising because they are so easy to cultivate, look beautiful when in blossom, are relatively easy to grow and will generally produce a reliable crop each year. They are a good investment too, as an apple or pear tree should last 30 years or maybe longer.

GROWING RESTRICTED FORMS

Apples and pears can be trained into many different shapes and grown on fences or walls, or on a system of horizontal posts and wires in small spaces. Some of the most popular shapes include:

* Cordons – single-stem trunks with short fruiting spurs at an oblique angle (about 45 degrees). Apples: M9, M26, M116 or MM106; pears: Quince C.
* Stepovers – only suitable for apples, as pears are too vigorous. As the name suggests, they are grown horizontally low to the ground, so they can be stepped over. Choose an M27 or M9 rootstock.
* Espaliers – series of horizontal branches opposite each other at intervals going up the trunk and trained against a wall. Apples: M26, MM106, M116; pears: Quince A or C.
* Fans – series of branches splayed out in a fan shape from the trunk against a wall or fence. Apples: M26, MM106, M116; pears: Quince A or C.

For an espaliered tree, tiers of horizontal branches are trained against a wall. Ideal for small courtyard gardens.

APPLE AND PEAR ROOTSTOCKS

Trees are grafted or budded onto rootstocks (a system of roots) to restrict their size. In other words, they do not grow on their own roots. When buying an apple or pear tree, always check what rootstock it has been grown on, to ensure it will fit your space. Size will also vary slightly according to the variety, as some apple and pear trees are naturally more vigorous than others. The fertility of the soil the tree is grown in will affect its size too. Unfortunately, apple and pear rootstocks have very unmemorable names, but here is a list of these in order of size, depending on the eventual height of the tree:

M27 - 1.2m (4ft)
M9 - 1.8m (6ft)
M26 - 2m (6½ft)
MM106 - 2.5m (8ft)
M116 - 2.5m (8ft)
M111 - 5m (16ft)
M25 - 6m (20ft)

Pear trees are grafted onto quince rootstocks and are slightly more vigorous than apple trees. The two most common rootstocks are:

Quince A - 2.5-3m (8-10ft)
Quince C - 3.5-4m (11-13ft)

The most popular rootstock for growing an apple tree in a container is M26. Apples grafted onto a dwarfing rootstock (M27) can be grown as 'stepovers' along the edges of paths or the sides of vegetable beds (as shown in the picture below).

POLLINATION

Apple and pear trees need to be pollinated by other fruit trees to produce fruit. This requires another variety that flowers at the same time, so pollinating insects can travel from one tree to another. When buying a tree, check the tree's pollination group. If there are no trees in the vicinity, you may need to purchase another tree from the same group.

CARING FOR RESTRICTED FORMS

Restricted forms should be pruned in late summer, with new growth pruned back to two buds. In winter, harder pruning can be carried out to remove some of the congestion on the older wood.

Apple trees trained as 'stepovers' are perfect for edging paths and flowerbeds.

STEP-BY-STEP TECHNIQUE

PRUNE AN APPLE TREE

The most common shape for an apple tree is as a bush or open-centred tree, consisting of four or five main branches coming off a central trunk, creating a 'goblet' shape. Prune apple trees once a year to encourage fresh growth, remove damaged and diseased shoots, and let more sunlight into the canopy, which allows remaining fruit buds to ripen. The best time to prune is the dormant period (late winter to early spring), when the tree has no leaves.

HARVESTING

You'll know when an apple is ready for picking by looking beneath the tree. If apples are starting to drop to the ground, then it is likely that they are ready for harvesting. To pick an apple, cup your hand underneath the fruit, lift it up and twist gently. It should come away easily with the stalk intact. If you have to tug slightly, the apple is not ready.

STORAGE

Apple trees are categorized into early-, mid- or late-season types, beginning to ripen from late summer to late autumn. Most early-ripening apple trees are not suitable for storing and should be eaten within a day or two of being picked. Trees that mature later in the season may need to be stored for a few days or weeks before they are ready to eat.

To store apples, check for rot and remove any infected ones, so they don't contaminate others. Wrap the apples individually in newspaper and place on a tray. Store somewhere cool and dark like a shed, garage or cupboard. Check regularly for signs of rot.

YOU WILL NEED

* Secateurs and gardening gloves
* Long-handled loppers
* Pruning saw

GO HORIZONTAL

When pruning, try to retain some lateral shoots, growing almost horizontally, with fruit buds along the stem. These are easy to spot because they have thick, fat fruit buds.

An apple tree about to burst into beautiful blossom.

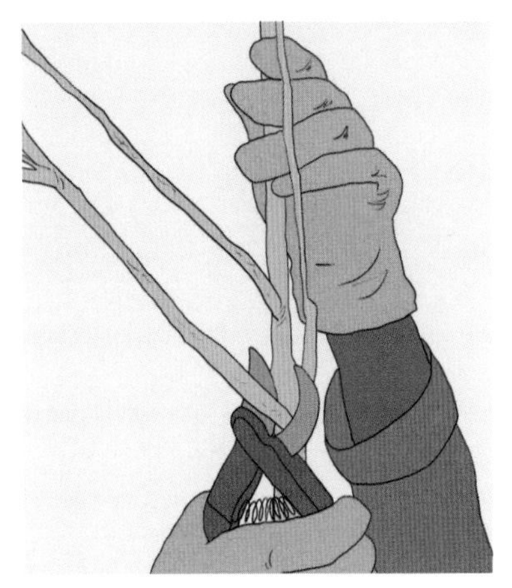

1. Remove any crossing or broken branches or those that look diseased. Aim to keep the branches nicely spaced out – usually about a hand's width apart, although this will vary depending on the tree's size.

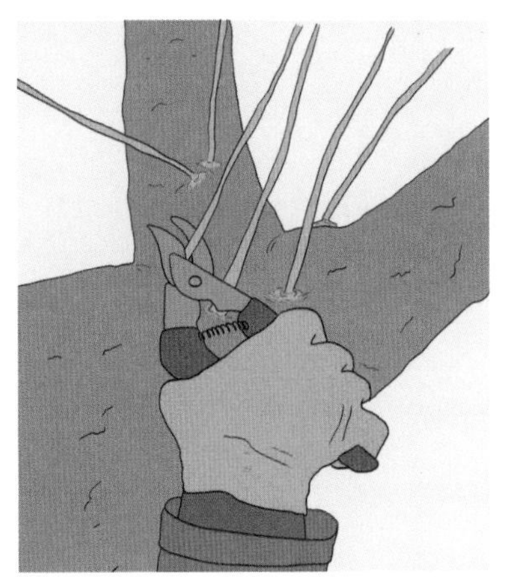

2. Use secateurs to prune back any water shoots (thin, wispy shoots) that are coming off the centre of the main trunk and causing congestion in the central area.

3. Use long-handled loppers to remove branches that are growing in towards the centre of the tree. Not only will these cast shade, but an overcongested centre restricts air flow, which can allow fungal diseases to take hold.

4. Remove any branches that are growing low down on the trunk, as these will divert energy away from the main tree canopy.

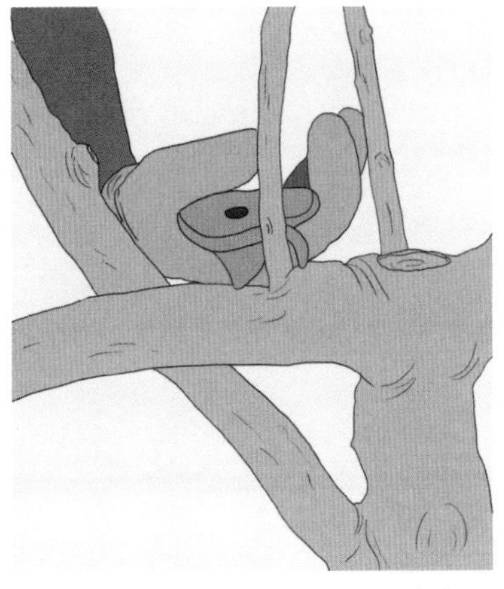

5. Remove any strong, upright, thick shoots because these are usually very vigorous and rarely bear any fruit.

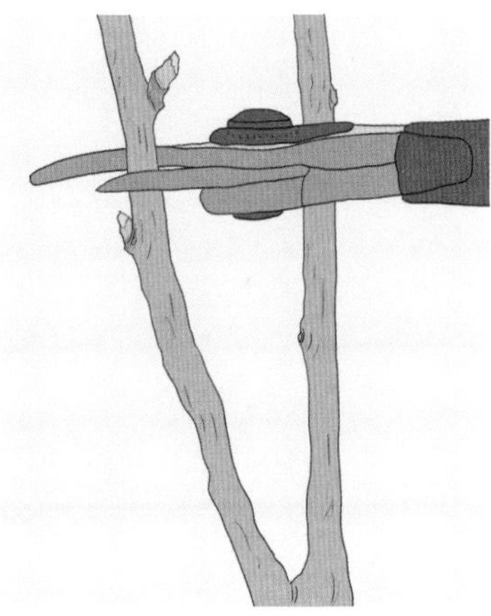

6. Prune back the 'leading' shoots on each branch to an outward-facing bud to ensure it continues to grow outwards.

Stone fruits

Some of the most delicious tree fruits belong to the 'cherry' family, which includes plums, damsons, peaches, nectarines, apricots and, of course, cherries. All of these are suitable for growing in small gardens as fans against a wall or fence. They can also be grown in large containers, which is ideal for those with a small space.

Peaches and nectarines may need protection with a suitable cover when the buds swell in early spring, to avoid a fungal disease called peach leaf curl later in the year.

None of the stone fruits featured here should be pruned in the dormant season (between late autumn and early spring). This is because the open wounds will not heal fast enough, leaving them susceptible to a fungal disease known as 'silver leaf' and bacterial canker. Instead, prune them when the sap is rising, from mid-spring until late summer.

PEACHES AND NECTARINES

These fruit trees are both slightly tender, so although they can be grown outdoors, train them on a warm, sunny, south-facing wall. Cover with horticultural fleece if a frost is forecast, as the early blossom can be susceptible. The most common training method is a fan. They fruit on wood formed the previous year, so remove some of the older wood and tie in new shoots. When fruits swell to hazelnut size, thin to 10cm (4in) apart, and 20cm (8in) apart when they are the size of a walnut. Peaches and nectarines are susceptible to peach leaf curl, a fungus that makes the leaves roll up and drop off, so cover with a clear waterproof cover in early spring as the buds begin to swell.

PLUMS

There are other plum varieties worth growing as well as the delicious 'Victoria'. Plums are mainly grown as freestanding trees, but can also be fan-trained on a south-facing wall or fence. They are easy to grow and require little pruning, just occasionally removing crossing branches to reduce congestion. Overcropping can, however, snap the branches. To avoid this, thin the fruit in early summer to a spacing of about 8cm (3in) per plum. Closely related damsons and greengages are grown in the same way.

APRICOTS

Although considered tender or even exotic, there are new, hardy varieties that are less susceptible to frost. Apricots are nearly as easy to grow as plums and are grown in a similar way, as fans on south-facing walls or as freestanding trees. Fruiting on the previous year's wood and on older stems, there are branches of different ages to consider when pruning. Thin fruit to 8cm (3in) apart when they are hazelnut size, so the remaining fruit can ripen fully and reach their proper size.

CHERRIES

Sweet and sour cherries have different growth habits. Sour cherries (like 'Morello') are suitable for north- and northeast-facing walls, although are happy with warmer aspects too. Grow as a fan or freestanding tree. They bear fruit like a peach, on wood produced the previous year, so remove some of the older wood and tie in new stems to encourage more fruit. Sweet cherries fruit on older spurs, similar to a plum, so prune back new shoots to a few buds each year. For maximum sweetness, they prefer more sunlight than sour cherries, so grow them in full sun, either as a fan on a south-facing wall or as a freestanding tree.

Net cherries when they start to ripen to stop birds eating the fruit before you do.

Gooseberries, currants and blueberries

Many soft fruit shrubs make beautiful garden features, as they have attractive, brightly coloured berries and can often be trained into decorative shapes on walls and fences. Most are fairly compact and can even be grown in containers. Best of all, you have delicious, fresh fruit growing just outside your back door. If you have a glut, most of the fruit can be frozen, so you can enjoy the fruits of your labours all year round.

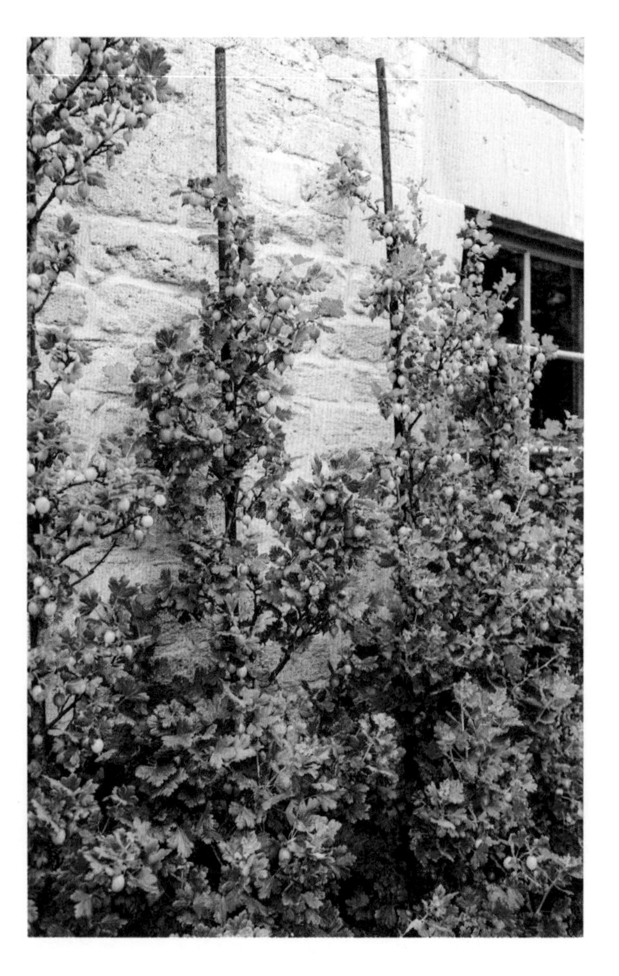

GOOSEBERRIES

You could be forgiven for thinking that gooseberries are unpleasant, sharp, hairy, acidic fruits that make your eyes water when you bite into one. This is because they are often sold in shops when they are unripe and have not fully developed their flavour. This is very unfair, though, as a ripe gooseberry is delicious, sweet and juicy. They come in a range of colours, including red, yellow, pink, white and green. Gooseberries can be grown as cordons or fans on a north-facing wall. Alternatively, they can be trained as bushes. To ensure the fruit ripens, thin them out, removing every other berry. The thinned fruit can be used for cooking and the remainder left on the plant to ripen fully. Gooseberries ripen on old wood and at the base of their young shoots, so prune new growth back to two buds in winter.

Left: *Gooseberries can be grown as upright cordons on north- or east-facing walls.* ***Opposite:*** *Grow blueberries in containers of ericaceous potting compost if you do not have acidic soil in your garden.*

REDCURRANTS/PINK CURRANTS AND WHITE CURRANTS

There are three types of currants – redcurrants, white currrants and blackcurrants (see below) – and these are essentially different varieties of the same fruit. Red and white currants look gorgeous grown on north-facing walls as a fan or cordon, especially when laden with brightly coloured fruit. They can also be grown as bushes or standards. Similar to gooseberries, they fruit on older wood and at the base of new shoots, so prune the new growth back to two buds in winter. It may be necessary to give the new growth a trim back to five or six leaves in summer to allow more light into the canopy.

BLACKCURRANTS

Confusingly, blackcurrants have a different growth habit to redcurrants, white currants and gooseberries, and so they are grown differently. They bear fruit on young stems, so prune back about a third of the older wood each year to near ground level with a pair of loppers, retaining plenty of young growth. Blackcurrants are grown as stool bushes, which means they need to be planted deep in the soil to encourage lots of new growth to shoot up from the ground. They're not really suitable for growing as a fan or cordon. They can be grown in a container if it is deep enough to accommodate the root system about 5cm (2in) below the surface.

BLUEBERRIES AND CRANBERRIES

These two closely related berries both prefer slightly acidic soil. If you don't have these conditions in your garden, then they can be grown in containers in ericaceous compost. Cranberries have a low, trailing habit and are suitable for full sun or dappled shade. They can also be grown in hanging baskets. They require little pruning, just the occasional trim of the ends when they get too straggly. They also tend to like fairly moist conditions.

Blueberry plants are larger than cranberries and have a more upright habit. They should be grown as bushes and are not suitable for being trained as either fans or cordons. Prune blueberries in winter or early spring by removing some of the older stems at the base, to encourage new shoots that will bear the fruit.

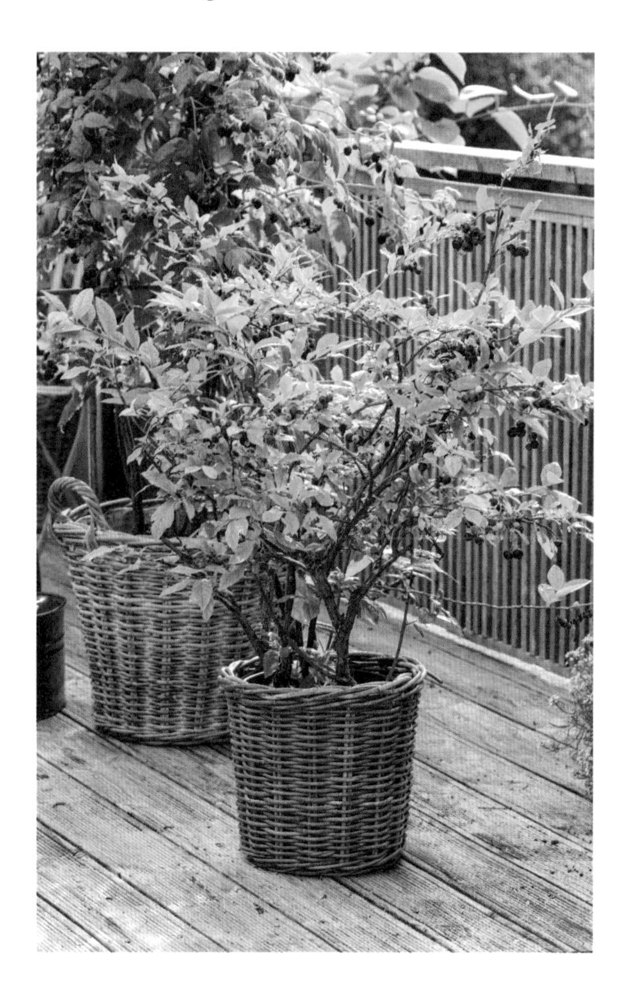

Strawberries, raspberries and grapes

There is nothing more delicious than homegrown fruit, and many of these can be grown in the tiniest of spaces. Grapevines can be trained on south-facing walls, while strawberries can be grown in patio planters and raspberries in containers. The joy of these plants is that delicious fresh fruit need never be more than a few metres from your back door.

Left: *Grapes are easy to grow and can be trained over archways to make the most of the available space.* ***Opposite:*** *Place straw under ripening strawberries to prevent them rotting on the soil.*

STRAWBERRIES

Most people's favourite fruit and so easy to grow, strawberries are low-growing perennials with a trailing habit, which makes them suitable for hanging baskets or containers. Or they can simply be grown in a strawberry patch at 30cm (1ft) apart. They are also ideal for patio planters with planting pockets or holes around the sides. If growing them in the ground, place straw underneath the berries to prevent them rotting on the soil surface.

There are two different types of strawberries. Summer-fruiting varieties bear large, juicy berries in mid-summer, while everbearing ones produce a few crops of smaller berries through the growing season. Both types are grown in the same way. Once plants have finished growing, trim back old foliage to allow new fresh foliage to emerge.

RASPBERRIES

Raspberries are upright plants that produce fruit on canes. There are two different types and it is important to know which one you are growing as they are pruned slightly differently. Summer-fruiting raspberries produce fruit on canes that grew the year before. So, once they finish fruiting, cut away the old fruiting canes and tie in the new growth, which will provide fruit the following year. Autumn raspberries produce their fruit on the current growth. All the canes are simply cut down to ground level in late winter or early spring each year, encouraging new shoots to grow and fruit later that summer. Summer raspberries will need a system of horizontal wires tied between two posts to tie the fruits onto. Autumn raspberries can be just left to sprawl on the ground, in a similar way to a bramble bush.

GRAPES

If you want to make your own wine, then you need to choose an outdoor variety of wine grape. Depending on where you live, dessert grapes may require a greenhouse or conservatory to ripen. Grapevines are climbing plants and so need something to grow on, such as a fence, wall or system of wires. They can also be trained over arches. It is possible to grow grapevines in containers if a suitable climbing structure can be provided. Grapes need a warm, sunny and frost-free site to ripen.

Prune established grapevines in winter by cutting all the new growth back to two buds. In summer, it might be necessary to trim back the new growth to about five leaves to prevent them from shading the rest of the canopy. Grapes should be ready for picking in the autumn.

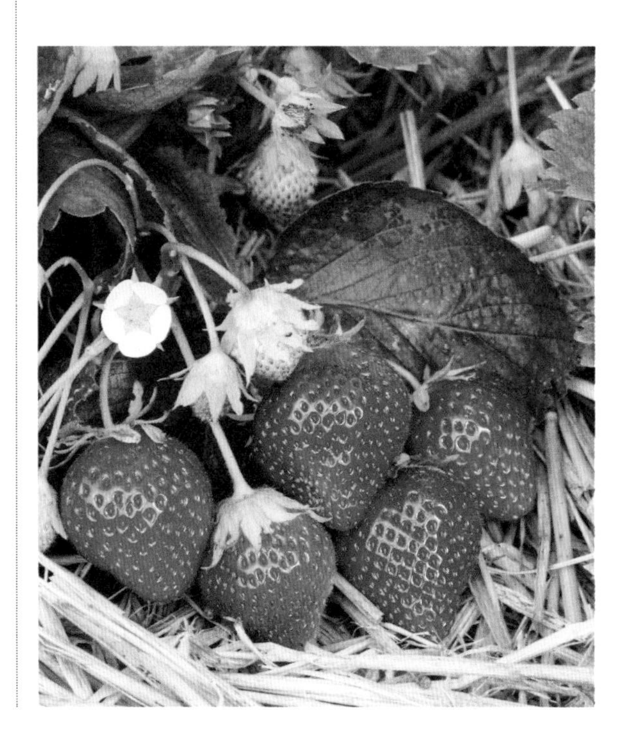

Other fruit to try

You can grow so many delicious fruits in a small garden that you really are spoiled for choice. Some of the lesser-known fruits are described here, all of which are easy to grow and should provide you with produce either to eat fresh or to use in the kitchen. Best of all, by growing your own fruit, you will be able to try varieties that you just cannot get hold of in the shops.

Left: *Figs are ideal for growing in pots as they produce more fruit when their roots are restricted.* ***Opposite left:*** *Hybrid berries like tayberries are easy to grow, taste delicious and are hard to find in the shops. Opposite right: Kiwi is a climbing plant and will therefore need to be grown on a training system such as trellis.*

FIGS

These Mediterranean plants are not as tender as you may think. There are varieties that are fairly hardy and will survive the harshest of winters. However, in order to produce ripe fruit, they benefit from being grown in a sunny location such as on a south-facing fence. Figs are one of the few fruits that will actually do better in a container than if grown in the ground. This is because when their roots are restricted, they tend to produce more fruits. If their roots have a free run, they can forgo fruit production and focus on producing lots of lush, vegetative growth. For this reason, if planting a fig in the ground, it is a good idea to dig a square pit, put patio slabs against each side of the hole and place some hardcore in the bottom in order to restrict the fig's roots.

HYBRID BERRIES

The term 'hybrid berries' usually refers to the plethora of delicious raspberry-related soft fruits. These include Japanese wine berries, tayberries, tummelberries, loganberries and boysenberries. Most of these examples fruit in a similar way to summer-fruiting raspberries, whereby they will fruit on canes produced the previous year. Cut back the old, fruiting stems after fruiting and tie in new shoots, which will then fruit the following summer. Many of these berries prefer a sunny location, although they will tolerate a moderate amount of dappled shade.

KIWI

The kiwi is a climbing plant with attractive foliage, producing sweet, juicy, green fruit in autumn. Most varieties require both a male and a female plant to produce fruit, although there are one or two self-fertile varieties available, which are more suitable for a smaller garden. Kiwi plants need a climbing structure on which to grow, such as a trellis, wall or archway. Pruning is carried out in winter by cutting all the new growth back to about 5cm (2in). Kiwis are fairly vigorous plants and will possibly need an additional trim in summer, with the new shoots cut back to five or six leaves.

Beans

There are so many types of beans, but the most popular are probably the tall, climbing runner and French beans and the shorter, squatter broad (fava) beans. They are all easy to grow and produce delicious beans. Another advantage of growing beans is that they are legume crops, which means they add nitrogen to the soil. So, once they have finished cropping, the roots can be dug in, meaning you do not need to fertilize the next crop.

RUNNER BEANS

Runner beans were first introduced as ornamental climbing plants because they have such pretty flowers. As time went by, people realized that the pods were tasty, and started to breed beans as an edible crop. Runner beans are grown as an annual. They are slightly tender, so do not get them started too early before temperatures are warm enough in late spring. Sow indoors in pots in late spring and then plant outside after all risk of frosts has passed. Or sow directly into the soil from early summer. Plants or seeds should be spaced 10cm (4in) apart. As runner beans are climbing plants, they require a wigwam or other support structure to grow up. They prefer a warm, sunny site with a fertile or rich soil. Add plenty of well-rotted organic matter prior to planting. As runner beans start to grow, they may initially need a bit of encouragement to attach to

Left: *Runner bean flowers are as pretty as the beans are tasty.* ***Opposite:*** *Broad beans are one of the hardiest members of the bean family and can be sown in winter for one of the first crops of the year in spring.*

the support structure. Once they have got a grip, however, they should scramble their way up to the top. Keep harvesting the beans as they appear. The more you pick, the more the plants will crop.

TIP ON TRAINING

Get the training structure in place before planting beans to avoid damaging the roots.

FRENCH/GREEN BEANS

These are very similar to runner beans, although there are also dwarf types that are perfect for growing in pots. There is a range of different colours, including purple and yellow varieties, as well as speckled (borlotti) and the usual green. Like runner beans, they are slightly tender, so plant or sow after all risk of frosts has passed. Grow in the same way as runner beans. French beans can be picked young and eaten in their pods or dried and shelled, and the beans used in salads and casseroles.

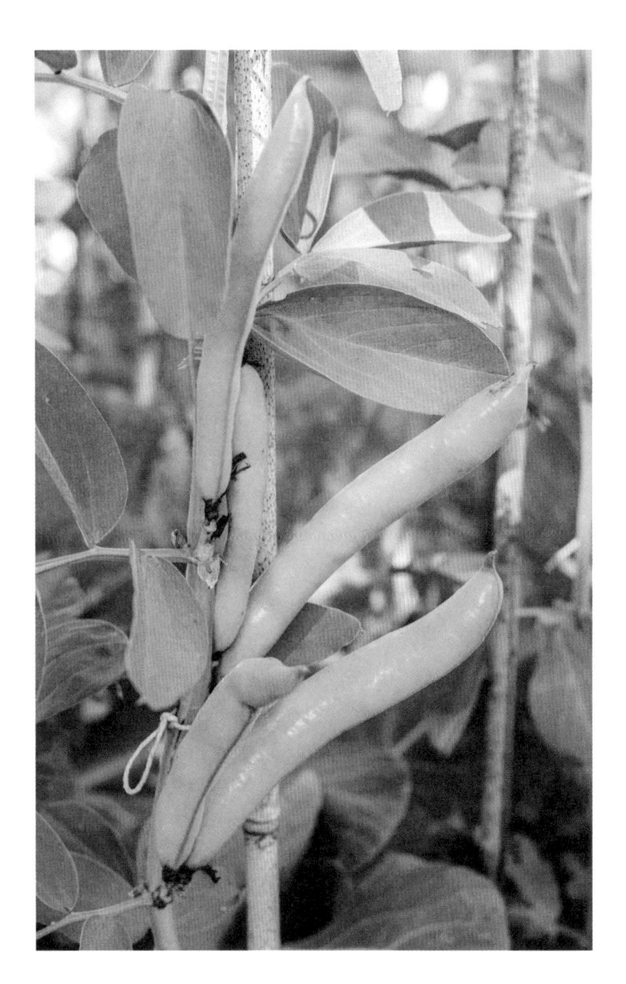

BROAD/FAVA BEANS

Much shorter than their cousins the runner and French beans, broad beans are also much hardier. Start them in autumn in modules or pots to get an early crop the following spring or plant in early spring. Plant directly into the ground at intervals of 8cm (3in). Insert twiggy 'pea sticks' along the row of beans to provide additional support unless you are growing a dwarf variety. Pinch out the tops in late spring once enough pods have formed. This encourages the plant to focus on developing pods and helps avoid the blackfly that attack growing tips.

Peas

Sweet, delicious peas are relatively hardy and also fun to grow. They are one of the toughest members of the vegetable world and a good choice of crop to sow in early spring if you want something in the garden to harvest early. Early sowings of peas can be made under horticultural fleece or cloches if you cannot wait for the soil to warm up fully.

***Left:** Growing peas in an old gutter is a good way to get them started early in the season if the ground is too wet and cold.* ***Opposite:** The roots of legumes (pea family) fix nitrogen to the soil.*

Peas need supporting with 'twiggy sticks', which are sometimes known as 'pea sticks'. Hazel branches are the most common, but anything with lots of lateral branches will do. Pea sticks should be about 1m (3ft) high, although there are shorter and taller ones. Peas prefer a warm, sunny location and fertile, free-draining soil. They are best grown in the open ground in rows, 8cm (3in) apart, in a zigzag pattern, but they can also be grown in containers in a good-quality, peat-free, general-purpose potting compost.

SOWING AND PLANTING PEAS

Sowing pea seed in gutters is a great way to get peas off to an early start. This is especially true if the soil in your garden is cold and wet. Once conditions have improved, the seedlings can be slid out of the gutter and planted in their final location. Peas prefer a fertile soil, so you may need to dig in some organic matter first. To sow seed in a length of gutter:

* Drill small drainage holes in the length of gutter, about 10cm (4in) apart.
* Clip 'gutter ends' to both ends of the gutter to stop the potting compost washing out.
* Fill the gutter with some peat-free, general-purpose potting compost.
* Sow pea seeds at a depth of 1cm (½in) in a zigzag pattern, approximately 8cm (3in) apart, down the centre of the gutter. Water in gently.
* Place the length of gutter in a greenhouse or even just on the patio while the seeds germinate.
* It may be necessary to place a net over the gutter to keep the birds off.
* Keep the seeds watered as they start to germinate.
* Once the seedlings are about 10cm (4in) tall, slide them out of the gutter, along with the compost, in one complete section.
* Dig a groove in the final planting place to the same depth as the gutter and slide the section of pea seedlings into it.
* Push in twiggy 'pea sticks' to support the pea plants as they grow.

HOW TO EAT

Peas are usually shelled before being consumed and can be eaten fresh from the pod or steamed or boiled. They are also suitable for freezing, so can be enjoyed all year round. In fact, peas are one of the few vegetables that benefit from being frozen, as it makes them taste sweeter. Sugar snap and mangetout/snow peas are sweeter and more tender, which means the whole pod can be eaten. In fact, the French name *mangetout* means 'eat all'.

NITROGEN-FIXING ROOTS

Like beans, peas 'fix' nitrogen in their roots. So once the plants have finished cropping, chop up the roots and dig them into the soil. The next crop planted in the soil will benefit from this boost of nitrogen.

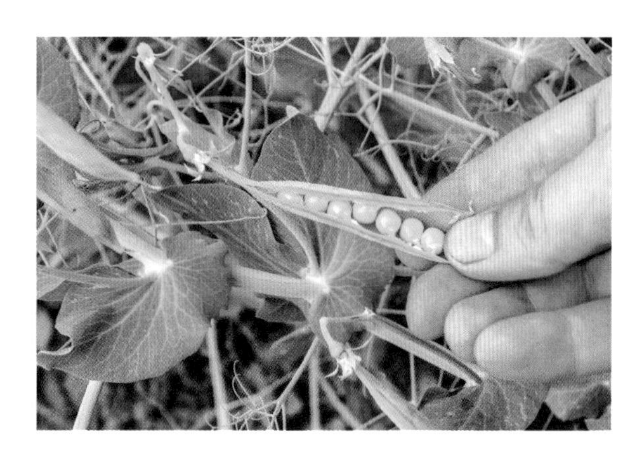

Onions and garlic

If you love cooking, then onions and garlic should be on your essential list of things to grow. They belong to the fairly large allium group which also includes leeks, chives, garlic, shallots, spring onions/scallions and bunching onions, as well as the familiar standard onion. They will all add a flavoursome bite to any culinary dish.

ONIONS AND SHALLOTS

Onions are closely related to the ornamental alliums often seen in flower borders. Not surprisingly, many onions and leeks develop a beautiful, purple-blue flowerhead if this is left to develop, which can be dried and used in flower arrangements. Onions are usually brown, but there are also delicious red and yellow varieties which taste sweeter.

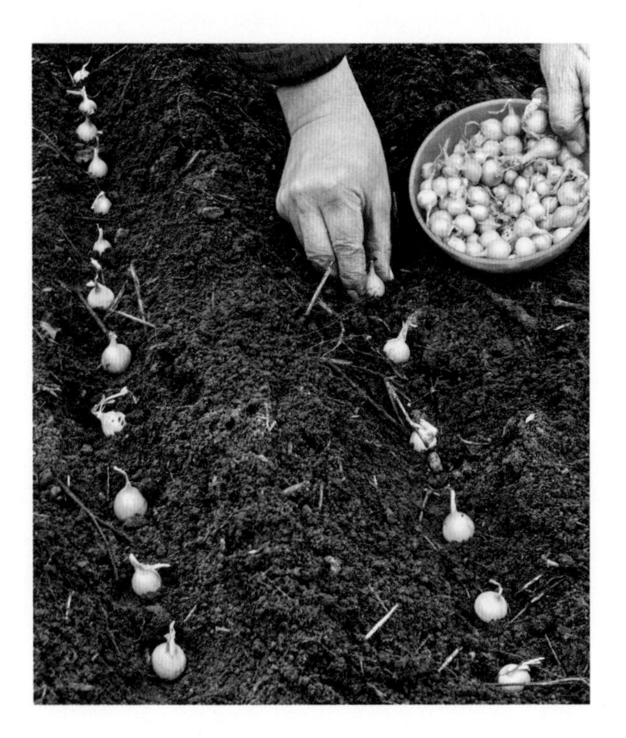

You can grow onions from seed, but it is easier to grow them from sets. These tiny onions are planted in autumn or spring and then swell to the size of a large bulb. They are ready to harvest about 80 days after planting, so you do not have to wait too long.

Plant onion sets 10cm (4in) apart in rows with 30cm (1ft) between each row. They require a well-drained soil, otherwise the bulbs tend to rot. Like onions, shallots are often grown from sets, but they usually develop into a cluster of small onions rather than a single larger bulb. They also take slightly longer to mature.

Harvest when the foliage starts to turn brown or yellow and wilts or flops over, ideally in dry weather. Leave in the sun for a couple of days, then store inside.

Left: *The easiest way to grow onions is from 'sets' which are baby onions that swell and grow larger.*
Opposite: *Leeks are often planted deep in the soil to 'blanch' the stem, making it white and slightly tender.*

LEEKS

Another very popular member of the onion family, leeks are grown for their succulent, onion-flavoured stems, which are a staple ingredient in so many soups and numerous other dishes and with roasted meats. One of the benefits of growing leeks is that they can be harvested in winter when not many other crops are available.

Leeks are usually grown from seed. They prefer a well-drained, yet heavy soil and full sun. The easiest way to grow them is to sow the seed in modules under cover and then prick them out when they are about 12cm (5in) tall before planting them out in spring, spaced 15cm (6in) apart. Their roots and tops can be trimmed when transplanting. Traditionally, leeks are planted using a dibber to make 15cm- (6in-) deep holes into which you drop the young plant. Once planted, water in, allowing the soil to wash around the roots. The idea is that these conditions allow the leeks to swell naturally and the depth of the soil will blanch the base of the stems. This technique is called 'puddling'. Alternatively, sow leek seed directly into drills, 1cm (½in) deep, and thin out to their final spacing.

Harvest leeks from late summer onwards, although they can be left in the ground during autumn and harvested when they are mature, digging them up with a fork as and when needed.

GARLIC

Like onions, garlic can be grown from seed, but it is far easier to start with small cloves. Garlic requires a long growing season and so is often planted in late autumn or winter. It prefers well-drained soil in a sunny position because otherwise the bulbs have a tendency to rot. Since they are shallow rooting, garlic is ideal for growing in a container too.

Garlic cloves should be planted 2cm (¾in) deep with the tip pointing upwards and the wider base at the bottom. Garlic is ready to harvest from mid- to late summer when the foliage starts to wither and turn yellow. It should be harvested in dry weather and left to dry out in the sun for a few days before either being stored or used in the kitchen.

CHIVES

These low-growing perennials are members of the onion family and are a wonderful addition to any garden. Their stalks can be snipped with scissors or chopped up with a knife and scattered over salads and other dishes to add a mild, oniony flavour. After two or three years, dig up and divide chive plants if they become congested. They have stunning, purple flowerheads that can be used to garnish dishes.

Pumpkins, squashes and gourds

This is one of the most exciting groups of vegetables, as there is such a large array of shapes and colours to choose from. Technically, pumpkins, squashes and gourds are fruits, but no self-respecting gardener would be without these in their veggie patch. Often referred to as cucurbits, the family includes courgettes (zucchini), marrows, pumpkins, squashes and cucumbers. Most of these are slightly tender and should not be planted or sown until all risk of frost has passed.

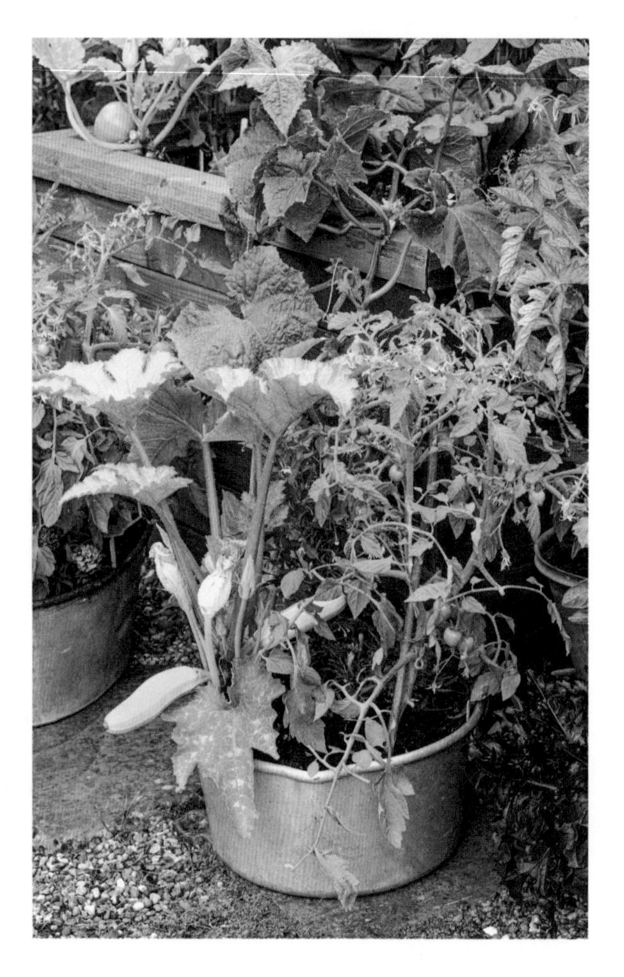

PUMPKINS AND SQUASHES

Halloween would feel incomplete without the iconic pumpkins adorning neighbourhood doorsteps and windows, yet they have far more exciting uses in the kitchen, whether in pumpkin pies or tarts or added to savoury dishes. Even pumpkin seeds can be roasted and enjoyed as a tasty, healthy snack.

Sow pumpkin seeds in pots under cover in late spring and plant them outside in rich, fertile soil in a sunny spot as soon as the risk of frost is over. They need quite a lot of space, so plant as much as 1m (3ft) apart, depending on the variety. Some can also be trained up fences, walls and trellises.

Pumpkins and squashes are hungry plants, so they may need a liquid feed every week when they start forming flowers and fruits. When ready for harvesting, they may benefit from being left to dry in the sun for a few days to cure/harden the skin.

Left: *Pumpkins can be grown in containers, but will need lots of watering and feeding if this is not big enough.* ***Opposite:*** *Cucumbers are climbing plants and will need to be grown on a training system.*

If you want to grow a really large pumpkin, then remove all the fruits when they are small except for one or two and allow these to develop to their full size. Make sure you choose one of the large varieties, as there are some small/mini pumpkins too.

COURGETTES/ZUCCHINI AND MARROWS

You will be amazed how many courgettes/zucchini a single plant can produce and also surprised at how quickly they can become 'marrow'-sized if not picked soon enough. Technically, marrows are giant courgettes, but specific varieties are more suited to growing to this larger size. So, if you want to grow a marrow, look for seeds labelled 'marrow'.

Courgettes/zucchini and marrows are grown in the same way. Sow seeds in pots in late spring or directly in the ground once the soil is warm enough. They are slightly tender, so do not plant or sow until all risk of frosts is over. They are Mediterranean plants and love to bask in warm, sunny conditions. They also produce a lot of foliage, so provide a well-composted or fertile soil. Also give them enough space, allowing about a square metre (a square yard) per plant. They can be grown in large containers or growing bags too. Keep harvesting to encourage more to develop and stop them getting too big. Expect three or four a week from each plant.

WHICH WAY UP?

Plants in the cucurbit family have large seeds. Sow the seeds on their edges, otherwise they can be prone to rotting if their largest surface area is facing upwards or downwards because water will collect on top.

CUCUMBERS

There are two types of cucumbers: indoor and outdoor types (the latter are sometimes called ridge cucumbers). Cucumbers are climbing plants, so need something to scramble up like a net or trellis in the greenhouse. Outside they can be left to sprawl on the ground or trained up a fence. Sow outdoor cucumbers in individual pots or modules in late spring. Indoor types can be sown earlier. Cucumbers have male and female flowers, with the latter developing into the fruit. Pinch out the tip once the plant has seven or eight leaves and encourage side shoots to develop where the fruits will form. Cucumber sizes vary according to variety – check the packet so you know when they will be ready to harvest. They are very thirsty plants, so water well and feed once a week from flowering time onwards.

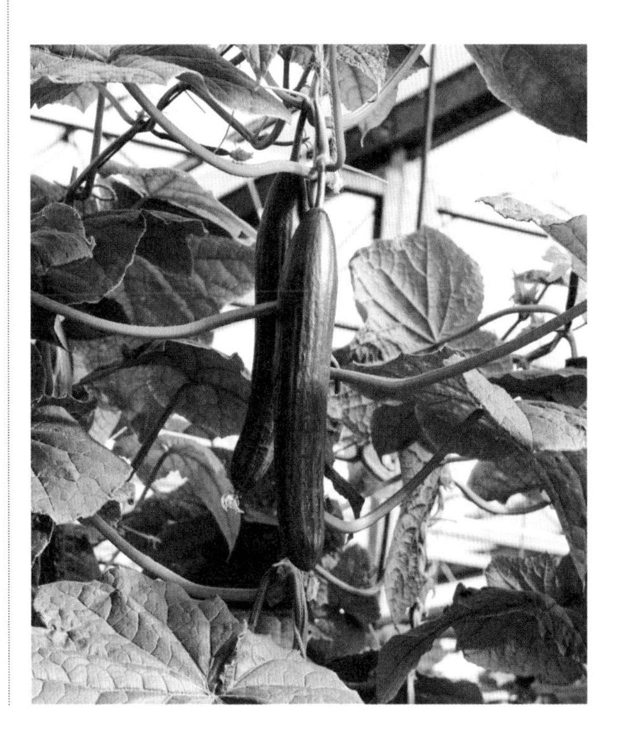

Tomatoes

A homegrown tomato picked fresh from the vine is juicy and delicious, and the taste is incomparable to that of those you can buy in the shops. Tomatoes are easy to grow and you do not necessarily need a greenhouse. If suitable varieties are chosen, all you need is a sunny, sheltered spot in the garden.

Tomatoes were originally introduced to Europe in the early 16th century as a decorative plant from the Americas. It was only much later that people started enjoying eating the fruit.

You can buy tomato plants as young plants in late spring, ready for growing at home. However, it is cheaper to buy tomato seeds, which should be sown under cover in late winter or early spring. There is also a wider choice of varieties if you grow from seed. In fact, one of the most exciting things about tomatoes is the large number of different varieties on offer, including rare heritage and heirloom varieties that you won't find in the shops. From tiny, sweet, cherry-sized tomatoes to large beefsteak types the size of cooking apples, there is a plethora of shapes and colours, ranging from gold, yellow, red and orange to purple and black. Some have streaky or stripy skins and can be plum- or cherry-shaped, while others are heavily ribbed. There are two types of tomatoes, which are grown differently:

CORDON (INDETERMINATE) tomatoes grow on a tall central stem and are usually trained upwards on a cane or length of string hung from the ceiling.

BUSH (DETERMINATE) tomatoes are wider and shorter than cordons and are usually staked, although some gardeners allow them to sprawl on the ground. Some bush tomatoes, such as 'Tumbling Tom', can even be grown in hanging baskets.

Left: *Tomatoes need regular watering and feeding to keep them cropping throughout the summer.*
Opposite: *Some trailing (determinate) types of tomatoes are suitable for growing in hanging baskets.*

 **TIP ON BLIGHT**

Tomato blight is a fungus that can quickly destroy a crop, but there are resistant varieties of tomato you can grow, such as Fantasio F1, Losetto F1, Legend and Lizzano.

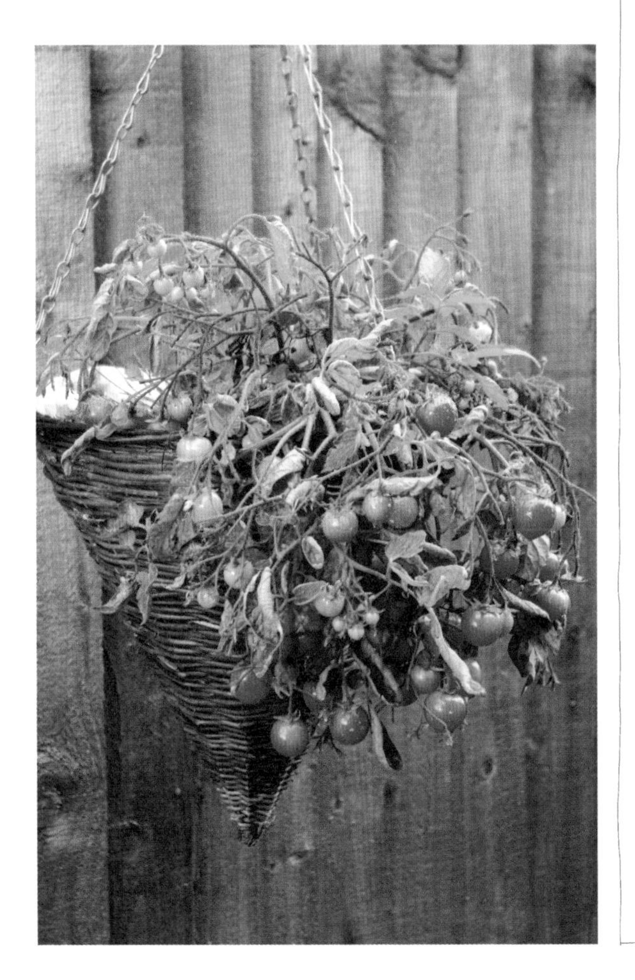

HOW TO SOW AND GROW

1. Fill 9cm (3½in) pots with general-purpose potting compost to just below the surface.
2. Place a seed on top of the compost in each pot, push it down just below the surface, then cover with compost.
3. Water the compost and place the pots on a sunny windowsill or in a propagator at a temperature of 12–20°C (54–68°F).
4. Plant the seedlings outside when they are 15cm (6in) tall and all risk of frost is over.

PLANTING OPTIONS

* Plant tomato plants directly into the ground, 45cm (18in) apart.
* Use growing bags, planting two tomatoes per bag. These contain a preformulated compost to get the tomato plants off to a good start.
* Grow in 15–50-litre (3–11-gallon) pots of general-purpose potting compost.

AFTERCARE

* Feed with an organic liquid tomato feed once a week as soon as flowers start to appear.
* Pinch out the laterals (side shoots) of cordon tomatoes to encourage fruit to ripen rather than branches to grow. Laterals appear between the main stem and the leaf.

The cabbage family

The cabbage family, also known as brassicas, is a large group of vegetables, which contains many of our favourite staple leafy crops such as kale, broccoli, cauliflower and Brussels sprouts. The group also includes some of the root vegetables, such as swede/rutabaga, turnip and kohlrabi (see page 166), as most people associate these delicious plants with root crops.

KNOW YOUR SOIL

Brassicas generally prefer a slightly alkaline soil to avoid a fungal disease called 'club root'. This causes swollen and distorted roots and stunted growth. Lime can be added to the soil to raise the pH levels.

Not only do homegrown cabbages and kale taste great, but their foliage also creates a rich tapestry of textures in the vegetable bed.

CABBAGES AND CAULIFLOWERS

If you like cabbages, then there is some good news – you can grow them almost all year round. The general pattern is 'spring greens' followed by the spring-sown summer cabbages. You then get the delicious winter cabbages, such as the famous dark-leaved Savoy cabbage which is fully hardy and can withstand the coldest of winter frosts, staying in the ground until ready for harvesting.

Cabbages like a firm and fertile soil, and although they prefer full sun, they can cope with some shade during the day. Sow seeds in a seed tray, then when the seedlings are 4cm (1½in) tall, plant them in their final position. Spacing will vary, depending on the variety, so consult the seed packet for details.

Bear in mind that cabbages can become top-heavy and may topple over. For this reason, you should grow them in firm soil. You may also occasionally need a stake to hold them upright.

Cauliflowers are grown in a similar way to cabbages, although these are slightly trickier because they are quite fussy about growing conditions. They require plenty of sunshine and water and also a slightly alkaline soil.

BROCCOLI AND CALABRESE

Just to clarify, the vegetable that we see labelled as broccoli in the supermarket is actually known as calabrese in the gardening world. And broccoli is referred to as purple-sprouting broccoli. The latter is often sown in spring and harvested the following year. It is a useful crop for filling the gap in early spring when there are no other vegetables to harvest. Calabrese is usually sown directly into the soil in spring and then harvested later in the year.

KALE

This is probably the toughest of all the brassicas, and that is saying something, as it's up against some pretty tough competition. Kale will survive almost anything winter can throw at it, and it is said that the cold can even slightly sweeten the more bitter leaves. Seeds should be sown in seed trays or modules and planted out when they are about 4cm (1½in) tall, at a spacing of about 45cm (18in).

Like many of the other brassicas, kale is a useful crop for filling in the winter gap when there is not much else available. They require a rich, heavy soil. One of the other benefits of growing kale is that some of the ornamental varieties have leaves in attractive shades, which can add structure and colour to the garden all through the year.

BRUSSELS SPROUTS

Perhaps not everybody's favourite, but Christmas dinner would not be complete without these contentious vegetables! Brussels sprouts are fairly easy to grow. Simply sow them in modules in spring and then plant them outside when they are about 8cm (3in) tall. They require a fertile, but firm soil in order to keep them upright and they may also need staking. They are winter hardy, and the sprouts can be picked throughout winter.

If you don't like Brussels sprouts because of their bitter flavour, then think again. There are now modern varieties available that have been bred to be sweeter and less 'sprout-tasting'. There are also some colourful varieties, including purple and red.

Perennial vegetables

Whereas most vegetable crops are grown as annuals, there are also a few perennials. It is worth giving extra consideration to where these are planted in the garden because once they are *in situ*, they should ideally stay there for a few years. They are a great investment in terms of time and effort since once you have sown or planted them, they are relatively easy to look after.

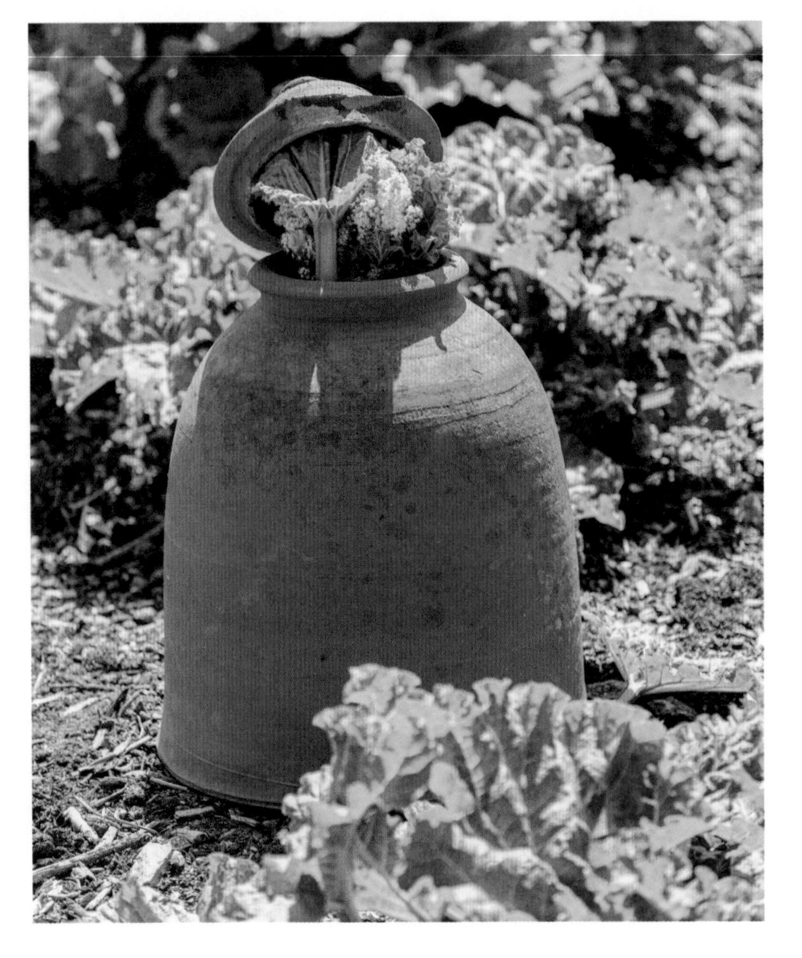

RHUBARB

Technically rhubarb is a vegetable, although many people associate it with fruit desserts, particularly rhubarb crumble. Not only does rhubarb taste great, but it is also a wonderful plant for anyone looking for something striking and beautiful for the garden because it has bright red stems and large ornamental leaves. Rhubarb plants are extremely hardy, and in fact require a cold period in order to go dormant and rest before growing again in spring.

Rhubarb can be 'forced' under a pot to produce an early crop with pink stems.

The easiest way to get started with rhubarb is to buy young plants. It is possible to sow seed in early spring, before planting out the seedlings in autumn or the following spring, although this will mean waiting at least an extra year before you can harvest a crop. Rhubarb prefers a rich, fertile soil, so add lots of organic matter prior to planting. The plants prefer a sunny location, but can tolerate some shade.

Harvest the red stems when they are about 25cm (10in) long and 2cm (¾in) across. Harvest the rhubarb by holding the stem at the base and gently tugging and twisting. Avoid cutting the stem with secateurs if possible as this can leave a stub which may lead to infection. Also, the gentle tugging motion is said to encourage the plant to send up more stems. Stop harvesting in mid-summer, to give the rhubarb plant enough time to recover before it goes dormant in winter.

APPLY SOME FORCE It is possible to force rhubarb for an early crop by placing a large pot over the crown in early winter. Shutting out the light in this way encourages the rhubarb to shoot out bright pink, sweet and succulent stems in late winter or early spring.

TOXICITY WARNING

The leaves of rhubarb are mildly toxic and so should not be eaten. In fact, some gardeners even boil up the leaves and use the liquid as an organic insecticide spray against blackfly and other pests.

ASPARAGUS

Nothing epitomizes the arrival of spring more than the appearance of succulent spears of asparagus in shops and restaurants. They are a luxurious treat and expensive to buy, yet they are easy to grow at home in the garden.

Asparagus is usually purchased as bare root crowns which can be planted out in spring at 30cm (1ft) apart. They need one or two years before they can be harvested to allow the plants to settle into their location. In the third year, use a sharp knife to cut the asparagus spears in spring when they are about 20cm (8in) tall. Allow the attractive, ferny foliage to develop over summer and cut it back in winter when it starts to die back.

Succulent asparagus in spring is one of the gourmet treats from the vegetable garden.

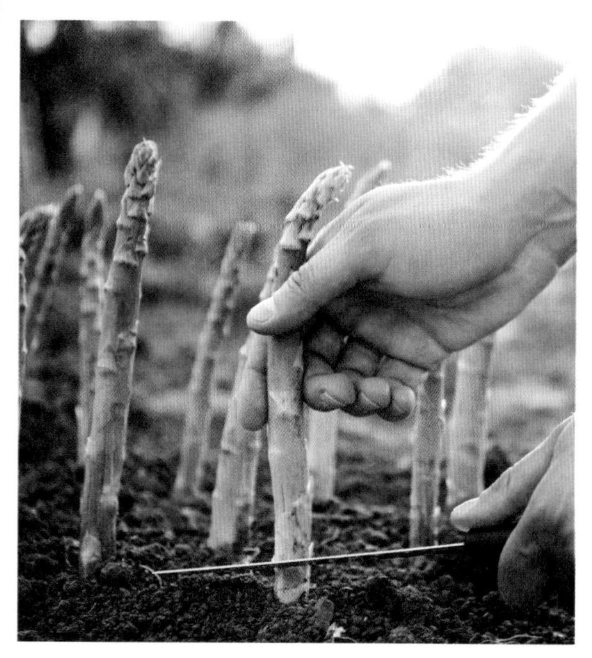

Lettuce, salad leaves and radishes

Lettuce is the staple plant in so many salads, as well as being a popular choice for using as a garnish. However, lettuce is only one of many leafy crops that can be grown. These include the hot and spicy rocket/arugula, sorrel, lamb's lettuce, and many others, including cut-and-come-again mixes. The word lettuce is thought to derive from the old French *laitues*, meaning 'milky'.

LETTUCE

There are four different types of lettuce leaves:

COS Sometimes referred to as Romaine lettuce, these have loose hearts and an upright habit.

CRISPHEADS Tightly folded and crunchy foliage, the most well known being iceberg lettuce.

BUTTERHEADS Soft, folded foliage and rounded hearts.

LOOSE-LEAF Lots of different types, but commonly categorized as 'cut-and-come-again'.

Left: *Lettuces germinate quickly, making them ideal for beginners.* ***Opposite left:*** *Radishes can be harvested after just a few weeks.* ***Opposite right:*** *Harvest winter or mooli radishes in autumn and winter.*

STOP THE BOLT

Lettuce and salad leaves can be prone to bolting (prematurely running to seed). Keep them well watered to avoid this if possible. Also keep weeds under control between the rows to stop them competing with your salad crops for vital nutrients.

Most salad crops are sown directly into shallow drills, about 1cm (½in) deep. Sow seed thinly, cover with soil and lightly water. If the seedlings are too close together, thin out to 2.5cm (1in) once they are about 4cm (1½in) tall. Space larger lettuce types every 25cm (10in), so they can mature fully. Don't thin out cut-and-come-again crops. Instead, harvest them regularly by cutting the leaves back to near the base and let them regenerate. It should be possible to do this a number of times in one season.

Sow regularly to extend the season even further. Harvest hearting types of salad leaves by cutting just below the surface of the soil with a sharp knife.

RADISHES

Radishes are not salad leaves, but are included here because they are often added to salads and grown with lettuce. As well enjoying the root, the leaves can be used in salads. Radishes are satisfying to grow since they are so quick and easy – there is usually just three to six weeks between sowing and harvesting. Sow in spring directly into the soil in shallow drills, then thin out after a few weeks to allow the remaining ones to grow. As they grow so quickly, many gardeners sow a new row every few weeks for a succession of harvests through the season. As well as traditional summer radishes, there are also winter and oriental ones (mooli/daikon). These develop slowly and produce larger roots later in the season.

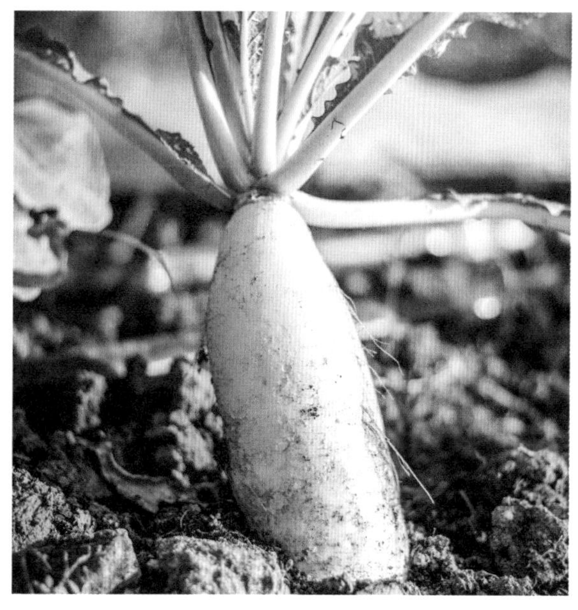

Potatoes

Who does not love potatoes in one form or another? Whether it is a delicious baked potato, roast potatoes, fries or mash, you would be hard pressed to find someone who does not enjoy the humble potato. Thankfully, they are easy to cultivate and if you do not have much of a garden they can be grown in containers or even large composting bags.

Potatoes are generally categorized as early, mid- or late, depending on when in the season they are ready for harvesting. If you have limited space, it might not be worth growing maincrop potatoes, as they take up a lot of room compared with other vegetables.

TIP ON PLANTING IN TRENCHES

* Dig out a trench, about 20cm (8in) deep, in a sunny position. Put the potatoes in the trench, with the eyes pointing up, at intervals of 35cm (14in) for early types, 45cm (18in) for mid-season types, and 65cm (26in) for late-season ones. Cover with soil, mixing plenty of organic matter into the trench. As shoots start to emerge, earth up soil against them. Not only does this prevent frost damaging the tubers, but it also stops them turning green and provides a larger growing space, as there is more soil for the potatoes to develop in.
* Harvest the potatoes once flowering has finished and the foliage starts to die back. Dig up with a garden fork, taking care not to spike too many potatoes with the spines.

TO CHIT OR NOT TO CHIT

To get potatoes off to an early start, they can be chitted. This technique involves placing the potatoes on a windowsill with the 'eyes' facing upwards for a few weeks before planting. When there are a few chits on the surface, the potato is ready for planting. Potatoes can be grown in a compost bag which is a great space-saving solution for small gardens. Place the bag in a sunny position for the best results, and do not forget to keep the bag watered as they grow.

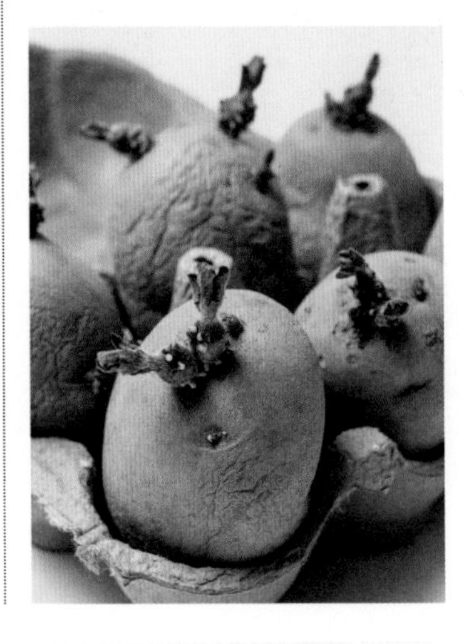

Exposing potatoes to light before planting – a technique known as chitting – can result in earlier crops.

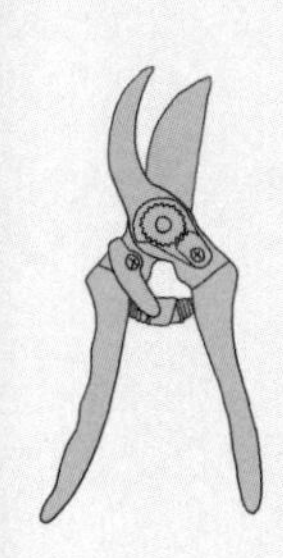

STEP-BY-STEP TECHNIQUE

PLANT POTATOES IN A BAG

YOU WILL NEED

∗ Large composting bag ∗ Sharp knife ∗ Peat-free general-purpose potting compost ∗ Seed potatoes

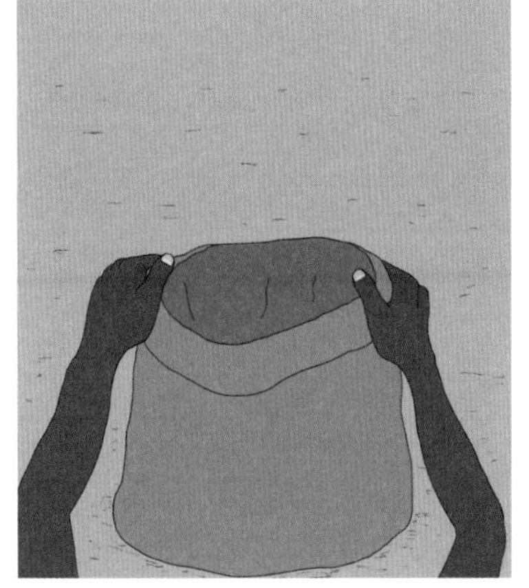

1. Use a sharp knife to cut a few drainage holes in the base of the bag and roll down the top by about two-thirds.

2. Fill the bottom of the bag with potting compost to a depth of about 15cm (6in).

3. Place a few potatoes on the compost surface with the rose end (where there are some buds) facing upwards.

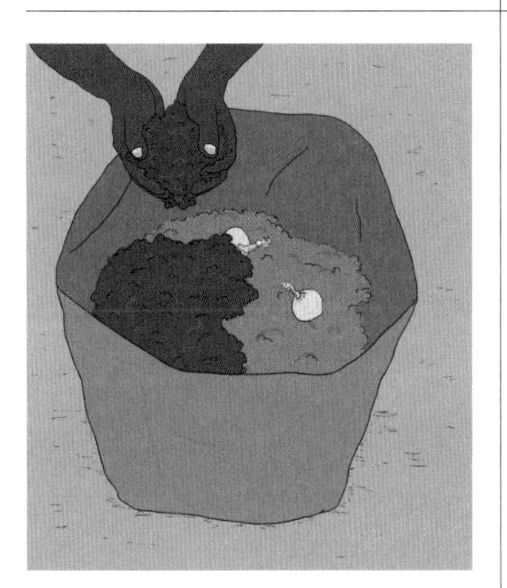

4. Cover the potatoes with 10cm (4in) of compost. Leave the bag in a sunny spot on the patio and keep it well watered.

5. As the potatoes start to grow and green shoots emerge, roll the bag up and add more compost. Keep doing this until you reach the top of the bag.

6. Once the flowers and foliage have started to fade, you are ready to harvest. To do this, simply split open the bag and pick out the new tubers.

Turnips, swedes and kohlrabi

Although turnips, swede/rutabaga and kohlrabi are all members of the cabbage family, unlike others in this group they are mainly grown for their tasty roots rather than the leaves. That said, young turnip leaves are also a gourmet treat. By growing all three of these vegetables, you can enjoy a crop nearly all year round: turnips are ready between spring and summer, while swede/rutabaga and kohlrabi can be harvested in autumn and winter.

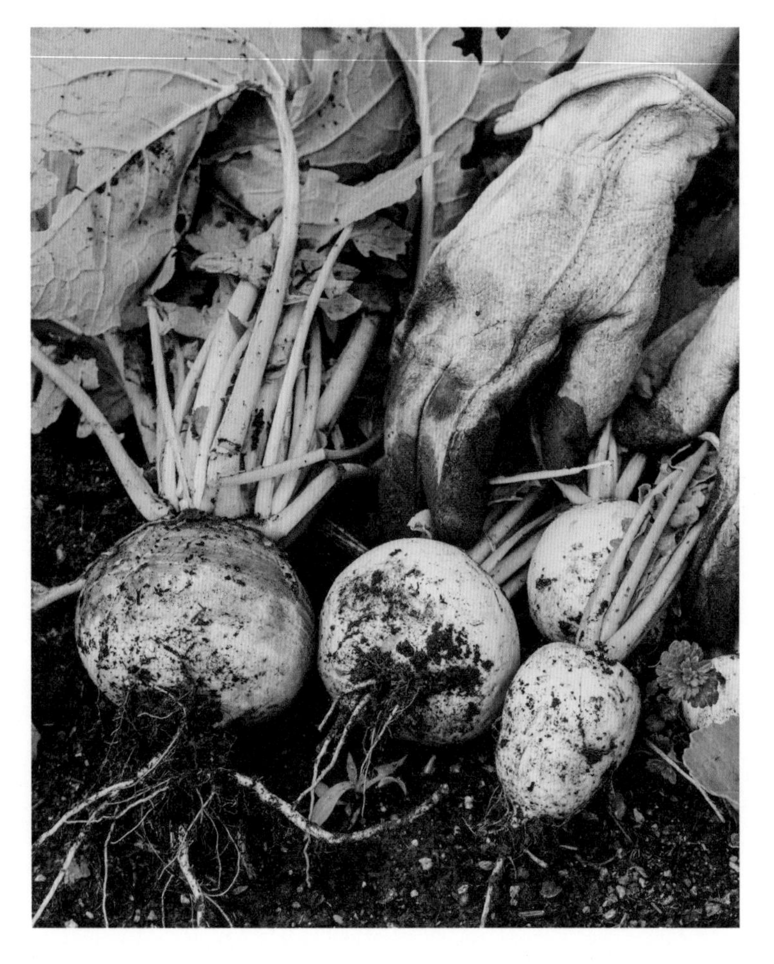

TURNIPS

Sow turnip seeds directly into well-prepared soil with plenty of added organic matter. Sow thinly in shallow drills, then thin out to about 10cm (4in) apart. Harvest when the turnips reach the desired size, but do not leave longer than three months because they can start to turn woody. They are ready when the leaves begin to wither and go over. Some turnips are hardier than others. Do not leave tender types in the ground once the temperature starts to drop in autumn.

Young or baby turnips are having something of a renaissance, with many chefs hoping to get hold of them. They are harvested just six weeks after sowing once they reach golf-ball size.

Left: *Harvest tender turnips before the first autumn frosts.* ***Opposite:*** *Kohlrabi is easy to grow and copes better with dry summers than swede/rutabaga or turnips.*

> **TIME THE PICKING**
> Turnips can also be grown for their tasty, tender leaves. Pick every few weeks from spring onwards. They still form roots below ground, but these will take longer to develop.

SWEDE/RUTABAGA

These delicious root vegetables have an undeniable sweetness and are delicious when roasted. They are ideal for using in the kitchen in winter, when there are few other crops available from the vegetable garden. Swedes prefer a fertile soil with plenty of added organic matter. Sow seeds thinly in spring in shallow drills and thin out to a final position of about 25cm (10in) apart. They take much longer to mature than turnips, and should be ready for harvesting from late summer and into winter.

DID YOU KNOW? Swedes are so called because their name is a shortened version of Swedish turnip. Things can get confusing, as some people refer to swedes as neeps, which is the abbreviated name for turnips and other root vegetables. To confuse things even further, turnips and swedes look fairly similar.

KOHLRABI

One of the lesser known members of the cabbage family, this vegetable is grown by gardeners for its delicious, swollen, ball-shaped stem. It is a very peculiar-looking vegetable, and if you have not grown it before, you might think initially that something has gone wrong. It consists of a small sphere with foliage spiralling outwards at random angles. However, apart from being a great talking point in the garden, kohlrabi is easy to grow and it has better drought resistance than turnips and swede/rutabaga.

There are two different types of kohlrabi. The green varieties are sown from early spring to early summer for picking in summer, while the tougher purple ones are sown in summer for an autumn and winter harvest. Sow seeds as you would for turnips, and harvest the swollen round stems when they are between the size of a golf ball and a tennis ball.

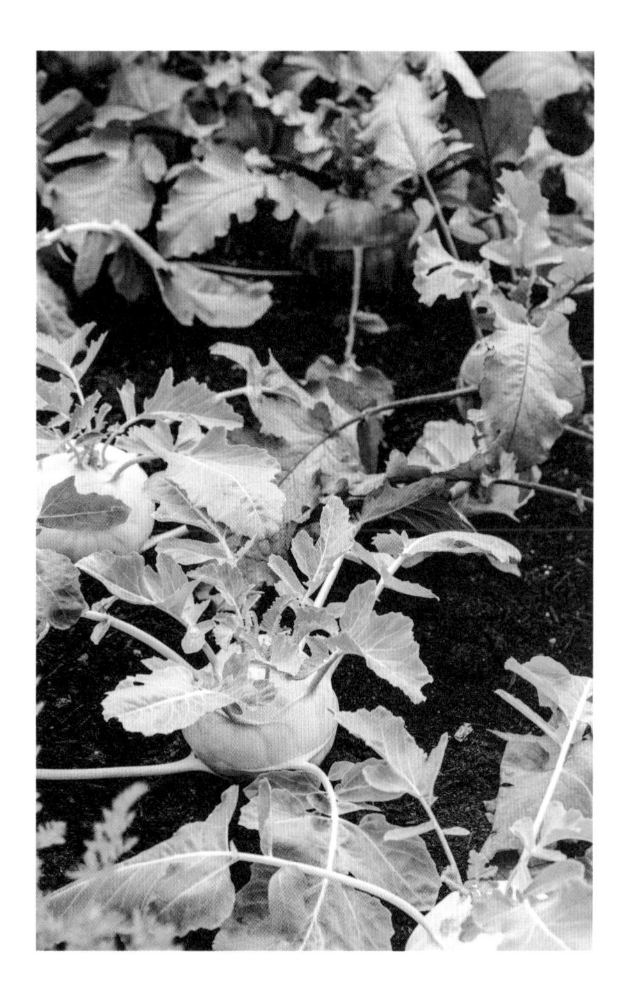

Carrots and parsnips

Carrots are versatile vegetables because the roots can be enjoyed raw when they are sweet and crunchy or used in a range of savoury or sweet dishes, whether grated, chopped into salads and soups, or baked in a carrot cake. Although parsnips need a longer growing season, they also have various culinary uses. Carrots and parsnips both prefer light, stone-free soils and if this is not possible, they can be grown in raised beds.

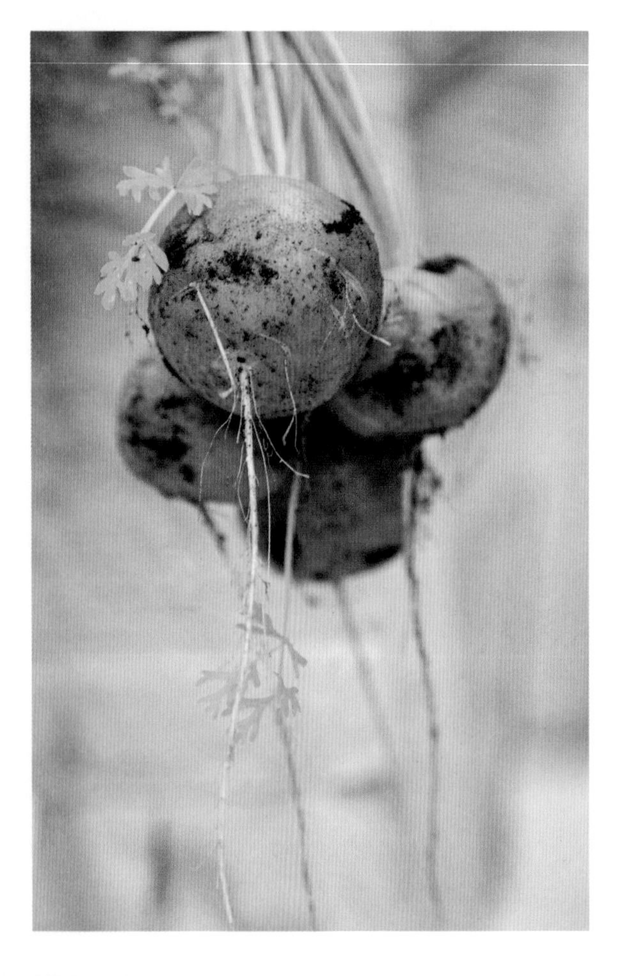

CARROTS

You do not need to settle for the traditional, long, pointed carrots. You can also grow round carrots, the size of a small golf ball, which are perfect for windowboxes or shallow containers.

* Carrots need a well-drained soil and a sunny site. If the soil is heavy, loosen with a fork first, so the root can grow downwards with minimal effort. Also remove any stones that may impede growth.
* Sow directly into the soil in spring in a drill, 1cm (½in) deep. Cover the seed with soil and water well.
* When the seedlings emerge, thin them out. Check seed packets for final spacing requirements.
* Water growing carrots well, or the roots may split.
* Lift carrots when they reach the desired size.
* Young carrots are best eaten fresh when they are sweet, crunchy and juicy.

Left: *Round carrots are an ideal crop to grow in shallow soil or containers.* ***Opposite:*** *Parsnips can take a long time to mature before they are ready for harvesting, so start sowing early in the season.*

COMPANIONS FOR CARROTS

Carrots are often grown closely with crops from the allium family, including onions, leeks and chives. This is to deter carrot root fly, the larvae of which burrow into the root and destroy the crop. Companion planting, as the technique is called, means the female carrot root fly is confused by the smell of the nearby onions when looking for the aroma of carrots to lay eggs and so goes elsewhere.

SUCCESSIONAL SOWING Make sowings every two or three weeks in spring and summer, as this will ensure a regular crop of carrots to harvest throughout the season.

PARSNIPS

Grown for their long, sweet taproot, parsnips are closely related to carrots. But although both have a fine seed and should be sown in shallow drills, parsnips take far longer to mature than carrots and will not be ready for harvesting until towards late summer. They are frost-hardy, however, and can be left in the ground over winter. In fact, it is said that the frost makes them taste sweeter.

NOTE Whereas some seeds will last for years, carrot and parsnip seeds tend to go off quite quickly. This is often the cause of poor or no germination. So only store carrot and parsnip seeds for a year or two and check their expiry dates.

DID YOU KNOW? Interestingly, carrots were originally purple or black. It is said that gardeners bred an 'orange' carrot to celebrate and support King William of Orange in the 17th century.

PARSNIP GERMINATION TRICK

Parsnip seed can be notoriously difficult to germinate. However, the seed can be 'chitted' or 'pre-germinated' by sprinkling it on a piece of damp paper towel prior to sowing. Once it looks as if the seeds are sending out shoots, very carefully sow directly into the soil.

Other vegetables to try

There are so many wonderful vegetables to grow, and two of the most popular ones are sweet corn and beetroot/beets. By growing a range of different vegetables, not only is it more interesting than just cultivating the standard types, but it will vary your diet considerably too. If you plan your vegetable garden well, you should be able to eat your own homegrown vegetables all year round.

Sweet corn plants are wind-pollinated, so they should be sown in a grid pattern rather than in straight rows.

SWEET CORN/CORN

This is probably one of the most enjoyable vegetables to grow because the ears of corn look so dramatic when they first appear. The plants can get fairly large, though, so you will need a bit of space if you want to grow this vegetable. Sow seeds in individual pots in mid- to late spring. Sweet corn/corn is slightly tender, so do not plant out until all risk of frosts has passed. Once the seedlings reach a height of about 8cm (3in), plant them in their final position.

Sweet corn/corn is pollinated by wind, so is best planted in a grid pattern, as opposed to straight rows – this increases the chance of pollen blowing from one flower to another. Space the plants 40cm (16in) apart –16 seedlings in a 4x4 arrangement is a good amount, but the more the better. Test whether it is ready for harvesting by peeling back the sheath and pushing your thumb into the corn. If it exudes a milky sap, then it is ready for picking.

BEETROOT/BEETS

Nothing beats (if you'll excuse the pun) the earthy flavour of beetroot/beets. Most are grown for the swollen roots but some are cultivated for their leaves too. Sow from mid-spring onwards. If frosts are forecast, it is worth covering the seed with some horticultural fleece. Thin out the seedlings, so there is about 10cm (4in) between each plant. Harvest young, succulent beetroots/beets when they are the size of a golf ball. Make successional sowings every two or three weeks, so you can continue harvesting it throughout the summer months. Don't just settle for the traditional red varieties. There are other wonderful colours out there too, including orange, yellow and even pink-striped ones.

THREE SISTERS GARDEN

This is a traditional growing system developed in North America by the First Nation peoples. In this three-vegetable system, climbing beans, sweet corn/corn and squashes or pumpkins are grown together as companion plants. This is also a great space-saving idea if you only have one bed for growing vegetables. The idea is that the beans scramble up through the corn, using them as a support system, while the sweet corn/corn plants are held upright by the beans. Squashes or pumpkins sprawl on the ground, providing shade and a mulch for the other plants.

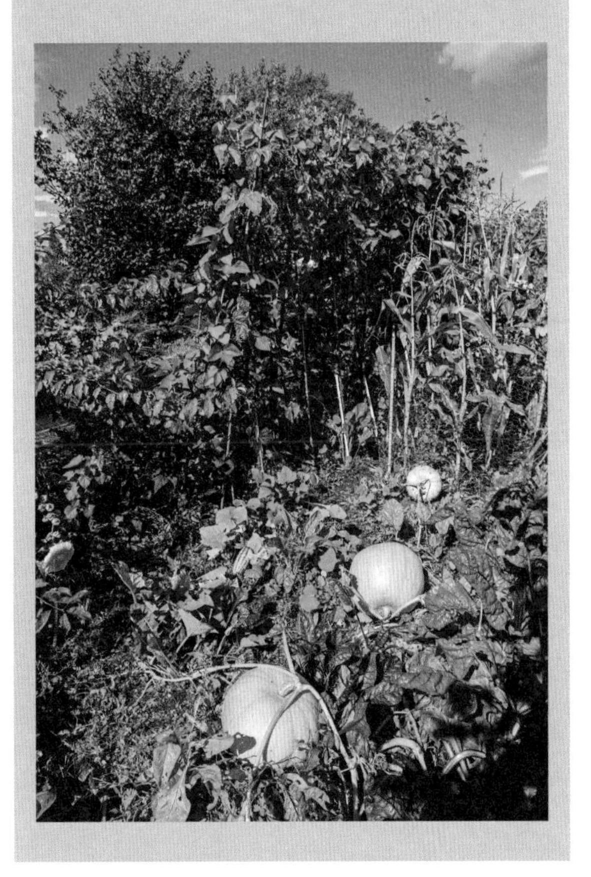

Herbs

Whether for medicinal or culinary reasons, herbs are satisfying to grow and look great planted in beds or containers. There are so many different types to choose from, and many of them are evergreen too, offering structure and texture to a flower border all year round. There is nothing more rewarding than rubbing the foliage of many of these aromatic herbs as you walk by to enjoy their wonderful aromas.

BAY

This herb is usually grown as an evergreen bush, although it is also often trained as a standard and used to adorn either side of a doorway or entrance. If left to their own devices, bay plants can be quite dominant, becoming large and unruly, so they may need the occasional trim to keep them in check. Bay is grown for its broad, aromatic, evergreen leaves which are used to infuse savoury dishes with flavour.

MINT

There are lots of different-flavoured mints to choose from, including apple, ginger and even chocolate. Underlying these flavours is the undeniably fresh minty aroma that exudes from their foliage. Mints are herbaceous perennials, so expect them to die back below ground in winter. Mint can be a bit of a thug in the border and take over an area, so it is worth growing it in containers.

Left: *Herbs are highly suited to raised beds, as most prefer well-drained conditions.* ***Opposite:*** *If your garden has heavy soil, try growing herbs like rosemary in pots.*

SAGE

One of the mainstays of the herb garden, sage is a popular evergreen shrub with attractive purple flowers. Some varieties have striking purple or multicoloured foliage. Sage is grown for its fragrant foliage which is used to flavour many savoury dishes, including casseroles and soups. It is, of course, the main ingredient in sage and onion stuffing.

ROSEMARY

There are both upright and prostrate forms of rosemary. It is a shrub with attractive, silvery green foliage. If you rub the leaves between your fingers, it is very difficult not to think of roast lamb, with which it is often cooked. Rosemary is very hardy and easy to grow, preferring light, well-drained soil. It requires very little maintenance, but plants may need cutting back in summer to prevent them getting leggy or if they outgrow their position.

THYME

This is an evergreen, low-growing shrub with tiny, aromatic leaves. There are a few flavour variations on the traditional aroma, including the very popular lemon variety. Thyme plants can get slightly straggly, so will benefit from an occasional light trim to tidy them up. Thyme requires a light, well-drained soil.

GETTING THE SOIL RIGHT

As a rule, herbs prefer a sandy, free-draining soil, so they are often better grown in raised beds or containers if you garden on heavy clay. Alternatively, dig in lots of horticultural grit to try to open up the soil.

BASIL

Very popular in Italian cuisine, basil is grown as an annual, although its life can be prolonged by growing it on a sunny windowsill indoors. Sow seeds between spring and summer for a succession of crops. Thin out the seedlings to individual pots when they have formed some 'true' leaves (the first leaves after the initial seed leaves or cotyledons). Like many Mediterranean plants, basil prefers a well-drained soil and a sunny location.

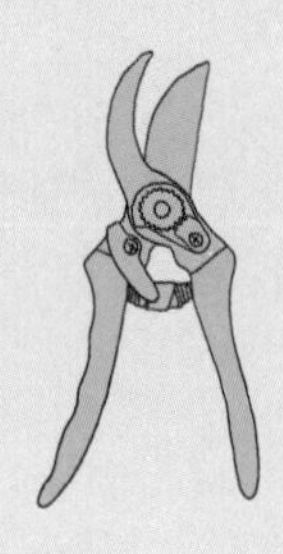

STEP-BY-STEP TECHNIQUE

GROW STRAWBERRIES IN A PLANTER

The trailing habit of strawberries makes them ideal for pots or hanging baskets. Even better are special strawberry planters as they can accommodate more plants. These planters are often made from terracotta and have planting pockets at various heights. They come in a range of sizes, but usually have five to nine pockets, as well as space at the top for a few more plants.

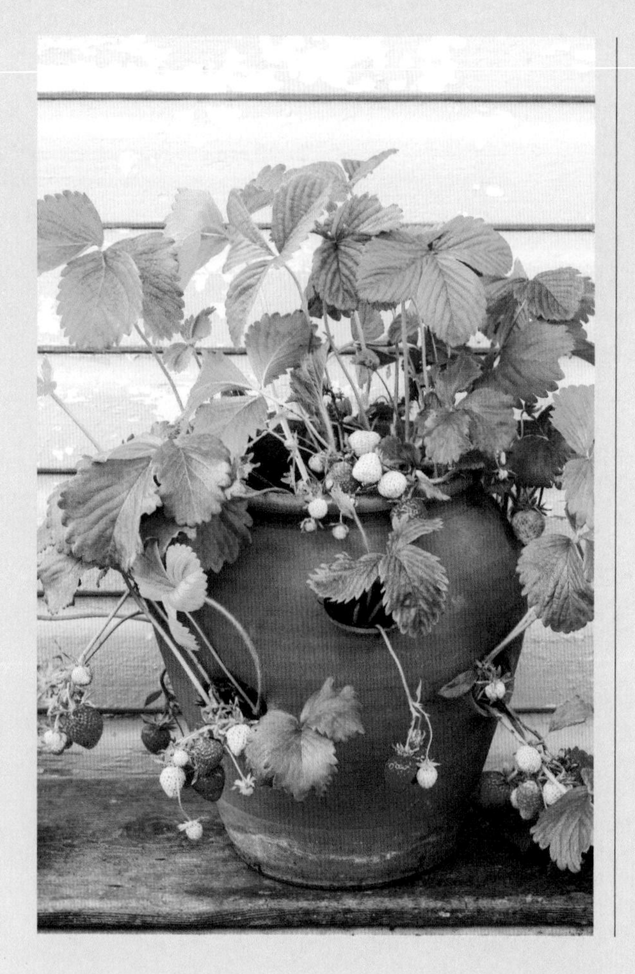

YOU WILL NEED

* Strawberry planter
* Broken crocks, stones or pebbles for drainage
* Peat-free general-purpose potting compost
* Strawberry plants

TIPS ON GROWING STRAWBERRIES

* Place the planter in full sun, turning it occasionally to ensure the plants on the other side receive some sunshine.
* Strawberries are perennial plants and should last two or three years in the same planter. To replace the plants, remove some of the runners hanging from the strawberry plants with secateurs. These are young baby plants, and if they are planted into individual pots, they can replace some of the older plants the following year.
* Grow herbs in planters too, as they enjoy the free-draining conditions.

Remember to turn a strawberry planter occasionally, so that every side receives some sunlight.

1. Place crocks, stones or pebbles at the bottom of the planter to improve drainage and stop the compost clogging up the drainage holes.

2. Add a layer of general-purpose compost to the bottom of the planter, filling up to the height of the first planting pocket.

3. Place a strawberry plant on top of the layer of compost and pull the plant through the hole, so the leaves are on the outside and the roots inside.

4. Repeat this process if there are more pockets at that level. Then add some more compost, filling the planter up to the next pocket and planting more strawberry plants.

5. Continue to plant the strawberries in this way, topping up with compost until you reach the top of the planter, stopping about 4cm (1½in) from the top.

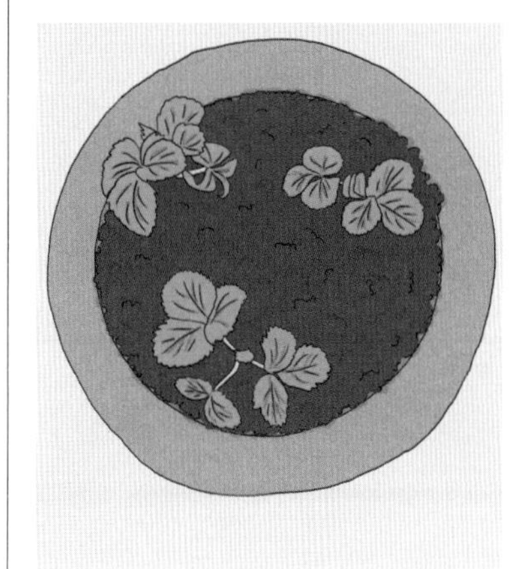

6. Plant one or two more strawberry plants in the top of the planter, depending on its size, and then add more compost so the roots are buried. Water thoroughly.

CHAPTER 9

LAWNS

In many gardens, especially medium to large ones, lawns understandably occupy most of the space. Where would we be without them? Often criticized and maligned for being hard work, lawns actually provide a wonderful, soft texture from which to enjoy the garden. In addition, they do not involve as much hard work as you may think. A green lawn also looks beautiful and contributes to our sense of well-being.

In this chapter, we examine the many benefits of having a lawn and explore how gardens can be designed and shaped using lawned areas. There is information on how to lay a lawn, with advice on the pros and cons of sowing grass seed and laying turf, as well as tips and advice on lawn care, including mowing, edging techniques and autumn renovation. So, if you have ever wondered what some of those bizarre 'greenkeeper' terms mean such as scarifying, thatch or aeration, here is a chance to learn.

There is also guidance on how to make your lawn wildlife-friendly, with suggestions for leaving areas uncut, and how to avoid using chemicals and artificial fertilizers.

Benefits of lawns

There are so many reasons to have a lawn, including improving air quality, reducing flood risk and enjoying the benefit that having access to green space has on well-being. Lawns have received a bad press of late since they are regarded as labour-intensive and not sustainable due to the amount of fuel needed for their use. But you can now buy lawn mowers and other machines that do not require petrol, meaning lawns can also be environmentally friendly.

CLEAN AIR AND OPEN SPACES

There are literally hundreds of grass plants in a square metre (square yard) patch of lawn, all pumping out oxygen and absorbing carbon dioxide. In fact, because grass is densely planted and has so many blades in a small space, the surface area is much higher and therefore more efficient than is the case with bigger plants that have large leaves. In cities with lawns, there are often open spaces. These draw people outside for picnicking, socializing and relaxing. As well as improving people's well-being, this also increases their exposure to vitamin D and all its benefits for good health.

NOTE Avoid plastic-based artificial lawns, as they are not biodegradable, do not help keep our air clean and require regular maintenance. In addition, in summer they become too hot and therefore unusable. Do not let your pets walk on artificial lawns in hot weather as they can burn their paws.

NATURAL BEAUTY

Whether you like the look of a freshly cut lawn with stripes or longer grass with wildflowers growing in it, there is no denying that both are beautiful. Seeing something that looks naturally lush and green is a far more pleasant experience than looking at concrete, patio, decking or tarmac.

FLOOD REDUCTION

Lawns have an important role in reducing flood risks in many areas. Since they absorb moisture over their large surface area, this reduces the risk of flash flooding in urban areas where tarmac and concrete dominate the landscape. If there were more lawns, there would be far less damage after heavy rainfall.

FRESHLY CUT GRASS

Almost all of us know and love the sweet and herbaceous smell of freshly cut grass. This fragrance is the result of a mixture of oxygenated hydrocarbons called green leaf volatiles (GLV). The great news is that if you have a lawn, then you can experience this wonderful smell on a regular basis in mowing season. When humans encounter this smell, it is said to release 'happy hormones' in the body because we associate it with springtime, weekends, trips to the countryside and relaxing.

PURE COMFORT

There is no better natural surface for sitting on or relaxing than a lawn. It is soft and comfortable, making it ideal for picnicking. For children, or adults who are young at heart, it provides the perfect surface for playing on. Grass is lovely and cool in the summer too. Alternative materials for covering a surface in the garden such as flagstones are uncomfortable and can become hot in summer.

Lawns provide a lovely, neutral foreground in the garden, helping to show off colourful plants in borders.

Designing with a lawn

There are plenty of ways to use lawns when designing a garden. Not only does the green colour create the perfect backdrop for plants but lawns can also be made into features in their own right by cutting them into various shapes and designs. Cleverly allowing the lawn to flow from one area of a garden to another can be used to unify or link different parts of the space.

DECIDE ON SHAPE AND DESIGN

Be bold and creative when designing your garden. Try to avoid the stereotypical 'centrifugal force' garden composed of a large, central, rectangular lawn and the flowerbeds pushed out to the extremities, as if they are caught up in some vortex. There are far more exciting ways to create flow, movement and structure in a garden. Cut large, dramatic curves in the lawn to create interesting flower borders, allowing the lawn to sweep down majestically in front of them.

When planning the garden initially, decide whether you want the lawn to be a feature or a backdrop to other highlights. Also consider whether it is going to be formal or informal. Look at the practicalities of connecting different areas together.

CREATE A FEATURE LAWN

Various shapes can be used to turn the lawn into the centre of attention. A circle is perhaps the most obvious and dramatic shape. In this case, keep the lawn cut and well edged to ensure it retains definition. Either create the lawn in the centre of the garden or over to one side, making it almost like a destination to be reached or a distinct area of the garden. Take this idea a step further by creating a figure-of-eight shape or series of concentric circles running down the garden. For those want to be really bold and creative, try personalizing the lawn by making it in the shape of a wine goblet or star.

Opposite: *The neutral colour of grass can link different areas of the garden.* ***Right:*** *Lawns can look lush and inviting, and so are still a popular surfacing material in most medium-sized and large gardens.*

MOW SOME STRIPES

Neatly mown stripes on a lawn can be used to very dramatic effect. Depending on which direction they are cut, they can make the lawn look either wider or longer. Diagonal stripes can also bring an otherwise dull area of grass to life.

ADD CONTRASTS

One of the most dramatic ways to use a lawn is to contrast short grass with long grass. To do this, cut swathes and patterns in long grass to create intrigue, making the experience very personal because it will feel as if you are walking through a meadow of wildflowers. Having different lengths of grass is also beneficial for visiting wildlife.

Choosing a lawn mower

Whether you want a finely mown lawn with stripes or a wildflower meadow, the grass will need cutting at some stage. While most of us mow less than in the past to benefit wildlife, grass management is still a crucial part of successful gardening. Lawns remain the key feature in the average garden, usually taking up most of the surface area, so they need to look good. Most mowers are either self-propelled or you have to push them, which is a lot of hard work for a larger lawn or one on a slope.

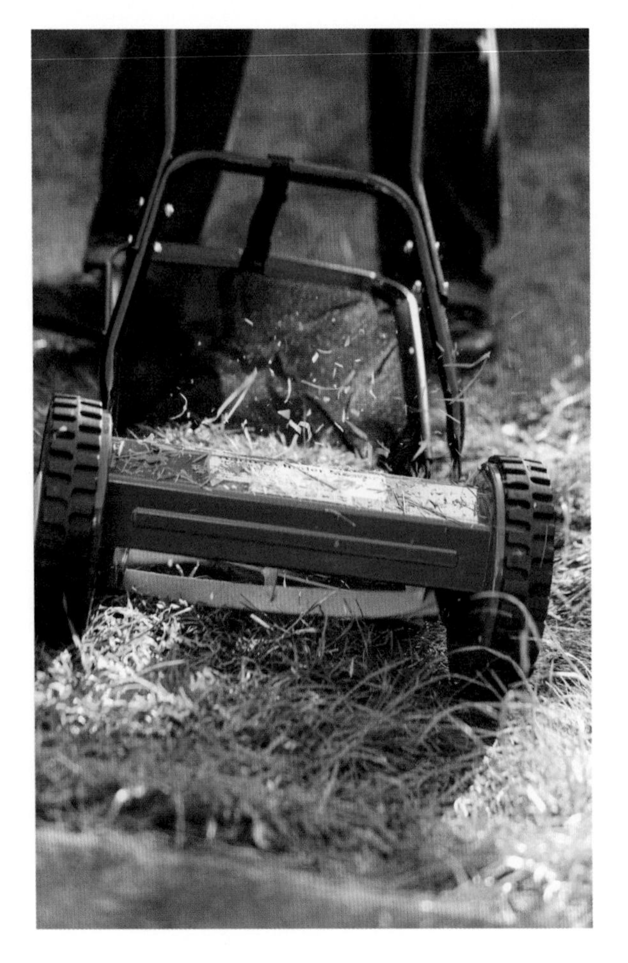

CYLINDER MOWERS

Used on fine lawns, these mowers operate by using a cylinder with blades that sit horizontally to the ground and spin, cutting against a static bottom blade. This type of mower is often used for sports surfaces, such as a cricket wicket, golf green, tennis court or bowling lawn, where a very fine cut is required. It is also used on formal lawns and is the best mower to buy if you would like to create impressive stripes or make a very low cut.

For those wishing to avoid using fossil fuels, traditional push cylinder mowers are also available. These call for a bit of muscle and sweat – which is great if you enjoy a good workout. They are also ideal for small areas and if you do not like the sound of a lawn mower engine.

Left: *A lightweight cylinder mower that is pushed rather than motor-driven is much quieter to use and also better for the environment.* ***Opposite left:*** *An electric rotary mower is the most popular type of lawn mower used in gardens.* ***Opposite right:*** *String trimmers are useful tools for cutting long blades of grass growing against fences and walls.*

COLLECT CLIPPINGS

Some mowers have a box at the back that collects the grass cuttings as you mow. If there is a lot of grass, it is worth collecting because otherwise it can smother the lawn underneath it. Clippings can be raked up and added to the compost heap if there is no box. If there are not too many grass clippings, leave them on the lawn as they return nitrogen to the grass which will help it grow.

ROTARY MOWERS

The most popular type of mower, they have rotating blades that spin a bit like those of a helicopter and slash through blades of grass. Although the finish is not as good as with a cylinder mower, if there is a roller on the back, a rotary mower will give a pretty good-quality finish with stripes. These mowers can be used on rougher or informal lawns. Most use petrol, but there are electric and battery-operated ones too.

HOVER MOWERS

These are a type of rotary mower, with rotating blades, but they 'float' on a bed of air, making it effortless to cut lawns in small areas.

STRING TRIMMERS

Sometimes called Strimmers®, these are not really mowers, but are useful for cutting tall grass. They operate by cutting the blades of grass with a spinning nylon string. Turned on their side, they can be used to edge the lawn instead of edging shears.

Mowing and edging a lawn

Those who take real pride in their lawns often like to add stripes. These are created by the roller at the back of the lawn mower flattening the blades of grass as you mow. Going in one direction, and then the opposite, gives an attractive striped effect. This can be done in various ways, such as diagonal or curvy stripes, but they are usually made by going up and down the length of a garden.

A GUIDE TO HEIGHT

If you would like a striped lawn, you will need to mow once or twice a week during the growing season. Go in the opposite direction to the previous time the lawn was cut to avoid 'ridges' appearing.

Season	Standard lawn	Fine lawn
Spring and autumn	30mm (1¼in) once a week	10mm (½in) once or twice a week
Summer	20mm (¾in) once a week	10mm (½in) once or twice a week
Winter	30mm (1¼in) as necessary)	15mm (¾in) as necessary)

* Raise the cutting height of the mower for the first few cuts of the season in spring. Then gradually lower it to the desired height as the season progresses.
* Edge a lawn after it has been cut. If it is done the other way round, then the mower pushes the blades back out over the beds, making them look straggly and messy again.
* Edging shears work like a pair of scissors. Try to keep one blade still and just use your right hand to move up and down to cut the grass. Keep your back straight when cutting.

TIP ON EDGING

If you have a large lawn to edge, use a string trimmer turned on its side in order to keep the edges of the lawn nice and tidy, instead of using edging shears.

Opposite: *If you would like stripes on your lawn, then you will need a roller at the back of the lawn mower.*

Avoid cutting grass when it is wet as this can clog up the lawn mower and make a muddy mess of the area. Also do not mow in periods of extreme drought, as this will stress the lawn. It has a better chance of surviving if the grass is left longer. Do not panic if the lawn starts to turn brown in dry periods in summer. It will often recover with little detrimental effect once the weather cools down. To conserve water at these times, try to avoid sprinklers and irrigating the lawn.

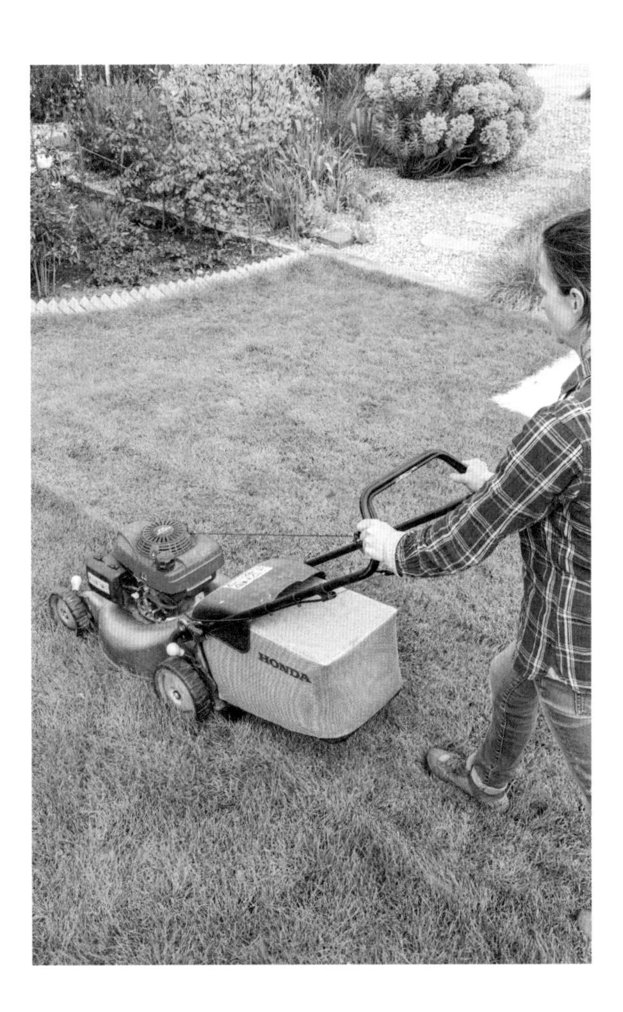

CREATE STRIPES IN A LAWN

You will need

A mower (cylinder or rotary mower) with a roller on the back.

1. Start at one corner and go across and back along the width of the garden at one end.
2. Go along the edge of the length of the garden to get to the other end.
3. Repeat step 1 by making two stripes at the other end of the lawn.
4. Run the mower back down the length of the lawn, next to the stripe you made in step 2.
5. Continue going up and down the length of the lawn in this way until you reach the other side.
6. Exit in the corner, avoiding going back over any of the stripes.

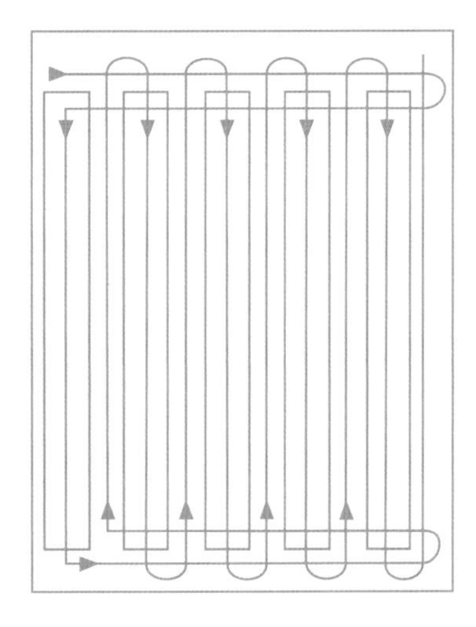

Creating a lawn

There are two ways of establishing a lawn. The first is by laying rolls of pre-seeded turf and the other is by sowing grass seed. There are factors to bear in mind when deciding whether to use turf or grass seed, including the time of year, your budget and how long you want to wait for the lawn to become established.

BENEFITS OF SOWING GRASS SEED

* Grass seed is much cheaper than rolls of turf.
* Seed is nice and light. Rolls of turf are heavy and require physical strength to move them.
* Seed keeps for ages, so if the weather is not suitable, it can be used another day.

Sowing grass seed may be cheaper than laying turf, but you will have to wait a while before the lawn can be used – a few weeks if sown in the middle of spring, but months if sown in autumn.

DISADVANTAGES OF SOWING GRASS SEED

* Birds love grass seed, so you may need to cover newly sown lawns with a net.
* Weeds grow just as quickly as grass seed, so some weed control might be necessary.
* Lawns can take a few weeks or even months to establish, depending on the sowing time.
* You may be looking at bare soil for quite a while until the seed germinates.
* Grass seed can only germinate between spring and early autumn.

BENEFITS OF LAYING TURF

* Almost instantaneous effect – laid turf looks great immediately after laying.
* Lawn can be used just a few days after laying.
* Turf can be laid almost all year round (avoid extremes of weather such as drought and frosts).

DISADVANTAGES OF LAYING TURF

* Turf is far more expensive than grass seed.
* There is more choice of lawn seed types.
* Laying turf is hard physical work. If you have to carry rolls from the front of the property around to the back, there is a lot of lifting.
* Turf has to be laid within a day or two of delivery/collection. If the weather changes or something unexpected turns up, and you do not have time to do it, you may lose the turf.

DIFFERENT GRASS SEED MIXES

A lawn is made up of different types of grass seed. Choose your seed mix carefully before applying because the wrong type of grass species might struggle in an inappropriate environment. If a lawn will have a lot of footfall, then very often rye grass and smooth stalked meadow grass is used. On fine lawns fescues and bent grasses are more common. Usually, grass seed is bought already mixed and labelled describing the conditions it prefers such as 'shade', 'hard-wearing' and 'fine', for example.

HOW TO LAY TURF

1. Prepare the ground thoroughly before laying turf by digging it over and removing any weeds. Rake the soil level and leave it to settle for a few days.
2. Start at the furthest end of the garden to avoid walking over your work. When laying turf, stagger the rolls like brickwork in each row. Make sure all the ends butt up closely to each other; otherwise, they can dry out. After laying the turf, tamp it down with the back of the rake head. Once the area has been covered, the final lawn shape can be marked out with string or sand and cut with a half moon edging tool. If the lawn is laid in a dry spell, keep it well watered.

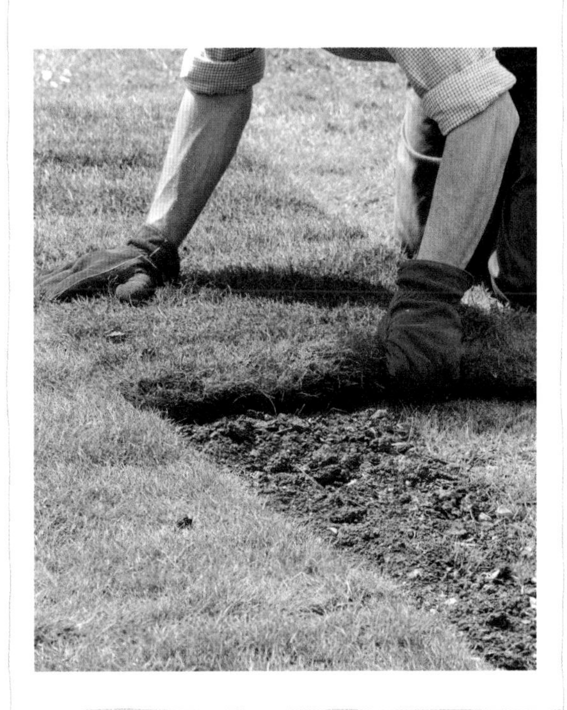

Wildlife-friendly lawns

Lawns can be a haven for wildlife if they are managed sensitively. Wildlife-friendly lawns do not have to look scruffy or neglected, but can be colourful and vibrant. They can incorporate grasses of different lengths to contrast with wildflowers and seedheads, which will not only be enjoyed by the local wildlife, but will also entice you outside to enjoy the beautiful surroundings.

BENEFITS OF LONG GRASS

If you have established a wildlife-friendly lawn, avoid cutting the grass too often. Instead, allow it to grow long because this will encourage flowers to grow in the grass, attracting bees, butterflies, moths, craneflies, sawflies, hoverflies and other insects. This in turn will encourage birds, bats and hedgehogs to feed on bugs that are attracted into your garden. You can expect to see a wide range of wildflowers appearing in the lawn, including dandelions, yarrow, daisies and buttercups. These plants will, along with greater plantain (*Plantago major*) and annual meadow grass (*Poa annua*) provide seedheads for

Left: *Leaving areas of long grass in a lawn not only looks beautiful, but the wildlife will benefit from it too.*
Opposite: *Leaving grass uncut can encourage wildflowers to appear.*

wildlife to forage on later in the year. Long grass also provides a quiet place in which birds can hide safely and insects can lay their eggs.

In addition, longer grass prevents the soil from drying out as it is shaded from the sun. This extra moisture creates an environment that will be enjoyed by insect larvae, worms and other soil invertebrates. This will bring a richer biodiversity to your garden, both below and above the ground.

Although leaving grass long encourages greater biodiversity in the lawn, some smaller areas can be cut short. This creates a clear feeding area for birds. For example, it is much easier for creatures such as blackbirds and song thrushes to pull out worms and find insects. The shorter grass and clearer areas also give them a better view for spotting predators.

TIPS FOR A WILDLIFE-FRIENDLY LAWN

* Cut the lawn less than usual.
* Leave some areas uncut throughout spring and summer.
* Mow paths or shorter areas to create a contrast with the long grass.
* Allow flowerheads to go to seed to provide food for wildlife such as birds.
* Remove grass clippings from the surface to stop it smothering the lawn.
* Avoid using chemicals and artificial fertilizers on the lawn as this will harm wildlife. Instead, look at alternative, sustainable methods of managing lawned areas and perhaps be more tolerant of the creatures you are sharing your outside space with.

Also, rain and moisture can penetrate the soil more easily, creating an environment that will be enjoyed by worms and soil-based insects.

Many different grass species make up a lawn, so include different types in the mix. A wider range of plants in the lawn is also better for biodiversity.

CLOVER LAWNS – IS THIS THE FUTURE?

If you do not want a standard lawn, you could opt for a 'clover lawn' instead. Reasons for having a clover lawn in your garden include the following:

* Needs less cutting than a standard lawn.
* Grows in poor soil.
* Does not need fertilizing.
* Is drought-resistant.
* The flowers are loved by bees.
* Unaffected by pet urine.
* Nice and soft for sitting on.

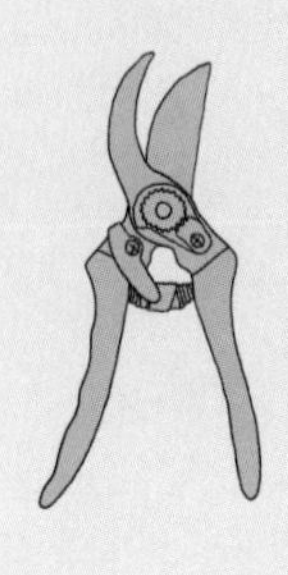

STEP-BY-STEP TECHNIQUE

LAWN CARE

If you would like your lawn to look good all year round, then this will call for some maintenance. Autumn is the usual time of year for an annual lawn care programme, when the garden is 'put to bed' before winter. On fine lawns some of the lawn care techniques such as scarifying, aerating and topdressing can be carried out every few weeks during the growing season.

WHY AERATE A LAWN?

Aerating a lawn does two things. First, it relieves compaction of the ground which gives the roots more room to grow and allows water and nutrients to percolate through the soil. Second, it breathes fresh air into the root zone, helping individual grass plants to develop and flourish.

HOLLOW-TINING A more elaborate form of aeration is to 'hollow core' the lawn. For this you will need a specially designed fork with hollow tines which can be hired. When the fork is pushed into the soil, it takes out a core or plug of soil. A topdressing can then be brushed into the holes.

WHAT IS SCARIFYING?

This removes the thatch – dead bits of grass and other plant debris – which smothers the blades of grass and prevents rain and nutrients reaching grass roots. It is more efficient to scarify with a spring-tine rake in two different directions, at right angles to each other, to remove as much thatch as possible. For large areas, buy or hire a scarifying machine.

TOPDRESSING

This is a mix of peat-free potting compost and sand which is incorporated into the surface of the soil. It can be lightly spread over the surface of the lawn and brushed in with a stiff broom. If rain is predicted, leave it to be washed naturally into the grass. Topdressing can also be used to fill in aeration holes.

YOU WILL NEED

* Hand tool such as a trowel to remove weeds
* Lawn mower
* Spring-tine rake
* Garden fork
* Aerating machine (for large gardens only)
* Topdressing and a shovel
* Stiff broom
* Grass seed

1. Check over the lawn first and use a hand tool such as a trowel to dig out any pernicious weeds like thistle, nettle or ragwort which will spread and dominate the lawn.

2. Cut the grass on a low setting. Short grass makes the autumn maintenance programme much easier. Remove any grass clippings and add these to the compost heap if you have one.

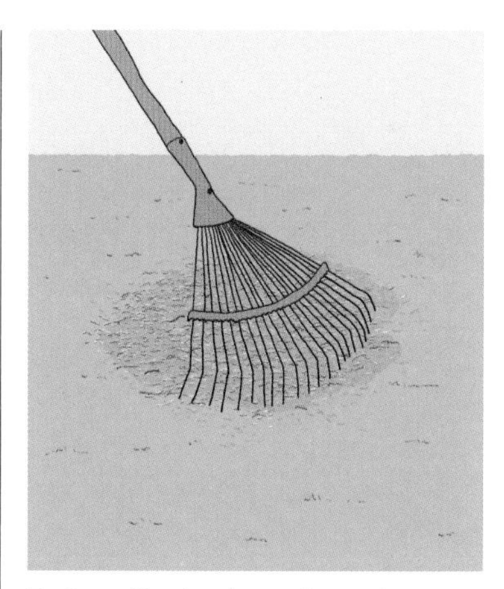

3. Scarify the lawn by using a spring-tine rake to scratch away at the surface of the lawn and remove the thatch. Gather up the thatch using either a mower with a box on the back or a garden rake. Add the material to the compost heap.

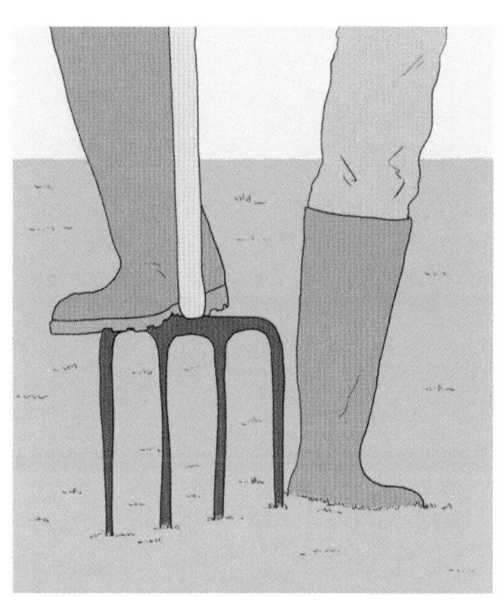

4. Aerate the lawn by pushing the tines of a garden fork about 10cm (4in) into the soil. Wiggle the fork around and then repeat this process at 10-cm (4-in) intervals.

5. For larger areas, an aerating machine which you walk behind can be purchased or hired. This makes the holes for you.

6. Spread topdressing lightly over the soil and use a broom to sweep it into the holes. Lightly sprinkle grass seed over any bare patches of soil at the rate recommended on the packet.

CHAPTER 10

WATER FEATURES

Water features are a key component in the design and structure of a garden. If you have room in your outside space, a water feature, whether this is a pond or a tiny container fountain, can completely transform it, bringing light, movement and sound. The presence of water will also encourage wildlife to visit your garden to drink, bathe and feed.

In this chapter, we look at the different types of water features you can have outside. These range from a dramatic waterfall or fountain to a tranquil wildlife pond. If space is at a premium, water features can also be mounted on a wall or the back of the house. There are also suggestions for the different types of plants that can be grown in a pond, including marginals, oxygenators and deep-water aquatics.

Finally, a useful step-by-step guide at the end of the chapter focuses on how to create an informal pond, so you can share your beautiful water feature with the surrounding wildlife.

Enjoy the sound of water

A water feature in the garden can bring the space alive. Waterfalls or just the sound of water from a simple water spout or bubble fountain can transform a garden into a vibrant and exciting place. The relaxing, splashing noise can be a welcome distraction in urban gardens from the sounds of traffic and neighbours. Water fountains without an area of open water are also the safest option if you have pets or small children who might run or fall into a pond.

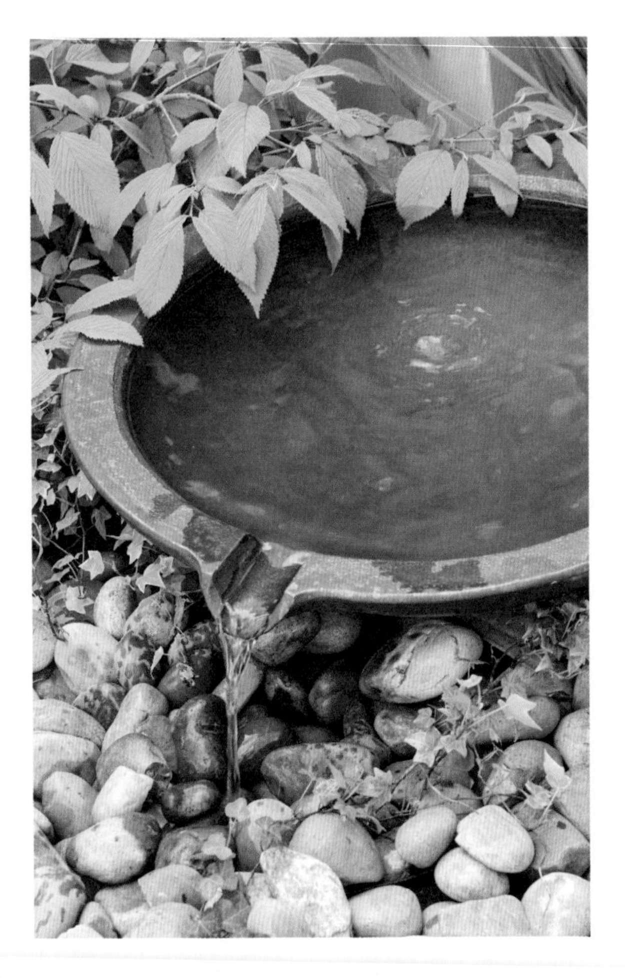

INSTALL A SIMPLE FOUNTAIN

Creating a water fountain is not as difficult as you may think, but you will need an outdoor power supply unless you are using a solar fountain:

* Dig a hole, about 30cm (1ft) wide and deep, for the fountain. Line the hole with a butyl pond liner.
* Put a water fountain attached to a pump in the bottom of the hole. These are available online and from garden centres.
* Ensure the fountain is just proud of the surface – you may need to use bricks or stones on either side to stop it moving when the water starts circulating.
* Place a length of chicken wire over the hole.
* It may be necessary to support the chicken wire with sturdy bamboo canes or sticks underneath and across the hole if the slate or stones are heavy.
* Cover the hole with slate or pebbles, ensuring the tip of the fountain is still protruding.
* Fill the hole with water up to the top.

A simple water feature brings a tranquil atmosphere to the garden and cools the air.

* Plug in the fountain. Alternatively, if it is a solar fountain, place it where it will receive full sun.
* Check the fountain works – the water should run back into the hole before being redirected up the fountain again. Adjust the water flow as necessary.

RAISED WATER FEATURES

A similar technique can be used for water features above ground. Often waterproof containers, urns and ornate vases can be used. Barrels cut in half make a rustic-looking sump for a water fountain. You can also add a rustic pump handle to the side of the barrel with water running out of it and splashing back into the barrel.

WALL-MOUNTED WATER FEATURES

In small gardens, wall-mounted fountains can be installed. These are often quite heavy, so not always suitable for a fence, although small, light versions might be fine if attached to a stout fence post. They are often attached to the back of the house. Once the feature is installed, keep the pump topped up with water, as water can be lost through evaporation.

SAFETY FIRST

Never run a fountain pump without water. If you are using an electric pump, ensure that it is plugged into a circuit breaker. A solar pump is a solution for powering a fountain if there is no power source.

If you are short of space, water features can easily be attached to walls or pillars.

Informal ponds

There is something magical about a natural-looking pond in the garden. It evokes a feeling of serenity and calm. If positioned near the house, an informal pond can even be enjoyed from the comfort of your armchair. In larger gardens, they can be placed just out of sight, to create a sense of intrigue as you come across the pond. This also provides some privacy for wildlife when you are not visiting the pond yourself.

There are two options when planting an informal or wildlife pond. One is to allow plant life to naturally colonize the water and surrounding area. It is surprising how quickly plants will seed and spread into the pond. However, this will need careful management to ensure nothing too invasive becomes established. Another disadvantage is you might not like the plants you end up with.

The second technique is to choose plants suitable for the pond. Although this approach involves an initial outlay, it does at least allow you to choose the plants and colours you like. You may find selecting aquatic plants unnerving at first, as there are so many to choose from. However, the two main factors to consider are the depth at which each plant should be planted and whether it requires sun or shade.

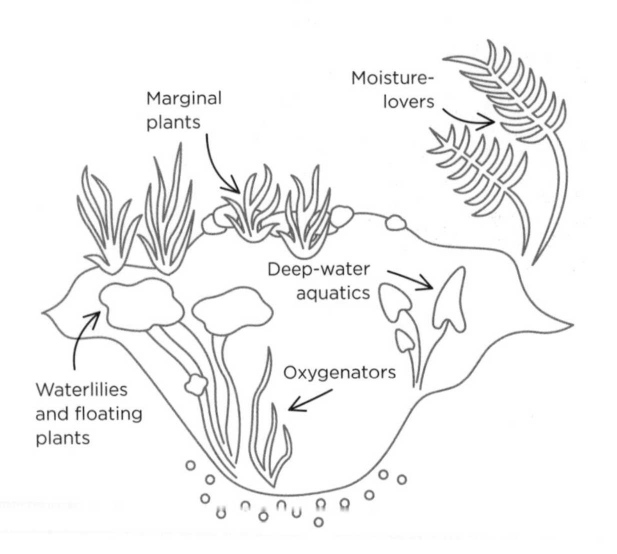

In small ponds, some aquatic plants, like deep-water aquatics (including waterlilies), marginal plants and oxygenating plants, should be planted in aquatic baskets to prevent them spreading. These 'containers' usually have latticed sides which allow for water and air movement around the roots. They usually need to be lined with some hessian/burlap or fine mesh to stop the compost washing out.

Use an aquatic compost when planting aquatic baskets. These specially formulated mixes use a medium- to heavy-grade loam combined with sand and nutrients. They will not make the water too fertile, which can encourage algae and other pond weeds. Place a layer of fine gravel, 1cm (½in) deep, over the surface of the rootball to stop the compost washing away. The best time to plant aquatic plants is spring when the water is starting to warm up.

There are five main groups of plants to consider when creating a pond. The category determines the depth at which they should be planted.

OXYGENATING PLANTS

These release oxygen into the water during the day, helping to keep the water clear. In small ponds they can be anchored in pots at the bottom. A few bunches per square metre should be enough.

FLOATING PLANTS

As the name suggests, these float on the surface and are not anchored. The most popular is *Hydrocharis morsus-ranae* which has white flowers with a yellow spot. Make sure that no more than 50 percent of the water's surface is covered. Float the plants on the water surface at a rate of 1 per sq metre (11 sq ft).

MARGINAL PLANTS

Marginals are planted around the pond edges and slightly submerged in the water. Ponds usually have marginal shelves around the edge which is where marginals should be planted. They soften the edges, provide shade and stop the water getting too warm and full of algae. If purchased in plastic pots, they should be transplanted into aquatic baskets.

MOISTURE-LOVERS

Moisture-lovers are similar to marginal plants, but are planted directly in the soil around the edge of the pond. They provide shade and cover for visiting wildlife. They can also be planted in bog gardens.

Disguise the edges of a pond with rocks or stones to make it look natural.

TIP ON WATERLILIES

If you grow waterlilies, make sure you choose species that are suitable for the depth of water in your pond. Depending on variety, this can range from 10cm (4in) to 1.5m (5ft).

DEEP-WATER AQUATICS

These are placed in the deeper sections of the pond. You may need to support the aquatic baskets with bricks to start with. Then, as the plants grow, the containers can be lowered gradually, so the leaves still reach the water surface.

SAFETY

If you have pets or small children, you may need to erect a fence around the pond to prevent them entering the water. Alternatively, although expensive, you can buy small, unobtrusive safety grids which are placed just below the surface of the water, stopping anybody from drowning if they fall in.

STEP-BY-STEP TECHNIQUE

BUILD A WILDLIFE POND

A pond not only creates a beautiful feature in the garden, but also attracts lots of fascinating wildlife, including a variety of birds, insects and some mammals. It is always worth making room for some water in a small garden, even if the pond is just a metre or so wide.

Ponds should ideally be positioned where they will receive a mix of dappled shade and some sunshine. Too much light can encourage excess green algae and pond weeds that can take over the pond, but some sunlight is good to entice creatures and plants to bask in the warmth.

CALCULATING THE SIZE OF POND LINER

The length needs to be twice the depth, plus the length, and the width needs to be twice the depth plus the width. Allow about 10cm (4in) at each end for the edge of the pond.

HOW DEEP? Most wildlife will use the shallower or marginal areas, but at least one-third of the pond should be more than 60cm (2ft) deep for fish or plants. This also stops the water freezing when cold. A ball floating on the surface can stop freezing too.

WHAT MIGHT I EXPECT TO SEE? A pond will attract lots of wildlife, including amphibians such as frogs, toads and newts. You may even see grass snakes. Bats and birds, such as swallows, house martins and herons, will also visit. Hedgehogs, badgers, deer and rodents may come down at night to drink, depending on the pond's size and location. Also look out for insects like dragonflies, damselflies, pond skaters, caddisflies and water beetles.

YOU WILL NEED

* Garden hose or large plastic bottle of sand
* Spade, spirit level and wooden plank
* Soft builders' sand
* Butyl pond liner
* Knife or scissors
* Rocks, stones and logs
* Selection of marginal and aquatic plants
* Rainwater or tap water

BEACH SIDE

Ensure there is a 'beach' or gently sloping edge at the side of the pond where creatures can approach to drink or access the pond without the risk of falling in and not being able to climb out.

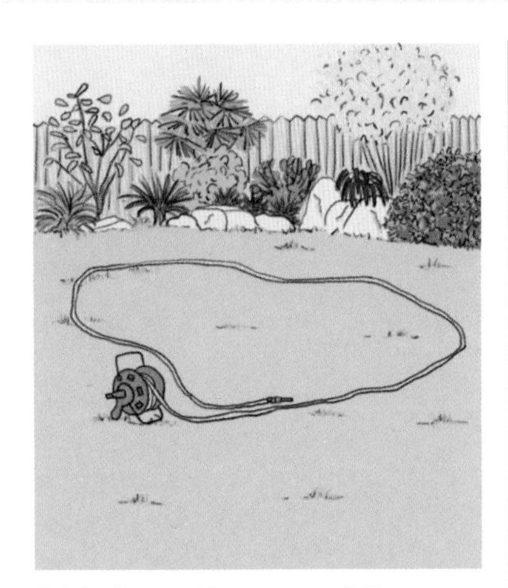

1. Mark out the area of the pond using a garden hose or a trail of sand from a large plastic bottle. Try to give the pond natural-looking contours instead of a shape that is too rigid and symmetrical.

2. Dig out the pond with a spade. Use a spirit level on a wooden plank placed across the hole to ensure the perimeter edges are all the same level. If not, the water will always be lower at one end, exposing the liner.

3. Make shelves around the edge of the pond to create an area for marginal plants. These should be about 10–15cm (4–6in) below the surface and about 20cm (8cm) wide.

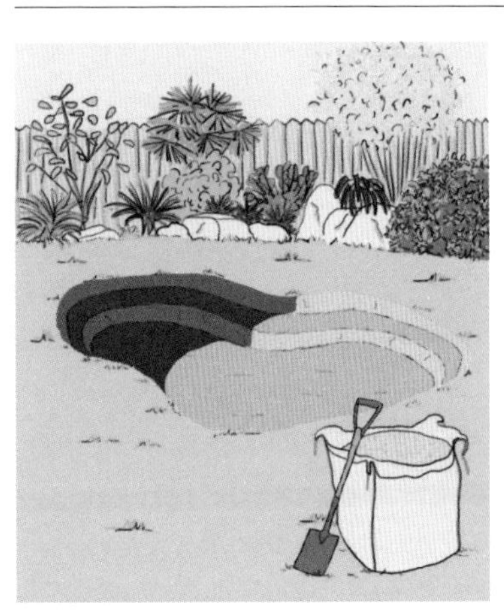

4. Remove any sharp stones from the bottom of the pond. Line the hole with a layer of soft builders' sand to a depth of 5cm (2in).

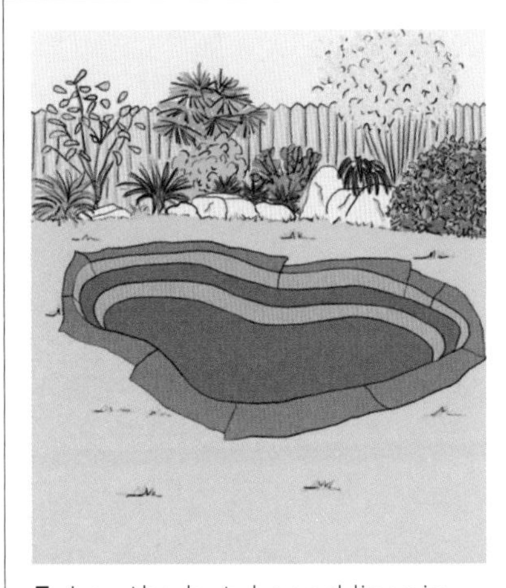

5. Lay the butyl pond liner in the hole, allowing an excess of about 10cm (4in) around the edge, trimming any excess with a knife or scissors. Dig out a small trench all around the perimeter of the pond and bury the edge of the liner in it.

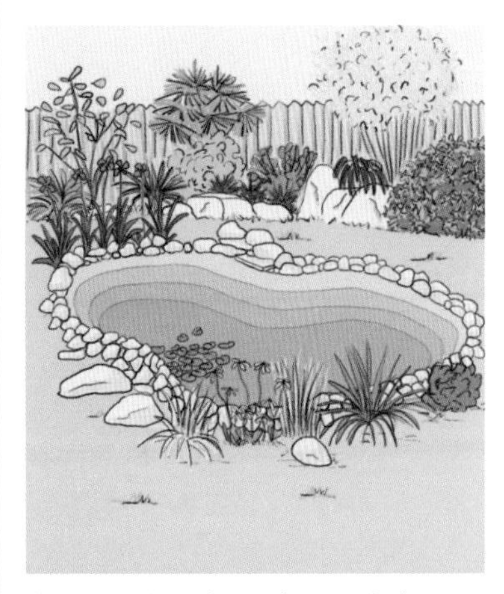

6. Disguise the edges of the pond with rocks, stones, logs and plants. This will also create habitats for wildlife. Fill the pond with water. Rainwater is ideal, but if not, tap water will suffice. Allow the water to settle for a couple of weeks before adding aquatic plants.

CHAPTER 11

PLANTS FOR FREE (OR ALMOST FREE)

Gardening need not be expensive. In fact, if you have the patience and a bit of know-how, you can quickly stock up your garden for free, or at least for very little money. Packets of seeds are very cheap to buy, and the only other thing you need to budget for is potting compost, although even that you can make yourself. If you have friends and neighbours with plants you like, it is easy to take cuttings and grow them in your own garden. Doing this will literally cost you nothing.

This chapter guides you through the various ways you can propagate your own plants, allowing you to save money while increasing the range of different types you grow. There is advice on how to sow seeds, take cuttings from stems, roots and leaves, and how to divide herbaceous perennials. It also explains how to propagate your favourite shrub simply by bending a branch down into the soil and layering it. Collecting and growing your plants on a budget has never been so easy.

Sowing seed

Seeing a plant grow that you have nurtured from seed is extremely rewarding. In addition, sowing seed is a cheap way of producing plants for your garden. In some cases, if you collect the seed yourself from either your garden or a friend's, it does not cost anything at all, particularly if you also make your own potting compost.

DIRECT SOWING OUTDOORS

Direct sowing is placing the seed straight into the soil, without growing the plants in pots, seed trays or modules first. The soil should be well prepared if you are sowing direct in this way. To do this, dig the soil over thoroughly to break up any compacted clods of earth and remove any weed roots. If you don't do this, the seeds will struggle to cope with the competition. Alternatively, if you are using a no-dig method (see page 98), make sure there are no weeds emerging and the compost is deep enough for the depth of seed and root systems of the new plants.

The most common way to sow seeds directly is in a 'drill'. This is a narrow and shallow trench into which seeds are sown and then covered with soil or compost. The easiest way to create a drill is to stretch some string taut from one end of the row to the other, then use a stick, bamboo cane or the edge of a hoe to draw out a shallow drill. Or, for shorter rows, a cane can be laid flat on the soil surface and pressed down to create a straight drill. Sow seed at the rates recommended on the packet. Often, they will need to be thinned to their final planting position. This involves pulling up the weaker and congested seedlings, leaving the remaining ones enough space to grow and flourish. Instead of sowing in a drill,

Direct sowing is one of the easiest methods of growing plants because you do not need to transplant them.

TIPS ON SOWING SUSTAINABLY

- Water seeds and seedlings with a 'rose' attached to the watering can, as the fine spray should not disturb the seed.
- If you are sowing very small seeds, such as carrot seed, it can be easier to mix them with sand in a bucket first and then spread the mixture lightly in the seed drill.
- Use seed compost for sowing seed in pots, modules and seed trays.
- Add some vermiculite to the surface of the compost in seed trays and pots at a depth of 3mm (⅛in) to help retain moisture. It can also be mixed in with seed compost for the same reasons.
- Always remember to cover seeds with more potting compost when sowing.

individual seeds can also be sown in their own holes using a dibber. This is usually easier for larger seeds such as pumpkins, courgettes/zucchini and beans.

SOWING INDOORS

To get plants off to an early start, seeds can be sown in pots or modules. This is suitable for plants that need a long growing season like tomatoes, chillies, and aubergines/eggplants, but it is still too cold to sow them outside. Seeds can also be sown indoors by broadcasting them lightly in seed trays. The seedlings are pricked out later into larger pots before being grown on and planted outside (see pages 106–7).

Propagators provide additional warmth, which is useful for getting seeds off to an early start in the season.

USE A PROPAGATOR

Some seeds require a bit of help to get going using a propagator. These are simply heated boxes that provide a warm environment to get germination underway. Some are simply plugged in and kept at a constant temperature, whereas more expensive ones have thermostats to alter the temperature. Some are just boxes with a lid to keep plants cosy. They are available in a range of sizes.

COLLECT YOUR OWN SEED

Seeds can be purchased each year, either online or from shops and garden centres. However, if you have established plants in your garden, it is possible to harvest your own, which can save money and guarantees that your favourite plants will remain in your garden (unless they are F1 hybrids which won't come true from their seeds). Wait until the seed is ripe, which is usually when the seed capsule or pod starts to split. Place the seed in a paper bag and store somewhere dark and cool until you are ready to sow. The seeds of some plants need stratification (a period of coldness) to break their dormancy – place them in the fridge for a few weeks prior to sowing.

Stem cuttings

Stem cuttings are a useful way of propagating plants vegetatively. This is often quicker than growing from seed. The other benefit of taking cuttings is that some plants do not come 'true from seed', meaning the resulting plant is different from the original plant, in the same way that a child does not look identical to his or her mother or father, but just has traits that are similar. By taking a cutting instead, you are practically 'cloning' the original plant (sometimes called the mother plant).

There are a few different types of stem cuttings that can be taken. The main three types are:

HARDWOOD CUTTINGS Generally taken when the plant is dormant, usually between late autumn and late winter. As the name suggests, this is carried out on plants with woody stems like trees and shrubs.

SOFTWOOD CUTTINGS Often called greenwood cuttings, these are taken early in the growing season, usually from late winter to mid-spring, from the tips of tender and herbaceous perennials.

SEMI-RIPE CUTTINGS These are taken later in the year from plant stems that have started to ripen but still have more growing to do in the season.

Some plants are easier to propagate than others, and it is worth doing a bit of research on this. Some also prefer to have the base dipped in hormone rooting powder before being planted in the potting compost. Others like to have a 'heel' retained when being removed as a shoot from the main stem.

Stem cuttings should be propagated as soon as they are removed from the plant. However, if there is an unavoidable delay – perhaps you have to travel home from a friend's garden where you took the cutting – the plant material should be put in a plastic bag

Roses are best propagated from softwood cuttings in late spring and early summer.

and kept as cold as possible. Hardwood cuttings can often be kept in the fridge in a plastic bag for a few weeks before being inserted into the compost.

Look for fresh, healthy new growth on the plant. Ideally, propagate from non-flowering shoots. With hardwood cuttings, ensure the wood has fully ripened. Use secateurs to remove a shoot with about five or six buds, although there may be more on shoots with tightly packed buds. The shoot can vary in length from 5cm (2in) to 15cm (6in), although hardwood cuttings can be up to 30cm (1ft) long, depending on the size of shrub. Softwood and semi-ripe cuttings are best taken in the morning when the plant tissue contains more moisture.

HOW TO TAKE A STEM CUTTING

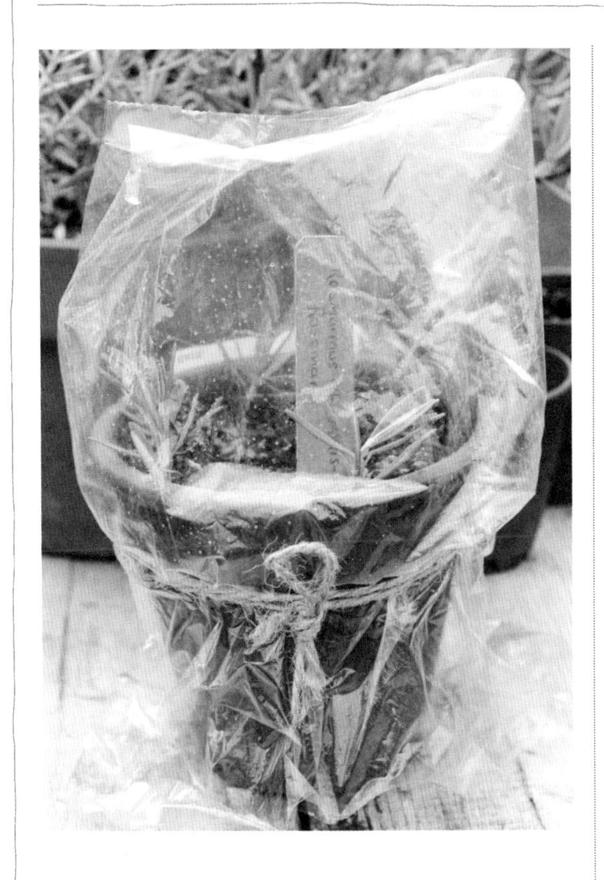

1. Make a cut at the bottom of the stem, just below a bud or pair of buds.
2. Remove the lower two-thirds of foliage. If the plant has large foliage, cut the remaining leaves in half to reduce transpiration (the loss of moisture through the leaves).
3. Insert the cut bottom end into hormone rooting powder, if recommended. Not all plants need this.
4. Insert the cutting into a free-draining seed or potting compost. Two-thirds of the stem should be below the surface, and the material with foliage (or potential foliage and shoots in the case of hardwood cuttings) above the surface. Often, a number of cuttings are inserted around the edge of a round pot. The reason for this is that it encourages roots to go downwards instead of outwards. Make sure the cuttings are not touching each other.
5. Keep the cuttings well watered, although not so damp that they start rotting. Leave in a warm, bright place but not in direct sunlight. Leafy cuttings will benefit from a plastic cover or bag placed over them to retain some humidity and moisture.

Division and layering

Division is one of the easiest methods of propagation because the plant is already established, which means that success rates are usually very high. Another advantage of this method is that plants benefit from being divided anyway if they have become mature and congested. Some plants are also suitable for propagating by layering stems.

DIVISION

This technique is used to propagate herbaceous perennials and involves splitting the root system into separate parts, each of which can then be planted individually. The best time to split summer-flowering perennials is in early spring, just as they are about to come into growth. It can also be done in autumn. Avoid dividing in the middle of summer when the plants are actively growing. Spring-flowering perennials can be divided after flowering in summer as they start to produce more roots.

The traditional method of propagating is to dig the plant up and place it on the surface of the soil. Insert two garden forks back to back over the plant and lever or prise the two sections apart. An easier method is just to slice down the middle of the plant with a sharp spade, or you can use an old but sharp gardening knife.

In some cases, it might be possible to simply pull small clumps apart by hand. Make sure each section has plenty of roots attached.

The two sections can then be planted individually or given to friends. You may need to discard the central crown of the existing plant if it has become too woody. The healthiest and most vigorous parts are usually those that come from around the outer edges of the original plant.

Small plants can be divided or split by cutting through the rootball with an old, but sharp, knife.

LAYERING

Usually carried out in spring or autumn, layering is a simple technique that is used on shrubs to create more plants. It works best on bushes that produce flexible shoots which do not take easily from cuttings. A shoot is pulled down towards the ground while still attached to the original plant. The shoot is then pegged down and soil or compost is placed over the part of the stem in contact with the ground. Alternatively, you can dig a small hole and cover the stem with soil again. It can help to inflict a small cut or wound on part of the stem to encourage rooting.

After about a year the layered shoot should have rooted. It can then be severed from the mother plant, dug up and planted elsewhere in the garden. Plants suitable for layering include:

- *Acer*
- Blueberry (*Vaccinium corymbosum*)
- *Camellia*
- *Chaenomeles*
- *Daphne*
- *Forsythia*
- Hazel (*Corylus avellana*)
- Jasmine (*Jasminum*)
- Lilac (*Syringa*)
- *Magnolia*
- Rhododendrons and azaleas
- Smoke bush (*Cotinus*)
- Witch hazel (*Hamamelis*)
- *Viburnum*

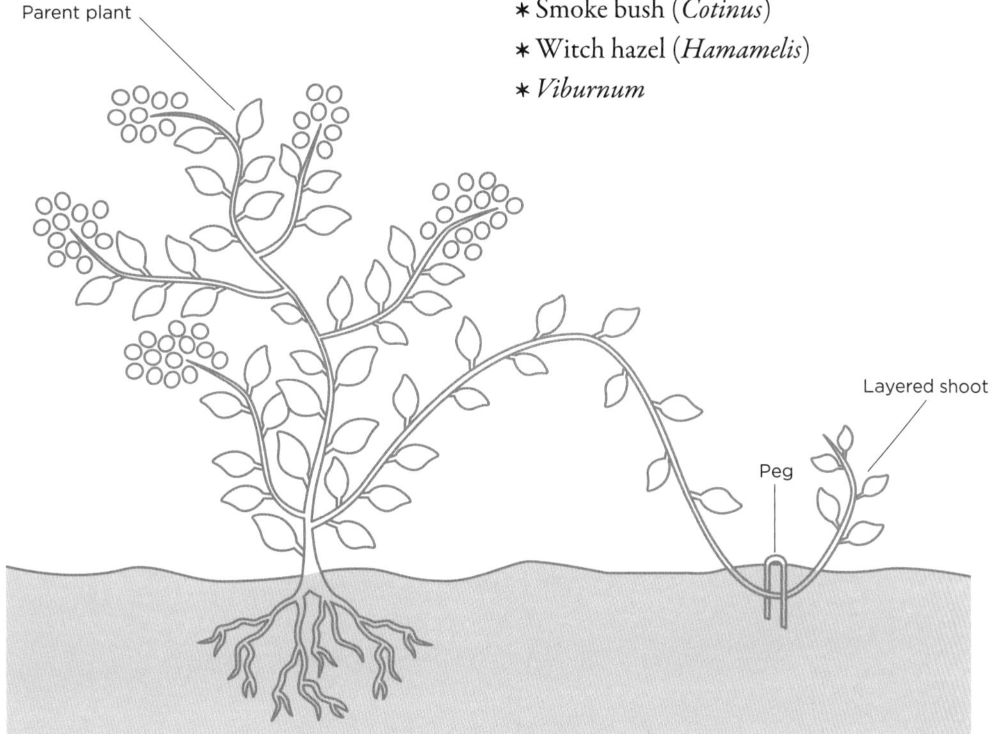

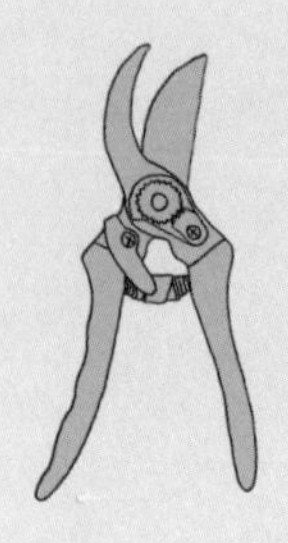

STEP-BY-STEP TECHNIQUE

TAKE ROOT AND LEAF CUTTINGS

Root cuttings and leaf cuttings are two easy methods of propagating your favourite plants for the garden. Use seed compost mixed with plenty of horticultural grit or sand to make it free-draining. Alternatively, add 25 percent vermiculite or perlite to the mix. Keep the rootings moist and within a few months you will have lots of brand-new plants to share with friends or add to your existing plant collection.

ROOT CUTTINGS

The best time to take roots cuttings is between late autumn and late winter. Most trees and shrubs that sucker naturally, such as *Aronia*, *Sarcococca* and species roses, are suitable. Other candidates include shrubs like *Aralia*, *Chaenomeles* and *Syringa*; climbers like *Campsis*, *Passiflora* and *Solanum*; and perennials like *Echinops*, *Phlox* and *Papaver orientale*. How to take a root cutting is explained in detail on the opposite page.

YOU WILL NEED

* Plant for propagating
* Garden knife or secateurs
* Pot, modules or seed tray
* Seed compost mixed with horticultural grit or sand, or a soil additive such as perlite or vermiculite

LEAF CUTTINGS

It is possible to take leaf cuttings of some plants. There are numerous techniques for doing this. Some involve using a whole leaf, while other plants require half a leaf or a section. Plantlets will appear growing from parts of the leaf which can then be carefully removed and potted on individually.

Leaf cuttings of some houseplants are easy to take and reward you with lots more plants.

1. Dig up the plant you wish to propagate or remove it from its pot. For really large plants where this is not possible, a section of the rootball can be exposed on one side, leaving the plant *in situ*.

2. Remove some of the roots for the cuttings from the plant using a knife or secateurs. The cuttings should be 5–10cm (2–4in) long and cut close to the crown of the plant, as this end of the cutting will send out roots.

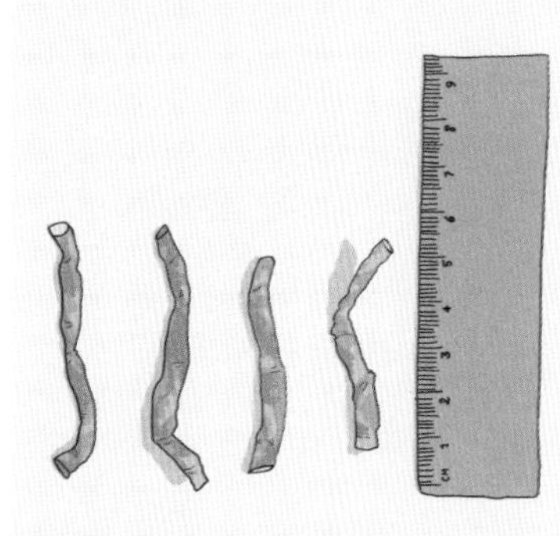

3. It is important to know which end was closest to the original plant, so place the cuttings on a table carefully, ensuring that you know which end is which.

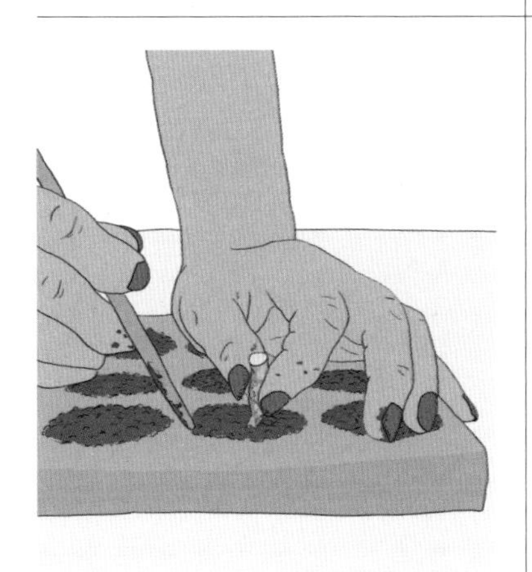

4. Fill a pot, module or seed tray to just below the top with free-draining compost. Insert the cuttings, taking care they are the right way up with the tips level with the compost (use deeper pots for longer cuttings). Space cuttings 3cm (1¼in) apart in a seed tray or add one per pot or module.

5. Keep the pot, modules or seed tray somewhere warm such as on a windowsill in the house or in a greenhouse or cold frame.

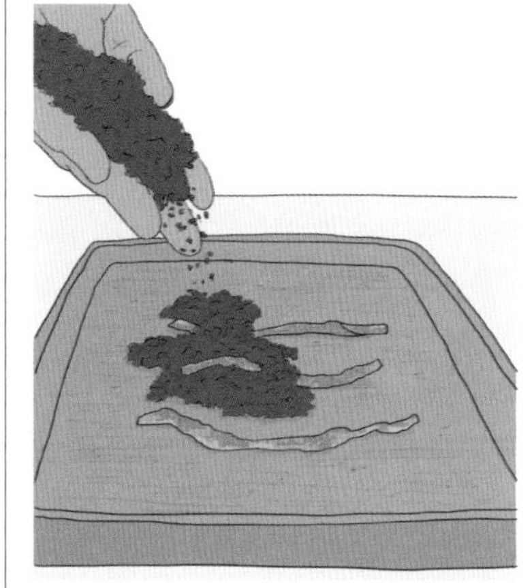

6. It is sometimes difficult to propagate skinny roots such as those from phlox with vertical cuttings. Instead, take longer cuttings, about 12cm (5in) long, then place them horizontally in a seed tray and cover them with seed compost.

CHAPTER 12

TACKLING PESTS AND DISEASES

At some stage while making the gardening journey to creating your horticultural heaven, you will almost certainly encounter plant pests or diseases in one form or other. Whether it is a nibbled leaf, rotting fruit or distorted stem, there is no need to panic since most of the time these issues will not kill your plant, and nature quite often has a natural solution for dealing with them.

However, by following a few simple guidelines, it is possible to reduce the chances of your plants succumbing to disease or attacks by pests. This chapter provides some tips on how to maintain a healthy and balanced garden ecosystem as well as how to encourage nature and wildlife to help manage any problems or imbalances in the garden.

There is also a list of some of the most troublesome or common pests and diseases, with advice on how to keep them in check, so they do not reduce your crops and leave your plants looking unsightly and ill.

Dealing with pests and diseases

One of the keys to successful gardening is keeping a vigilant eye out for pests and diseases. By regularly monitoring your plants, you will be able to nip the problem in the bud, if you will excuse the pun. On the other hand, do not panic if you discover pests or diseases. In many cases, nature will deal with these if there is a wide range of plants and you have encouraged wildlife into your garden.

REDUCING PEST AND DISEASE PROBLEMS

* Prevention is always more successful than cure. Good plant husbandry should help reduce the chances of problems occurring in the first place.
* If buying plants from a garden centre, check them for pests and diseases first. Some plants such as potato tubers should be certified virus-free, so avoid ones that do not come with this claim. Also, be wary of collecting material, including seedlings, cuttings and seeds, from a friend's garden and check the plants do not have diseases before bringing them home. It's not just above ground you need to check either. Many diseases, such as honey fungus (*Armillaria mellea*) and sudden oak death (*Phytophthora ramorum*), can be transmitted in the soil, while pests like vine weevil can be carried on plant roots.
* A weak plant is far more susceptible to problems than a healthy plant. So make sure plants are not deficient in nutrients by feeding them and keeping them watered. Mulch the soil around plants to suppress weeds and keep the roots moist. If a plant is suffering from drought stress or nutrient deficiency, it will easily succumb to other

problems. Do make sure the mulch comes from a reliable source, though, as even mulches can carry soil-borne pests and diseases.

* Keep the surrounding area free of weeds, as these will take moisture and nutrients from plants that need these to survive pest and disease attacks.
* Have a balanced garden full of biodiversity. By encouraging wildlife and having a range of plants, pests and diseases will not be able to get a hold. For example, small pests can be controlled by encouraging birds, hedgehogs and bats.
* Many fungal diseases like grey mould (a disease caused by *Botrytis cinerea*) and mildew can be controlled by creating good air circulation around plants. Prune shrubs and trees with an overly dense canopy. Reducing the congestion and allowing in sunlight can help prevent plants from succumbing to problems.
* Choose pest- and disease-resistant varieties if possible. Not all plants are fully resistant, but many have good 'resistance'. For example, some gooseberries are resistant to mildew and some carrot varieties have resistance to carrotfly.

BARRIERS Whether it is birds you are trying to keep off your seedlings or cabbage whitefly off the cabbages, using protective barriers such as netting or fine mesh is a great way to stop 'pests' from destroying your crops.

BIOLOGICAL CONTROL It is possible to control pests by using natural predators to help reduce their numbers. One of the most popular techniques is to introduce ladybird larvae (these can be purchased online) to reduce aphid infestations.

Opposite left: *Mulching helps retain moisture, keeping plants healthy.* **Opposite right:** *Remove weeds to increase the availability of nutrients, making plants better able to combat disease.* **Right:** *Ladybird larvae can control aphid infestations.*

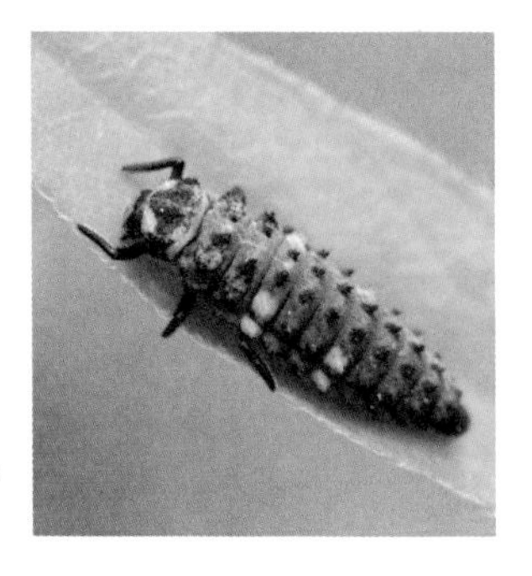

Common pests and diseases

There are thousands of pests and diseases to which plants are susceptible, although some are very specialist in terms of the plants they target and where they occur. However, a few of the most common ones you may encounter are covered here. It should be possible to control these pests and diseases without resorting to chemicals. The key is to be vigilant and practise good husbandry to keep your plants fighting fit.

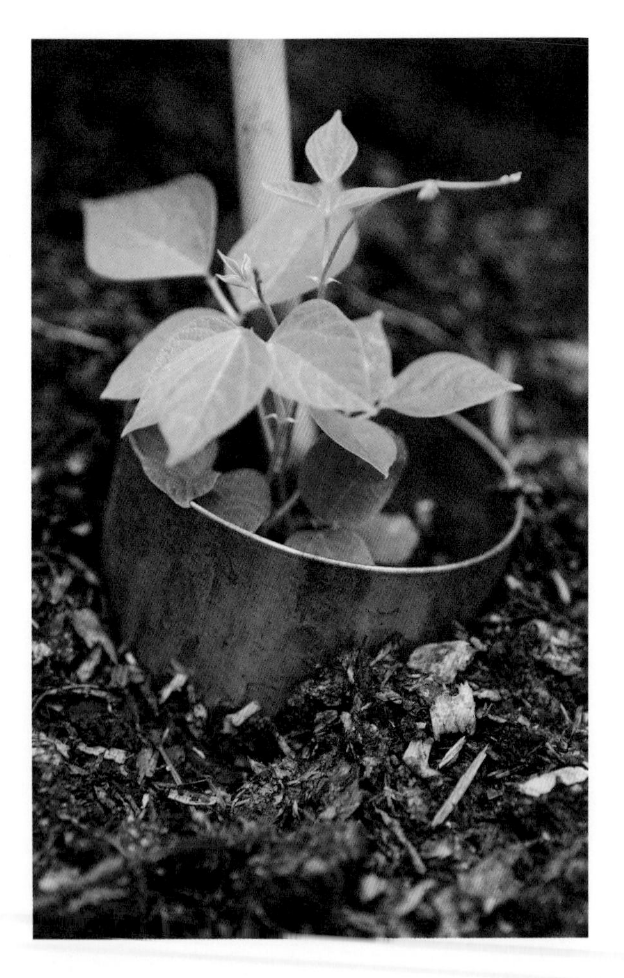

SLUGS AND SNAILS

Definitely the gardener's main enemy, there are various ways to deal with slugs and snails, but most of these will only help to reduce numbers.

BEER TRAP Plunge a glass or jar into the soil near a susceptible plant, top it up with beer and the snail or slug will fall in and be unable to get out.

NEMATODES These are microscopic round worms that eat slugs. They can be bought in a packet, mixed with water in a watering can and then watered onto the plants and soil where there is a problem.

BARRIERS Put copper bands around plants as slugs and snails do not like to cross them. You can also put very thorny branches around seed trays and raised beds to act as a barrier. Although this will have a limited effect, it will deter some slugs and snails.

PICK THEM OFF To reduce numbers, pop outside in the evening with a torch when they are most active. Pick off with gloves and move them away from plants.

DID YOU KNOW? Not all slugs are baddies. For example, the Leopard Slug (*Limax maximus*) will eat other slugs, helping to control infestations. It also feeds on decomposing plants, helping you recycle garden waste and convert it into organic matter.

BIRDS

The most effective method is a barrier such as a net. Erect a fruit cage around taller crops like soft fruit bushes. Special 'buzzing' strings can be tied tightly between two posts and the noise will deter birds, or string up CDs, shiny paper or foil to scare them away.

APHIDS

These can be a real nuisance, especially when there is a heavy infestation, and they generally feed on new shoots and leaves. They can be controlled by hand (use a glove as they can make a mess) by rubbing them off the plants. Or spray them off with a garden hose. In some cases, such as the growing tip of a broad/fava bean, the most effective method is to remove the tip to create a bushier, aphid-free plant.

VINE WEEVIL

Adult weevils create notching on the edges of leaves, but it is their larvae that cause the most problems. These white grubs, about 1cm (½in) long, like to eat the roots of plants, particularly those grown in containers. The most effective method of controlling the larvae is to spray the plant's rootball with microscopic nematodes which will feed on them.

Opposite: *Surround plants with copper bands to deter slugs and snails.* ***Right:*** *String up old CDs to keep birds away from ripening crops.*

POWDERY MILDEW

This looks like a white dusting on leaves and shoots. It occurs when conditions are too dry. Remove infected foliage and keep plants well watered and their roots mulched. Choose resistant plant varieties.

POTATO BLIGHT

Affecting tomatoes too, blight turns foliage brown and makes tubers or fruit rot. Choose resistant varieties and destroy infected material. Grow tomatoes in a greenhouse to stop spores blowing onto foliage.

CLUB ROOT

Affects many brassicas, causing swollen roots and stunted growth. Add lime to soil to increase pH as it prefers acidic conditions. Choose resistant varieties.

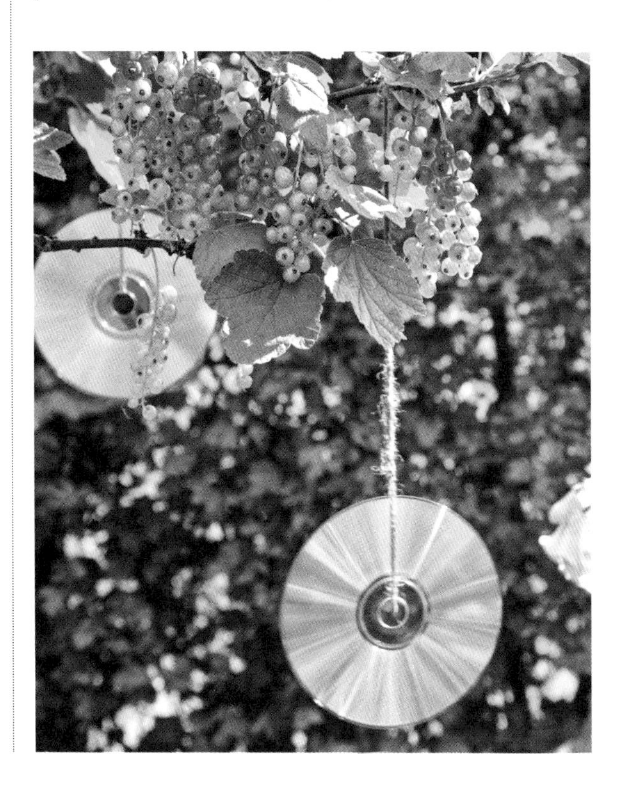

Glossary

ANNUAL – A plant that lives, flowers and dies within one year.

AERATION – A process that allows air to circulate in the soil. Often used in lawn care by pushing a fork into the ground to promote healthy growth. It is also used in composting to speed up decomposition by 'turning over' the compost with a fork.

ASPECT – Used to describe the direction in which a garden faces, such as north or south.

BIOLOGICAL CONTROL – Using a natural predator to reduce the numbers of a garden pest, such as using ladybird larvae to reduce aphid infestations.

BOLT – When a plant prematurely goes to flower and seed. Often caused by stress such as lack of watering. There are resistant varieties.

BIANNUAL – Produces flowers twice a year.

BIENNIAL – Flowers or bears fruits every other year.

BROADCAST SOWING – Sowing seed by scattering it across an area.

COLD FRAME – A structure kept in the garden, usually made of glass, to protect young plants and get crops off to an early start. Like a small version of a greenhouse.

COTYLEDON – These are the first leaves produced by a seed and are not considered a 'true' leaf. Often called a seed leaf.

CROCKS – Small, broken bits of crockery or old pots placed over drainage holes to stop compost leaching out. Today, stones, slate or even recycled polystyrene pieces can be used to cover the holes.

DECIDUOUS – A tree or shrub that loses its leaves when the temperature drops and the plant goes into dormancy.

DEADHEADING – Removing flowers after a plant has bloomed to encourage more flowers later in the season. If a plant is allowed to go to seed, it may stop producing flowers.

DIRECT SOW – Sowing seeds straight into the soil, as opposed to sowing them into pots first.

DORMANCY – When a plant is not actively growing. This usually occurs during winter when it is too cold for many plants to grow.

SEED DRILL – A narrow and usually shallow row made in the soil into which seeds are sown. Drills are usually made in a straight line.

ERICACEOUS PLANT – A plant that prefers acidic soil (low pH). Includes most heathers, camellias, rhododendrons, azaleas, blueberries, enkianthus and most magnolias.

ERICACEOUS COMPOST – Used as a medium for planting acid-soil-loving plants (ericaceous plants).

EVERGREEN – A plant that keeps it foliage all year round. The leaves do not necessarily have to be green. They can also be variegated, white, red, and so on. Most conifers are evergeen.

GERMINATION – When a seed breaks dormancy and sends out its first shoots.

HARDY – A plant that can survive cold temperatures and frosts. There are different levels of hardiness, including fully hardy, frost-hardy and half-hardy.

HARDENING OFF – Before being planted outside, plants are placed in a cold frame or porch for a few days to acclimatize to colder temperatures compared with the original growing conditions.

HORTICULTURAL FLEECE – A material used to cover plants to protect them from frost and cold.

HORTICULTURAL GRIT – Small stones added to potting composts to improve drainage. Particularly useful for growing cacti and succulents.

MULCH – Used to cover bare soil to prevent weeds germinating and to retain moisture for the roots of plants. It is usually organic material such as garden compost or wood chips, but it can also include pebbles, slates, shells, and so on.

PERENNIAL – A plant that lives for more than one year.

PERLITE – Produced from a type of volcanic glass, these white, tiny and lightweight pieces look like tiny polystyrene balls. Used in potting composts to improve drainage and add air to the mix.

RACEME – A long stem with lots of individual flowers on short stalks growing along its length.

ROOTBALL – The root system of a plant when it has been grown in a container and has therefore become ball-shaped.

ROOTSTOCK – Some plants are grown on a system of roots called rootstocks. This is done to restrict a plant's size, such as that of apple trees, or to give them resistance to a particular pest or disease, as in the case of grapevines and phylloxera.

SCARIFICATION – A process used in lawn care to remove the dead material (thatch) around the base of grass blades to encourage healthy new growth. Also a process used in propagation to scratch the surface of seeds to improve germination rates.

SEED DRILL – A long, shallow groove created in soil or potting compost to make rows for sowing seed.

SEEDLING – A young plant before it reaches maturity.

STRATIFICATION – Some seeds require a cold spell in nature to break their dormancy. This can be replicated artificially by placing seeds in the fridge.

SUBSOIL – The layer of soil below the topsoil. Usually compacted and hard to cultivate.

THATCH – The dead organic material found around the base of grass blades. Usually an accumulation of dead grass, foliage from surrounding trees and other natural debris that has settled in among the blades.

'TRUE' LEAF – This is the 'proper' set of leaves that appear after the cotyledons.

TILTH – When the top surface of the soil is broken down into a crumbly texture, which is ideal for sowing or planting into.

TOPDRESSING – A mix of loam and organic material such as compost (sometimes also includes peat) which is added to the surface of a lawn to improve the growing quality.

TOPSOIL – The top layer of soil in a garden or field. If the soil is of a poor quality, fresh topsoil is sometimes incorporated into the existing soil.

VERMICULITE – Used in potting composts to improve moisture retention, particularly when propagating plants. This fine, flaked mineral is either mixed in with the compost or placed on the surface to lock in moisture.

Index

PICTURE CREDITS

Alamy Stock Photo: Anne Gilbert 167, a-plus image bank 156, ArchivalSurvival 164, Bailey-Cooper Photography 170, Chris Clark 32, Clare Gainey 92, David & Micha Sheldon/Mauritius 144, David Hunter 203, Deborah Vernon 64, 200, 205, Diane Randell 124, Enterline Design 138, fotoshoot 168, Jacky Parker 55ar, Jenny Lilly 59, John Glover 137, Kathy deWitt 17, 73, Linda Cooke 157, Maggie Sully 171, Matthew Noble Horticultural 47, Matthew Taylor 150, mediasculp 123, Pollen Photos 182, SJ Images 98, Steve Taylor ARPS 76, Thomas Smith 97l, Tim Gainey 114, Volodymyr Nadtochii 147r; **Claire Takacs:** 31, 42, 68; © **Clive Nichols:** 180; **Dreamstime.com:** Aga7ta 72, Alexmak72427 75, Catalina Zaharescu Tiensuu 13al, Elena Luria 13cl, Graham Corney 105, Lijuan Guo 116, Maximilian Feszler 67, Mirekova 38, Paul Maguire 13bl, Rbiedermann 95b, Schlegelfotos 61l, Volodymyr Muliar 81, Yana Tatevosian 22, Yurporada 151; **GAP Photos:** 58, 109, 110, 125, 141, 172, 183r, 185, Abigail Rex 13br, 52, 189, Anna Omiotek-Tott 28, Anna Omiotek-Tott - Designer Matt Keightley 4, BBC Magazines Ltd. 206, Carole Drake 136, Christa Brand - Weihenstephan Gardens 84, Claire Higgins 145, Clive Nichols - Design Angel Collins 188, Designer Luke Heydon, Sponsor Thetford businesses and residents 66, Elke Borkowski 11, 45, 55al, 194, 215, Friedrich Strauss 129, 143, 173, Gary Smith 10, 153, Hanneke Reijbroek - Design Esther de Graaf - Escape Tuinarchitectuur 122, Heather Edwards 85, Howard Rice - Rhadegund House 55br, 82, Howard Rice - RHS Gardens, Hyde Hall 61r, J S Sira - Design Philippa Pearson 6br, Jonathan Buckley 102, 108, Jonathan Buckley - Demonstrated by Carol Klein 208, Jonathan Buckley - Design Alan Titchmarsh 86, Jonathan Buckley - Design John Massey 70, Juliette Wade 174, 178, Lynn Keddie 57, Mark Bolton 35, Mark Bolton - Roy Barker and Christopher Stock 6l, Martin Hughes-Jones 106, 204, Matt Anker 214, Michael Howes 96, Modeste Herwig 16, Nicola Stocken 29, 49, 60, 120, 154, 181, 195, Paul Debois 37, Paul Debois - Designer Caro Garden Design 48, Rachel Warne 30, Ray Cox - Garden Lynbrook 46, Rebecca Bernstein - Design Gordon Beale 142, Richard Bloom - Adrian's Wood, Bressingham Gardens 77, Robert Mabic 53, Sarah Cuttle 107l, Stephen Studd 158, Tim Gainey 183l, Visions 146, Zara Napier 187; **Getty Images:** Betsie Van Der Meer 78; **Giulia Hetherington:** 62; **iStock:** aloha_17 112, Anneliese Gruenwald-Maerkl 88, Artur Henryk Bialosiewicz 25, Bouillante 197, brytta 74, Daisy-Daisy 8, Diane Labombarbe 155, DLeonis 163l, Hana Richterova 95a, kororokerokero 213, L Feddes 80, Liudmila Chernetska 161, lucentius 212r, MarkoDzeletovic 186, MichelR45 71a, mtreasure 148, Nosyrevy 169, Obradovic 23, Orest Lyzhechka 140, RiverNorthPhotography 126, Rossella De Berti 6ar, Sarawutnam 163r, SbytovaMN 97r, svehlik 101, 162, Volokhatiuk 176, vvvita 55bl, whitemay 104, YuriyS 152, ZAKmac 149; **Jason Ingram:** 6al, 26, 202, RHS 132; **Sadolin:** Superdec in Mid Green, www.sadolin.co.uk. Photographer Max Attenborough 130, **Shutterstock:** Anastasiia Murko 210, Cia Marsh 71b, Cora Mueller 33, Dean Clarke 13cr, Debu55y 36, Dmitry Naumov 118, iMarzi 24, jmb 69, Johan Kusuma 107r, Jon Rehg 212l, Keith 316 160, M. Schuppich 147l, Nadia Nice 166, Serhii Brovko 13ar, Sever180 94; **Simon Akeroyd:** 131; **The Garden Collection:** FP/Garten Fräulein 50, FP/Jürgen Becker 192.

ACKNOWLEDGMENTS

I would like to thank Alison Starling, Sybella Stephens and Juliette Norsworthy at Octopus Publishing for their help and support in writing this book. Thanks also to Rachel Cross, Claire Rollet and Claire Huntley for the design and beautiful illustrations, Giulia Hetherington and Jennifer Veall for the picture research, and Lucy Carter and Nic Jones in production. Also a big debt of gratitude to Caroline West for her talented editing skills and her impressive gardening knowledge. Thank you also to Simon Maughan at the RHS for his horticultural advice and comments.